THE MIDDLE AGES SERIES
Ruth Mazo Karras, General Editor
Edward Peters, Founding Editor

A complete list of books in the series
is available from the publisher.

The Salian Century

Main Currents in an Age of Transition

Stefan Weinfurter

Translated by Barbara M. Bowlus
Foreword by Charles R. Bowlus

PENN

University of Pennsylvania Press

Philadelphia

Originally published in 1992 as *Herrschaft und Reich der Salier: Grundlinien einer Umbruchzeit*, by Stefan Weinfurter
Copyright © 1991 by Jan Thorbecke Verlag GmbH & Co., Sigmaringen

English translation copyright © 1999 University of Pennsylvania Press

10   9   8   7   6   5   4   3   2   1

Published by
University of Pennsylvania Press
Philadelphia, Pennsylvania 19104-4011

Library of Congress Cataloging-in-Publication Data
Weinfurter, Stefan.
 [Herrschaft und Reich der Salier. English]
 The Salian century : main currents in an age of transition /
Stefan Weinfurter ; translated by Barbara M. Bowlus ; foreword by
Charles R. Bowlus.
  p. cm.
 Includes bibliographical references and index.
 ISBN 0-8122-3508-8
 1. Holy Roman Empire—History—Franconian House, 1024–1125.
2. Germany—History—Franconian House, 1024–1125. 3. Franconian
House. I. Title.
DD143.W46 1999
943'.023—dc21

99-25597
CIP

Frontispiece: Genealogical table of the Salian dynasty in the *Chronicle* of Ekkehard of Aura. (Havelberger version, now in the Staatsbibliothek Berlin, Stiftung Preußischer Kulturbesitz, Cod. lat. 295, fol. 81v) probably based on an earlier version in the Recensio II of 1106/1107.

Contents

Foreword

Charles R. Bowlus

IN THE PAST HALF CENTURY German medievalists have done much to reevaluate their history. The nationalistic overtones that characterized so much of earlier historiography have vanished to the point that John B. Freed, an American medievalist, has criticized his German contemporaries for overlooking almost completely that which is distinctive about medieval German history, making their subject more and more similar to the histories of France and England during the same era. In one essay, written well before the Maastricht treaty, Freed accuses his colleagues of writing the prehistory of "the common market."[1] Freed is correct. Many German historians have indeed placed their subject squarely in the mainstream of medieval European history.[2] Whether or not this distorts the German or European past is open to question.[3] In any case, Weinfurter's work does not fall into this category. It is unabashedly "German" medieval history. *Reich* in the German title of his book refers to Germany, then generally called the "East Frankish kingdom,"[4] including much of what is now Belgium, Holland, and France. Burgundy, which was also under Salian rule, and even Italy come rarely under Weinfurter's scrutiny. *The Salian Century* is about the internal political dynamics of the German realm during the eleventh century.

As political history, this book may be subjected to yet another of Freed's criticisms: modern German medievalists are still excessively concerned with political history, so much so that they have neglected social history as it has been practiced notably in France by scholars associated with the *Annales* school.[5] German historians have been especially concerned with the problem of Germany's failure to produce a strong centralized monarchy during the High Middle Ages. On this point Weinfurter is guilty—if it is guilt that we are trying to establish. Throughout his study the author attempts to explain why the Salians failed to translate their remarkably clear concept of royal authority into the reality of a centralized kingship.

I would argue, however, that in attempting to explain this persistent problem of political history, Weinfurter is using the methodologies and results of social and cultural historians to elucidate more clearly political structures.[6] His is not an old-fashioned political history that dwells excessively upon surviving administrative documents. Using refined techniques of analysis, Weinfurter attempts to penetrate the minds of the Salians, to understand their *mentalité*, and to delineate indirectly their concept of regal authority from a myriad of sources. Drawing on concrete examples, he illustrates this dynasty's concept of kingship in the art of the Salian era, especially illuminated manuscripts and frescoes that were produced under royal patronage. Most significantly he interprets the monumental architecture of the cathedral church in Speyer, one of the largest churches in Christendom, for the construction of which the Salians mobilized enormous resources, as the ultimate expression of their rulership. In its unity and linear directness the architecture of Speyer characterizes the uncompromising sense of purpose that Conrad II and his heirs set upon to realize their royal mission. Of primary importance is Weinfurter's insistence that the Salian monolithic concept of royal authority was not always compatible with disparate forces of social change that were unleashed during the eleventh century. Thus, *The Salian Century* is political history within the framework of what is called social and cultural history.[7]

Although Weinfurter deals with a traditional problem in German historiography—the failure of a centralized monarchy to emerge in the Middle Ages—his answers to this perennial question are very different from those of his predecessors and some of his contemporaries. Traditional German historians believed, for example, that the dynasty's fascination with the Roman imperial crown and its conflicts with the papacy prevented these rulers from concentrating on their most essential task, state-building in Germany. The Salians' adventurism in Italy, however, was not the problem. In Weinfurter's view, the Salian concept of authoritarian rule, of a highly structured hierarchical transpersonal polity directly linked to the dynasty, contained inherent contradictions, making its implementation impossible in the long run. Moreover, the concept was so strong in the minds of the members of this dynasty that compromises proved difficult to achieve. Rather than frittering away their energies on meaningless diversions such as interventions in Italy, the Salians pursued energetically, in Weinfurter's view, an ideal of a structured command kingship (*Befehlsherrschaft*) that ultimately could not be translated into reality. This royal ideal of the Salians, Weinfurter argues, originated with Conrad II, the founder of the dynasty, a ruler who has been relatively neglected. The author's treatment of Conrad II, one of the most cogent portions of his book, will become the starting point for all future discussions of Conrad's rule and the Salian dynasty.

A second traditional interpretation that Weinfurter disputes is that the German monarchy ultimately failed because of the anarchical behavior of the princes of the realm who, in the pursuit of their own selfish interests, took advantage of every opportunity that came along (the minority of Henry IV, the Investiture Conflict, etc.) to undermine royal authority. Weinfurter argues, however, that the high aristocracy also had a concept of the unity of a realm that it was intent on preserving. Following the death of the last Ottonian ruler, Henry II, the princes elected Conrad II king precisely because many magnates perceived that he embodied the concept of institutionalized kingship in a kingdom threatened with dissolution. Although Henry II had himself been a strong ruler, he failed to provide for the transfer of power to the next generation, and consequently his demise conjured up the specter of political chaos. Rather than promoting anarchy, the princes chose stability in this case. Nevertheless, the aristocratic concept of a realm in which they were full participants in governance came ultimately into conflict with Conrad's monolithic idea of regal authority, one positing that God Himself had bestowed power on the Salian dynasty. Thus, much of what has been condemned as particularism by earlier scholars was in reality justifiable reaction to the authoritarian inclinations of the Salians. The problems of the dynasty may well have been rooted in the Salians' determination to impose a hierarchical command structure throughout the entire realm.

Traditionally historians treated Henry III very well. Because he died unexpectedly at the age of thirty-nine, leaving only his six-year-old son, Henry IV, as his heir, it has been speculated that had the elder Henry lived until the younger reached his majority, the German nobility might have retained its sense of obedience and discipline, and the reformers associated with Hildebrand (later Pope Gregory VII) might never have gained control of the Roman curia. The "evils" of particularism and religious conflict that plagued Henry IV's reign thus could have been avoided. Weinfurter's analysis casts doubt on these hoary notions. Henry III, who had been well schooled in Conrad II's concept of authoritarian monarchy, had by his arbitrary practices already succeeded in alienating most of the high nobility of the realm, so that revolt would have been likely had he not suddenly been removed from the scene. Rather than endangering Salian kingship,

Henry III's death, coming when it did, may have preserved the rule of the dynasty for two more generations.

One of the most persistent notions in the historiography of medieval Germany is that the reformed papacy and the Investiture Dispute played central roles in the declining fortunes of the Salians following the death of Henry III. Once again Weinfurter develops powerful arguments against the traditional view. Upon reaching his majority, before the beginnings of his conflict with Gregory VII, Henry IV, like his father and grandfather, attempted to implement a hierarchical command structure throughout Germany. Once again the realm tottered on the brink of rebellion. "The verdict against Henry IV and his tyrannical rule," Weinfurter maintains, "had in essence been rendered long before he became subject to the unrelenting wrath of the reform papacy." As for the investiture issue, it became the focal point of the disagreement only during the pontificate of Paschal II and the reign of Henry V, long after the crisis had first emerged.

Another point concerns the reign of Henry V. Traditional German historians castigated him for abandoning his father to side opportunistically with the king's opposition, betraying the ruler and even imprisoning him. Opportunism may well have been involved in the younger Henry's actions, but it was not the crass personal opportunism that modern critics of his reign have implied. Weinfurter demonstrates that Henry V moved against his father only *after* he realized that drastic action on his part was necessary to salvage Salian kingship, an ideal to which he remained faithful to the end.[8] Following Henry IV's death, the son went to great pains to rehabilitate his father, who was under excommunication at the time of his demise, seeing to it that he was eventually laid to rest in the cathedral church at Speyer, that splendid monument that the Salians erected for themselves. Thus Weinfurter shows that there was a remarkable degree of continuity in the royal ideals of Salian rulers, a major and novel thesis for most Anglo-American medievalists.

The Salian Century is likely to attract the attention of English-speaking scholars for yet another reason. Since the publication of Susan Reynolds's recent scholarship, the subject of feudalism has become a hotly debated one among Angloliterates.[9] Although the issues raised by Reynolds have sparked little perceptible discussion in Germany, it must be noted that the image of a "feudal system" is rarely conjured up in the pages of Weinfurter's book, and for good reason. Feudalism played no role in the regal concept of the Salians, as it had been formulated by Conrad II and rigorously pursued by his successors. The Salians' power base, which provided them with the means to become eligible for the royal office in the first place, rested upon a foundation of allodial holdings and advocacies over ecclesiastical institutions. They encouraged the clearing of forests and the development of wastes on their private possessions, thereby creating new wealth for themselves and their dependents. Pre-royal Salian lordships provided a model that other aristocratic families used to increase their wealth and power in the course of the eleventh century. As kings, the Salians treated dukes, counts, and other dignitaries from the high aristocracy as officials, not as vassals. They appointed and dismissed them according to the royal will, and allowing their appointees little or no room for initiative, they tolerated no breech of royal prerogatives. As has been known for some time, Salian kings relied heavily upon military retainers called ministerials to enforce their will.[10] Although these men possessed the expensive equipment necessary for warriors at this time, they were not really knights, nor were they considered vassals, and the properties that they held could be easily alienated. In fact they were legally unfree, servile dependents of the king. Imperial ministerials, executing royal commands that were perceived as arbitrary, did much to enhance the view among the high aristocracy that the Salians were tyrants. Feudal suzerains they certainly were not.

Only at the end of the Salian century, during the reign of Henry V, does Weinfurter see the beginnings of a process of "feudalization," which occurred because the last Salian was forced to accommodate himself to the enormous social changes that had taken place during the course of the eleventh century. Whether or not the term "feudalization" properly describes this process will no doubt be a subject for future debates. It might be pointed out, however, that the power of those aristocrats, who in the end successfully challenged the Salian concept of royal authority, themselves had created their wealth and power by supervising the clearing of lands, the founding of cities, and the granting of municipal charters, as well as the using of unfree military retainers in their military and administrative entourages.[11] Whether or not the dynamics of this development can be summed up under the rubric of "feudalism" demands further discussion.

In the closing words to his book, Weinfurter, who is working on an analysis of the Hohenstaufen kings, the eventual successors of the Salians, posits that the latter dynasty attempted to accommodate the Salian concept of kingship to the "feudal" realities of the twelfth century, a premise that is sure to spark further discussion. Was the Salian era a disaster for Germany? Weinfurter thinks not. Although rulers were finally forced to share power with the nobility, institutionalized kingship was on a firmer foundation at the demise of Henry V than it had been when Henry II died a century earlier. The end of the Salian male line brought with it little concern about the survival of kingship per se.

All in all, the Salian period was a century of intense dynamism. It was an era of tremendous social, economic, political, and cultural upheaval. The work of Stefan Weinfurter, because of its intense focus on medieval German kingship within the context of this maelstrom of change, offers scholars who deal primarily with other parts of medieval Europe a model for fruitful comparative work. Students on various levels will find *The Salian Century* a stimulating introduction to and interpretation of a formative period in European history.

Introduction

A RULER SITS MAJESTICALLY on his throne. The writing above his head announces his name, Emperor Conrad (II). In his left hand he holds the orb. His right arm is stretched out and holds a medallion that contains the bust of an additional ruler, Emperor Henry (III). Below, suspended by connecting lines, follows a medallion bearing the image of Emperor Henry (IV) who, in turn, is connected to his children, a daughter Agnes to his right—here, for unknown reasons, named Adelheit—and beneath him sons, King Conrad and King Henry (V). The entire composition is framed by sections of wall and battlements, which suggest a palace or fortified house (see frontispiece).

This remarkable picture has been passed on to us in a copy of Ekkehard of Aura's *Chronicle*, dating ca. 1130.[1] It employs striking imagery to introduce the viewer to the Salian dynasty, the royal house, which ruled from 1024 to 1125. Recent research has established that the original manuscript on which this drawing is based, although no longer extant, probably was composed in 1106 or 1107.[2]

The miniature conveys a sense of singular unity and intimacy that ties the members of the royal house to each other; the houselike architecture framing the scene further emphasizes this intensified feeling of identity. The enthroned Emperor Conrad, the founder of the Salian house, dominates the picture and provides dynastic support and a firm foundation. Energy and vitality flow from his image into the succeeding generations and seem to provide strength and lasting stability for the entire dynasty.

Surprisingly though, the political situation in the realm reflected a very different reality in this period. The adolescent son of Henry IV, Henry V, depicted on the last medallion, had joined a conspiracy of princes in the winter of 1104–1105. In 1105 and 1106 he ruthlessly sought to wrest the royal power from his father, subjecting him to the deepest humiliation in the process. How can these events be reconciled with the harmony con-

veyed by the Salian family tree? The famous depiction of the Salian house
belongs to a group of miniatures originating within the sphere of the
young king (Henry V) who had rebelled against his father. But from the
very beginning, as the iconographic program of the Salian family subtly
indicates, the son's struggle for power was motivated less by personal
greed than by a desire to bond with his father on a level of higher dynastic
unity. The continuity of the dynastic mission seemed seriously imperiled
when the princes were no longer willing to follow Henry IV, who had
been severely weakened by his excommunication. These circumstances also
threatened the son's chances for royal succession. Henry V may have felt
compelled to act in the interest of the dynasty when he usurped his father's
power—an idea that will have to be examined more closely. Somehow the
strength and bond of the dynastic concept had transcended the rights of
the individual ruler.

The Salians' program of transpersonal, dynastically based kingship
was a new phenomenon in the East Frankish–German kingdom, and it
signals a new level of legitimating royal rule and authority. This departure from earlier norms leads directly to a concept of kingship that the
Hohenstaufens later espoused. They believed that their family represented
the last link in an imperial dynasty that had existed from the very beginning and held the only legitimate claim to rulership. How this concept of
kingship evolved during the Salian era and which ideological and constitutional changes played a role in this process will be a major theme of the
present study.

Scholars have frequently overlooked the sheer energy that the Salian
rulers devoted to shaping dynastic consciousness. Such references, if they
occur, are more apt to be found in older publications as, for example, in
Karl Hampe's classical work *Germany Under Salian and Hohenstaufen Emperors* (1908).[3] "It is hardly an exaggeration to claim that no other dynasty
in all of the German Middle Ages could compete with the Salians' genuine talent to rule," he wrote. "Despite extensive, corrosive struggles and a
decline in central authority," Hampe continues,

it could not be said that the realm's vitality was deteriorating at this time; its
military prowess was unshaken. Politically it was still the leading power, notwithstanding its problems. As the landed nobility began to retreat from an active role
in economic life, the lower strata of society, ministerials and peasants, were drawn
into a brisk economic upturn. Emerging towns absorbed the superfluous man-
power from the countryside and multiplied and enriched economic life. Growth
and mobility was everywhere! In the intellectual domain we can hardly speak of

a "Salian" culture in the same way as we refer to an Ottonian or Hohenstaufen one. While the Salian age brought forth great historical narratives and astounding works of architecture, it somehow lacked the introspection that is essential for generating extraordinary cultural feats. On the other hand, one should not underestimate the significance of the Salian era for the intellectual maturing process of the nation; the flourishing lay culture of the Hohenstaufen period would be unthinkable without the development that preceded it.[4]

If one ignores Hampe's turn-of-the-century nationalism, it is striking how his rough sketch already pinpoints the social forces that emerged side by side with the Salian kingship and how it grasps the dynamism of the Salian century. This era brought about fundamental changes that were neither initiated nor guided by the king, changes that would have a lasting impact on the realm and its people: "Growth and mobility everywhere!" Karl Hampe scratched only the surface of these phenomena, however; since he wrote, numerous extensive studies on the political, social, legal, economic, and religious aspects of the Salian period have appeared. Through detailed analysis scholars have arrived at a clearer and deeper understanding of the nature of the movements and social shifts that transformed eleventh-century society. Especially the ecclesiastical and monastic reform movements have been thoroughly investigated, foremost among them the investiture conflict, which can be roughly delimited by the years 1076 and 1122. Several comprehensive works of recent vintage scholars, emphasizing different aspects, provide an excellent overview of the latest insights into this era. Books by Hagen Keller and Egon Boshof cover the entire Salian period while those of Horst Fuhrmann, Friedrich Prinz, Alfred Haverkamp, Hermann Jakobs, and Eduard Hlawitschka either extend to or begin in the middle of the eleventh century.[5]

These diverse scholarly achievements show clearly that the history of the German realm during the Salian period must be understood as a composite of a great variety of forces, interacting with and counteracting each other on many different levels. In this context it is essential to be familiar with the circumstances that gave rise to various developments and to be aware of the consequences resulting from shifts within a network of connections, influences, and dependencies. Besides the king and his dynasty, the magnates of the realm, such as bishops and abbots, dukes, counts, and advocates, were major actors in the transformation of society. We further need to consider the altered patterns of noble lordship and the fundamental changes in the practice of ecclesiastical office. In addition, we must also focus on the rise of newly constituted groups, such as town dwellers ("burghers"), servile warriors, and peasants. Among these, the ministeri-als, a new class of military retainers and administrators, who, though of servile status, enjoyed special rights and privileges, eventually gained great prominence in society. Last but not least, new perceptions of the function-ality and role of Church and clergy need to be taken into consideration, as well as the functional ordering of society, the increasing precedence of "truth" over "custom," and the dichotomy of harsher punishment and obedience of dependent subjects. The investigation of each of these topics leads more deeply into the inner workings and social interactions of Salian society. The king and the ruling dynasty represent only a small segment within this intricate nexus of forces. The following monograph is meant only as a brief introduction to the Salian period and cannot possibly treat the realm and the social circumstances of its people exhaustively. But it will attempt to view the Salian kingship and its concept of royal rule within the complex context of social change, to outline the main currents of this tran-sitional age, to explore the nexus of forces through various examples, and to convey a sense of the fundamental changes that transformed the realm and the society during the Salian century.

I

Origins and Lordship of
the Salian Dynasty

ON 4 SEPTEMBER 1024, a new German king was elected in Kamba, a locality (long since vanished) on the right bank of the Rhine across from Oppenheim (see fig. 4). This new ruler, Conrad II, was a descendant of the noble family whose members later came to be called the Salians.

Who were the Salians? The term *reges salici* itself sheds little light on this question since it does not appear in the sources until the beginning of the twelfth century and hardly seems to reach much further into the past. The appellation could possibly have been derived from *sal*, an old German word for "lordship," on the basis that the Salian rulers favored hierarchical structures of governance (*Befehlsherrschaft*), a phenomenon that was already noticed by contemporary observers. More plausible, though, is a reference to the most distinguished "tribal" group among the Franks, the Salian Franks. Through an early Frankish legal code, the *lex Salica*, this name was preserved in the common memory over centuries. The Salian rulers were (Rhenish) Franks; the fact that Wipo, Conrad II's biographer, traces the family's maternal lineage to the Frankish royal houses may explain why the name *Salian* was transferred to Conrad II's dynasty. Strictly speaking only the sequence of emperors from Conrad II to Henry V (1024–1125) should be called Salian. However, scholars have long since expanded this term to include the tenth-century ancestors of this noble family, and I will continue this practice in the present study.

Wipo, though, never mentions the term *Salian* in his biography of Conrad II, dating circa 1044/45. He describes the emerging royal family as follows: "There were two men named Conrad. One was called Conrad the Elder because of his greater age; the other was known as Conrad the Younger." This opening refers to the two cousins who had become the final two candidates at the election of Kamba. Wipo continues:

Both were distinguished noble lords from Rhenish Franconia, and they were the sons of two brothers. Their fathers were named Henry and Conrad, respectively. These two fathers, in turn, were the sons of Duke Otto of Franconia who had two additional sons: Bruno and Wilhelm. Bruno became pope and assumed the name of Gregory.[1] Wilhelm, as bishop, had a lasting impact on the church of Strasbourg (1029–1041). But the two Conrads not only descended from the highest nobility on their paternal side, as mentioned earlier; their maternal lineage was hardly less illustrious. Conrad the Younger's mother, Matilda, descended from a daughter of King Conrad of Burgundy. Conrad the Elder's mother, named Adelheid, came from a distinguished noble family in Upper Lotharingia. She was the sister of the counts Gerhard and Adalbert who were constantly feuding with kings and dukes and were hardly more subdued during the reign of their relative, King Conrad [II]. Adelheid's ancestors supposedly descended from the ancient royal house of Troy whose kings had put their necks under the yoke of faith at the time of the confessor Remigius.[2]

Wipo thus invokes a connection with famous royal houses and infers that Conrad II, through his mother Adelheid, could trace his ancestry to the Merovingians, the Frankish dynasty that derived its legitimacy from Troy. In 496 the Merovingian king Clovis received the holy baptism from Bishop Remigius of Reims (ca. 462–533). What is striking about this genealogical construct, whose origin is associated with the inner circle of the Salian court, is the absence of any reference to familial ties with the Ottonians, the previous royal dynasty, notwithstanding the fact that Conrad II's great-grandmother, Luidgard, was a daughter of Otto the Great (936–973). Equally curious is the fact that the paternal line is only traced back to Duke Otto of Franconia, but not to the latter's illustrious father, Conrad the Red, who, as Otto the Great's son-in-law, had risen to fame and influence at the Ottonian court. There can be no doubt, however, that these genealogical connections were common knowledge during Wipo's lifetime, especially since Conrad the Red and his descendants were buried in the family vault in the cathedral church of Worms where their memory was nourished and preserved. These observations indicate that the first Salian rulers consciously kept their distance from the Ottonian kingship and that they attributed their paternal line's powerful position to its very own noble tradition and ducal foundation. We will scrutinize these matters more closely in connection with Conrad II's election.

Scholars, of course, have never been satisfied with Wipo's curtailed genealogical derivation of the Salians' paternal lineage. Numerous studies have concluded that the Salian ancestors must have belonged to the Widonen family,[3] an aristocratic clan whose appellation is based on the "leading name" Wido. The term "leading name" (*leitname*) refers to names that occur frequently in certain families and hence become associated with them. Members of the Widonen kindred, whose origins have been traced to the Moselle region of Upper Lotharingia (see Figs. 2, 3), appear in the sources as prominent supporters of the Carolingians as early as the seventh century. They held high administrative offices and intermittently occupied the episcopal see of Trier. Early on they founded a proprietary monastery at Mettlach on the Saar River in Upper Lotharingia; a second proprietary foundation, the monastery of Hornbach in the Bliesgau, was established in the same region around the middle of the eighth century[4] and was given to the great Irish-Frankish missionary Saint Pirmin, the founder of such famous monastic centers as Reichenau on Lake Constance in Swabia and Murbach in Alsace. The original power center of the Widonen was located in Upper Lotharingia and encompassed the upper reaches of the Moselle River and the watershed of its tributary, the Saar.[5] The first step toward an eastward expansion occurred with the foundation of the monastery of Hornbach and its large endowment of royal donations in the Wormsgau. These circumstances allowed the Widonen to extend their authority eastward across a vast belt of forests onto the plain of the middle Rhine region, a favored place for settlements since time immemorial (fig. 1). Around 760 a small monastic center, Saint Philipp, sprung up at Zell on the Pfrimm River west of Worms; as a subsidiary of their proprietary monastery at Hornbach, Saint Philipp was subordinated to the Widonen as well.

Toward the end of the eighth century the Widonen kindred split into several branches that created their own respective power centers in Brittany, around the lower ranges of the Loire River, and in the Italian duchy of Spoleto. Duke Wido of Spoleto, in fact, developed grandiose ambitions. In 888 he sought to attain the kingship of Burgundy and even managed to be crowned Roman emperor in 891. This lineage of the Widonen kindred was called the Lambertiner because of its "leading name" (*leitname*) Lambrecht.

One branch of the Widonen remained, however, in Upper Lotharingia and the upper Rhine region. Using the proprietary monastery of Hornbach in the Bliesgau as a base, this family expanded its dominion considerably in the course of the ninth century. To the west it controlled large holdings on the Saar River, despite the loss of Mettlach to the bishop of Trier; to the east it made substantial inroads toward the Rhine into

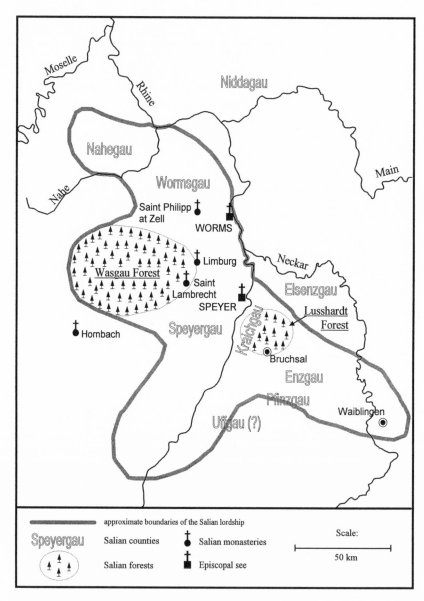

Moselle

Rhine

Niddagau

Nahegau

Main

Nahe

Wormsgau

Saint Philipp
at Zell

WORMS

Neckar

Limburg

Elsenzgau

Wasgau Forest

Saint
Lambrecht

SPEYER

Lusshardt
Forest

Hornbach

Speyergau

Kraichgau

Bruchsal

Enzgau

Pfinzgau

Uffgau (?)

Waiblingen

approximate boundaries of the Salian lordship

Speyergau   Salian counties   Salian monasteries

Scale:

50 km

Salian forests   Episcopal see

1. The Salian lordship at the beginning of the eleventh century.

the Wormsgau and Speyergau. At the beginning of the tenth century we encounter a certain count Werner in the Speyergau; from the time of his appearance in the sources the Salian lineage can be traced without interruption. Although the genealogical linkage between the Widonen and this Werner has not been firmly established, the fact that he held the same lands and offices and was connected to the same proprietary monastery, Hornbach, makes a familial relationship highly plausible.

This count Werner had the good fortune to wed a woman from the royal house of the Conradines, probably the sister of King Conrad I (911–918). Through this marital alliance the new leading name Conrad came into the family. But there were deeper implications to this marriage. When the Conradines lost their struggle against Otto the Great in 939, they also lost their preeminence in the middle Rhine region. A substantial portion of their previous power was now, undoubtedly with the king's consent, transferred to Count Werner's family, in particular to the latter's son Conrad, who, in addition to other advantages, could base his claims on kinship as well.

In 941 this Conrad, nicknamed "the Red," appears in possession of his father's counties in Nahegau, Wormsgau, and Speyergau; in addition, he held the county in Niddagau north of Frankfurt. In 947 he reinforced his close relationship to the Ottonian royal house by marrying Luidgard, the daughter of Otto the Great; but already before this wedding, in 944 or 945, the king had made him duke of Lotharingia. These events show clearly how the interests of the king and of Conrad the Red were closely intertwined. Otto promoted the preeminence of the Salian family in the middle Rhine region, while Conrad assumed the responsibility for Lotharingia, a duchy that was notoriously unreliable as a political partner. Conrad's task consisted in fostering this region's ties to the realm and in controlling its vast territory which reached from Alsace to the mouth of the Rhine, encompassing approximately the area between the Rivers Meuse and Rhine.

Therefore, it was a hard blow for Otto I when Conrad the Red joined a group of rebellious nobles in 953 who posed a serious threat to Otto's kingship. According to his chronicler Widukind,[6] the king complained bitterly about the ingratitude of his son-in-law: "He, whom I loved most, whom I promoted from a mediocre station to the highest dignity, to an exceptional position of power and official responsibility, he has my only son [referring to Otto's rebellious son Liudolf] on his side against me." The rebellion was put down and Conrad the Red lost the duchy of Lotharingia

Salians Buried in the Cathedral of Worms

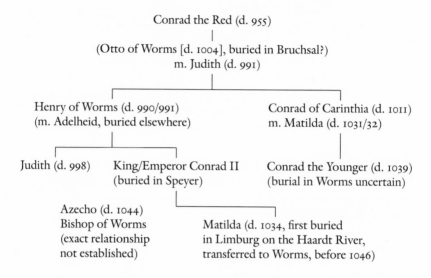

Conrad the Red (d. 955)

(Otto of Worms [d. 1004], buried in Bruchsal?)
m. Judith (d. 991)

Henry of Worms (d. 990/991)
(m. Adelheid, buried elsewhere)

Conrad of Carinthia (d. 1011)
m. Matilda (d. 1031/32)

Judith (d. 998)   King/Emperor Conrad II
(buried in Speyer)

Conrad the Younger (d. 1039)
(burial in Worms uncertain)

Azecho (d. 1044)
Bishop of Worms
(exact relationship
not established)

Matilda (d. 1034, first buried
in Limburg on the Haardt River,
transferred to Worms, before 1046)

in 954. Yet he submitted to the king and in 955 he joined him in the battle against the Hungarians on the Lechfeld near Augsburg.[7] Widukind reports: "Duke Conrad, the foremost of all in combat, suffering from battle fatigue caused by an unusually hot sun, loosened the straps of his armor to catch his breath when an arrow pierced his throat and killed him instantly. Upon the king's command his body was raised up with full honors and transported to Worms. This man, who was great and illustrious through the virtue of both his soul and his body, was buried there, accompanied by the tears and lamentations of the Franks."[8]

This report conveys clearly that Conrad the Red was an impressive individual in the opinion of his contemporaries, that he possessed all the virtues expected of a valiant warrior, and that the king, after his submission, looked upon him with special favor once more. After his death on the battlefield, Otto the Great honored him with a glorious funeral in Worms; there he was laid to rest in the crypt of the cathedral where he still reposes next to nine other members of his family. The choice of this grave site is indeed significant because in those times burial in an episcopal church was as a rule restricted to bishops or kings, in other words, to persons who had been consecrated. The remains of ordinary mortals, even those of powerful princes, were normally excluded from these holiest places of divine worship. Without a doubt, the honor and distinction bestowed on Conrad the Red enhanced the prestige of the Salian family in the long run and imbued it with a sense of confidence and mission.

Worms, consequently, assumed the character of a princely center for the Salians. On the same spot where the canonry of Saint Paul was later built, stood the comital residence of the Salian lords; this location was probably identical with that of the old Carolingian palace.[9] Further, it was in this locality where Werner and Conrad the Red had created the core of a territorial complex by combining allodial holdings with substantial portions of fiscal properties. Worms had become the center of Salian power (fig. 2).

The brilliant rise of the Salian house was hardly interrupted by Conrad the Red's death. King Otto I now directed his favors and attention toward Conrad's small son, his grandson, who also bore the name Otto. In 956, while still a minor, this Otto (henceforth referred to as Otto of Worms) already appears as count in the Nahegau. Eventually he combined the Wormsgau, Speyergau, Niddagau, and several other counties between the Rhine and Neckar Rivers into a nearly contiguous territorial complex in the middle and upper Rhine region.[10] When Otto II (973–983), the uncle of Otto of Worms, became king, however, he sought to curb the powerful position of his Salian relative on the middle Rhine. By making his nephew duke of Carinthia in 978, the king hoped to divert his energies to the remote southeastern region of the realm. A year later, on behalf of the bishop of Worms, he further pressured the Salian into giving up certain jurisdictional rights and revenues from immunities and tolls within the city.[11] The Salian prince only came to terms with these losses in 985, during the regency of Otto III, when he was formally compensated with the large Wasgau Forest and the important royal palace of Lautern,[12] crucial properties for the westward expansion of the Salian dominion. Around the same time Otto of Worms renounced the duchy of Carinthia, and in exchange apparently was rewarded with fiscal property and jurisdictional rights over the influential monastery of Weißenburg in Alsace.

Particularly instructive for the creation of Otto of Worms' dominion are two religious foundations, a canonry and a monastery, that can be traced to his initiative. In 975/76 the abbot Adalbert of Hornbach, at Otto's command (*iussu*), began restoring the monastery of Saint Philipp at Zell west of Worms. This locality, which we have encountered earlier, lay in ruins at that time.[13] The revived monastic center was designed as a chapter

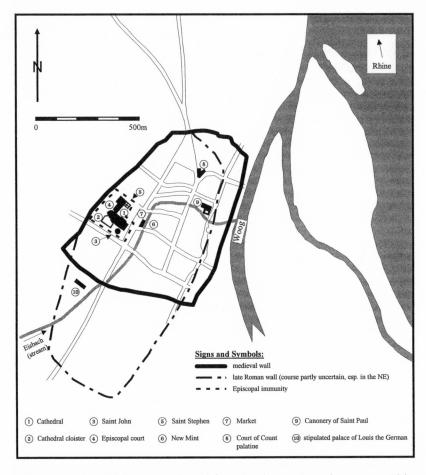

2. Worms in the Middle Ages (adapted from P. Classen, *Bemerkungen zur Pfalz-forschung*, 1963, ND 1983, p. 501).

house for canons who were to assume pastoral duties in the surrounding countryside; beyond its spiritual function though, the foundation would allow for a concentration of holdings and for a more effective mode of agricultural management. There is no doubt that the Salians or their representatives held the advocacy, that is, the secular administration, of this foundation, adding considerable strength to their authority in the region. The example of Saint Philipp vividly illustrates the type of power concentration that Otto of Worms pursued in the second half of the tenth century.[14]

The foundation of the monastery of Saint Lambrecht on the Speyer-bach in 987 (not 977), located above Neustadt on the Wine Road west of Speyer, may be even more important. Its interesting foundation charter, apparently crafted at a later date on the basis of earlier records, emphasizes the fact that this institution was established with the consent of the emperor Otto III.[15] This reference indicates that his permission actually had been required, as generally was the case when fiscal lands were involved in such a foundation. The document provides a meticulous description of the monastery's substantial property concentration which—at least partially—consisted of fiscal lands. Several other rights which are mentioned also seem to derive from royal rights. The charter further states that the advocacy, that is, the jurisdictional and administrative authority (*Gesamtheit der Herrschaftsrechte*), over the new monastery shall always be held by the oldest member of the Salian family in agnatic succession. Heretofore neither the king (!) nor any other prince or secular authority could lay claim to any jurisdictional rights whatsoever.[16]

A close analysis of this document's content reveals an interesting scenario: allodial holdings and fiscal lands were being merged through their transfer to the monastery and combined into a unified advocacy. Since this advocacy thus in principle was indivisible, this move was obviously designed to tie the secular authority over Saint Lambrecht irreversibly to the Salian family. The adherence to the principle of seniority, that is, primogeniture, the granting of priority rights to the eldest son, further promoted the concentration and stabilization of their lordship. This does not mean, however, that the spiritual motivation should be discounted; the investment in the salvation of the soul was no doubt a dominant concern in the life of medieval people. Still, jurisdictional and administrative considerations played a significant role and were consciously interwoven with religious motives. Such an approach, termed patrimonialization of properties and rights, became typical in the formation of "modern" territorial lordships in the eleventh and twelfth centuries. As has been shown, however, the Salians pursued these political strategies and policies as early as the tenth century. This factor is crucial for evaluating the way this family perceived itself and its mission later on. Starting with Otto of Worms a marked trend toward the establishment of an autonomous lordship emerged, a type of lordship that existed independently of any royal favor or commission. The Salians' conviction that their family's prominence had risen up from its own roots and innate rights must have gained increasing significance during this time; for Wipo, as has been shown, traces the male lineage of the Salian genealogy back no further than Otto of Worms.

The powerful position that Otto of Worms had established in the middle Rhine region was already recognized by contemporaries and led to the unusual circumstance that the crown granted him the title of duke (*dux*) even when he did not yet hold a duchy. Modern scholarship has demonstrated that this titular duchy, the first ever documented in German history, rested upon a mighty complex of dominions and counties that were concentrated around Worms.[17] The designation *Wormatiensis dux Francorum* describes this situation quite accurately; since a Franconian duchy no longer existed at this time, this phrase should appropriately be translated as the Frankish Duke of Worms. Worms had practically become identical with the family name. *Dux* establishes the rank of the family within the structure of the realm. *Francorum* could be seen as a reference to the former duchy of Franconia, but more likely it relates to the Frankish origin of the Salians since their duchy was based solely on the newly acquired Salian patrimony at the turn of the millennium. Their ducal rank had arisen by virtue of its own strength and eventually had to be recognized by the crown. Otto of Worms used his powerful position to restructure his dominion internally as well; there is no doubt that he—just as the Bavarian duke around that time—installed counts in his middle Rhenish counties, among them the Emichonen, the later counts of Leiningen. These should not be called "sub-counts," as some scholars have done, because they were definitely subordinates of the "duke" and stood in a feudal-type relationship (*feudalrechtlich*) to him.

It is important to keep these particular characteristics of the Salians' noble and ducal lordship and their dynastic consciousness in mind when we consider the further development of their princely house and the eventual emergence of the Salian kingship. It must have been a crucial element to the way Conrad II, the first Salian king, perceived himself that his father, Henry, was the eldest son of Otto of Worms. This Henry of Worms was to assume the leadership in the family and his marriage to Adelheid, whose ancestors hailed from the Merovingian royal house according to Wipo, was appropriate to support this role. But Henry died prematurely before his father Otto, probably around 990/991, in any case before the year 1000, which meant that his seniority rights were transferred to his younger brother, Conrad of Carinthia (see genealogical chart).[18] At the beginning of the new millennium these unforeseen events seem to have caused considerable tension among the members of the Salian house at Worms. For Henry's young son, whose name was also Conrad (the Elder) and who would become King Conrad II, rebelled against the setback of his line. Taking advantage of this family dispute, Bishop Burchard of Worms (1000–1025) took the eleven or twelve-year-old Conrad under his tutelage in order to break down the unified front of the Salian house.[19]

At this juncture the newly elected king Henry II (1002–1024) entered the scene. As soon as he assumed the kingship, Henry began to assert his royal authority by implementing a program of unusually intensive governance encompassing the whole realm. He energetically sought to monopolize royal power politically as well as ideologically and to permeate the realm as thoroughly as possible with his claims to royal sovereignty. Presenting himself as *vicarius* and *typus Christi*, he emphatically and with deep conviction embraced the idea of the Christian kingship as a legitimation for his actions. He claimed undivided, unrestricted royal power throughout the entire realm (*sine aliqua divisione*).[20] The programmatic concept of viewing royal authority as a divinely ordained mandate and a manifestation of God's will had already emerged under Otto the Great and had been vividly formulated in the coronation ceremony of Mainz around 960. Henry II, however, was the first king who sought to enforce this principle systematically throughout the kingdom and to subject all ecclesiastical and secular princes to its rigor. For the first time in the history of German kingship one can observe a trend toward a constitutional order that places the king at the apex of the hierarchical pyramid. Of course, no constitution in the modern sense of the word existed at that time and no such thing had been set down in writing. The term *constitution* must, therefore, be understood as a set of unwritten rules which governed the interaction of the various cooperating and opposing forces within the power structure of the realm.

It should not come as a surprise that a ruler with such a strong sense of mission and authority[21] would move energetically against the attempts of a noble family like the Salians who unusually early had begun to build an independent base of power. To undermine the Salians' progress in building an autonomous lordship, Henry II decided to oust them from their center of power at Worms where Otto of Worms had ensconced himself. Although one easily can understand that the king could count on Bishop Burchard of Worms as a faithful ally in this endeavor, it seems amazing that he was able to persuade Otto of Worms in October 1002 to give up the Salian possessions and the fortified family residence within the town of

Worms. The underlying reasons for these events remain subject to speculation. It is conceivable that the aging Otto, who died two years later, had simply become too weak to put up an effective fight. We also need to consider that the Salian "duke" received substantial holdings in exchange for his losses. The king compensated him with the important royal palace in Bruchsal with its extensive properties and the royal forest of Lußhardt. In material terms these estates were much more valuable than those that had been given up in Worms, a fact that might have mitigated the loss of the old power center. Otto of Worms may even have been buried in Bruchsal, perhaps an indication that he had already contemplated the formation of a new power center.

In spite of Henry II's success in this one instance, the Salians remained adversaries of his concept of royal authority throughout his reign. They did not comply with his wishes and pursued political schemes that suited their own purposes, a situation which led to constant conflicts and mistrust on the part of the king. During this time Conrad the Elder, the future King Conrad II, assumed overall responsibility for the Salian family affairs and took on custody of his cousin Conrad the Younger whose father, Duke Conrad of Carinthia, had died unexpectedly in 1011. The Salians experienced this period as a time of humiliation, as an ordeal from God. In any case, that is how Wipo presents these years in his biography of King Conrad II.[22] These observations are crucial because they confirm once again that Conrad the Elder's unusual confidence and remarkable sense for the Salian family's noble mission, as we have traced it up to the time of his royal election, was not in any way connected to his predecessor's kingship. This may also be the reason why the names Otto and Brun, which had been adopted from the Ottonian royal house, completely disappear from the Salian dynasty at this time. The new leading name, Henry, in contrast, probably was perceived as a Salian name already and was derived from the first Salian king's father, Henry of Worms.

Conrad the Elder's marriage to Gisela in 1016 must have been of great significance for his self-perception as well. She was the daughter of Hermann II of Swabia, who had emerged as a viable rival of Henry II's in 1002. We can even assume that Hermann might have been the favorite in a regular election, but had proved inadequate to challenge Henry's iron will. For a short time though, at least until he submitted to the new ruler, Hermann could consider himself a king in his own right and could foster a sense of royal rank and aura in his family. Gisela's mother, Gerberga, was the daughter of King Conrad of Burgundy (937–993), whose ancestors, as Wipo correctly noted, "had come from the family of Charlemagne." In these terms, Conrad the Elder was married to a royal princess; and his bride brought not only important Conradine holdings in Swabia into the marital alliance, but also could contribute to the rank and prestige of the Salian house. How Gisela's presence affected Conrad the Elder's position is hard to determine; but if we consider her crucial role during Conrad II's kingship, we must conclude that her influence was considerable.

2

The Dynamic Beginnings of the New Royal Dynasty

EMPEROR HENRY II DIED on 13 July 1024 without any male offspring and without a designated successor. He had evidently lived with the idea that his kingship would revert to God after his death, and this belief had motivated him to designate the Church as his heir. Henry II's creation of the new bishopric of Bamberg in 1007 and his subsequent transfer of vast land holdings to this see might also be connected to this notion. In these actions kingship and the powers inherent in it appear very personal, almost individualized.

Henry II's passing, and the demise of king and kingship in one person, caused great consternation among the powerful elite and throughout the realm. We must remember that the "German Reich" was by no means a stable, well-defined entity at that time, in spite of Henry II's efforts to improve the unity of the realm. For better or worse, only the king could muster enough power and prestige to integrate and unify far-flung regions and interests. If the king died without making provisions for a successor, it jeopardized the whole polity of the realm, threatened it with dire unrest and discord, possibly even total disintegration. Especially in Italy, where Otto the Great had extended his suzerainty even south of Rome, efforts to break away from the German crown apparently materialized at once. Abbot Bern of Reichenau (1008–1048) implored his colleague, Abbot Alberich of Como (1010–1028), in an extremely concerned letter to employ the whole weight of his influence to forestall hasty decisions in Italy. For the sake of imperial unity, he pleaded for clear minds to prevail: "You, as responsible members of your realm, should bide your time until we will again be united in the blissful community of a common king, until his authority will direct us, until his political skills will once again bring forth the type of brilliant men who refuse to be separated by the harshness of the Alps or to be split apart by public or private affairs."[1] In any case, the letter urged that no action should be taken until the election assembly at Kamba had taken place.

The situation in the realm was very unsettled; and this crisis evidently released a flurry of activities among the imperial princes. Bishops, dukes, counts, and other notables assumed joint responsibility for terminating the looming interregnum without delay. Wipo, the chronicler, characterizes the events as follows: "Convinced that there was no better and faster way to avert the menace, the [mentioned] bishops, dukes, and other nobles labored diligently and with remarkable perseverance to end the troubled polity's condition of being without a ruler [that is, to find a new ruler as soon as possible]."[2] Within a few short weeks—remarkably fast considering the communication network of those times—many intricate negotiations were conducted, and in the beginning of September, barely six weeks after Henry II's death, the concerned parties had agreed to convene an election assembly at Kamba on the Rhine. On 4 September 1024, the electors reached a consensus: the Salian prince Conrad the Elder was chosen to be the new king.

This royal election raised many questions, the most obvious being, "Why did the choice fall on a member of the Salian family?" Scholars generally defer to the Salian family's bloodlines and legitimate claims to the throne as the main reason; indeed one has to begin with the assumption that hereditary principles must have played an important role. As previously mentioned, the Salians were directly related to the Ottonian dynasty through Luidgard, the daughter of Otto the Great. But did that relationship determine the succession? Did the electors of 1024 basically restrict themselves to determining the closeness of hereditary rights of the respective candidates?

The description in Wipo's *Deeds of the Emperor Conrad II* provides us with detailed information about the election proceedings.[3] However, scholars generally agree that this report was embellished and tendentious in its nature. Specialists suspect that the author deviated from the actual events because he was intent on portraying the election as a manifestation of the collective will. Guided by divine inspiration, the leading magnates, representing all regions of the realm, chose the one who was most suited to wear the crown. Wipo's tendentiousness is readily apparent when he asserts that Saxons and other specific persons and groups had participated in the election at Kamba in spite of their documented absence. For these reasons, most scholars have come to the conclusion that Wipo must have described a fictitious election.

Despite the fact that specific details of this judgment can hardly be contested, we must consider whether Wipo's account may not reflect the predominant sentiment among the assembled princes at Kamba; Wipo may simply have relied on the prevailing mood to convey a somewhat idealized version of the actual events. This raises several questions. Is it plausible to assume that the electors of 1024 as well as the society at large may have had definite ideas about the type of characteristics and attributes that were desirable in their future king? Could it be that the search for these qualities would have favored Conrad II's candidacy independent of his hereditary prerequisites? In this context we must recall the sense of imminent danger that had gripped the imperial polity during the weeks preceding the election. Unifying the realm and finding means to secure permanent stability were matters of great urgency, matters that could not be resolved by a kingship that was restricted to *one* individual king. It is possible, therefore, that people expected the Salians with their highly developed dynastic consciousness and their "modern" concept of lordship to be more suited for these tasks. The electors made their choice, so to speak, in anticipation of the realm's future stability. Such a hypothesis would explain why Wipo had literally the entire realm participate in the election and, especially, why he held the opinion that not one individual person but an entire noble family, the house of the Salians, had been elevated to the kingship in 1024.

Following intricate negotiations and the elimination of additional unnamed contenders (whose existence has been questioned by some scholars), two candidates remained according to Wipo: the Salian prince, Conrad the Elder, and his cousin, Conrad the Younger, the son of Conrad "of Carinthia." The elder was probably about thirty-five, the younger twenty-two years old at this time and jointly they represented the Salian "house." However, the younger Conrad controlled the main portion of the Salian patrimony because seniority rights had been shifted to *his* father around the turn of the millennium after the death of his uncle, Henry "of Worms," Conrad the Elder's father. Wipo's report reads as follows: "Between these two, the elder and the younger Conrad, the remaining nobility could not reach a decision. In secret council almost all of them chose the elder Conrad, ardently desiring him, because of his valor and his righteousness; yet because of Conrad the Younger's powerful position, they withheld their opinion to prevent the two men from quarreling amongst themselves over their striving for the highest honor." Finally, according to Wipo, Conrad the Elder saved the day by taking his younger cousin aside and saying to him:

I feel with joy how my inner strength is growing since the two of us were the only ones who were unanimously nominated by this great assembly so that one [of us] may be elevated to the kingship. . . . Whatever persuaded the others that we may be better suited for this task, for this let us render thanks to God, our creator. Since we have been found worthy of consideration for such a high honor through the consensus of others, we must take care that we do not dishonor this favor through a family quarrel. . . . The collective desire, will, and consent of Franks, Lotharingians, Saxons, Bavarians, and Swabians combined to favor us, the shoots of one root, of one house (*domus*), of one indissoluble domestic community. No one will suspect that two men who are joined through so many bonds could become enemies.

Conrad the Elder then suggested: "If I sense that the spirit of the people wants you, that it desires you as their king and lord, by no perversity will I divert this good from you; in contrast, I will vote for you even more joyfully than the others because I believe that I am closer to you than they are. If, however, God should favor me, I have no doubt that you will be equally obliging on my behalf." The younger Conrad supposedly answered that he was in complete agreement. "When these words were spoken, as was observed by many, the elder Conrad bent down ever so slightly and kissed his cousin, and this kiss was the first indication to the assembly that they had reached an agreement."

This version of Conrad the Elder's speech was, of course, crafted by Wipo; but that the conference between the two cousins actually occurred has never been doubted. Since the Salian house had been singled out for the kingship, a clear mutual understanding between the two contenders had become indispensable, at least for the moment, for later Conrad the Younger indeed joined his older cousin's opponents. After the conclusion of this "domestic" agreement, Archbishop Aribo of Mainz (1021–1031), the presiding official, finally could proceed with the vote. In the context of this election we have the earliest documentation of the archbishop of Mainz's right to vote first (*Erststimmrecht*), and this tradition actually may have been established on this occasion. Because the opposing faction of Lotharingians had left the assembly early, Conrad the Elder was now chosen in an unanimous decision as the "new ruler and protector of the realm." An early departure of those who held divergent views was typical at the election of a medieval king. The voting itself became simply a confirmation of the prevailing opinion and was understood as a manifestation of the divine will; the decision was unanimous because it was preordained by the Christian world order.

This manifestation of the collective will (*Kur*) along with the acclamation of the people legitimized kingship. Following the election, the empress Kunigunde, widow of Emperor Henry II, presented the royal insignia to the new king. The chronicler Wipo commented: "I believe that the favor of heavenly grace, indeed, was not absent from this election since men with extraordinary power, among them many dukes and margraves, bare of envy and contention, chose one who by birth, virility, and allodial goods was any body's equal, but who, compared to his peers, held few beneficies and powers from the realm." Once more we are reminded that Conrad II did not owe his prestige and thus his kingship to the promotion of the previous dynasty but rather to his personal virtues. His status of power and rank had grown up independently and was first and foremost rooted in the Salian house itself.

The election at Kamba, as indicated earlier, took place under the auspices of Archbishop Aribo of Mainz. He followed in the footsteps of Archbishop Willigis (975–1011) who had played a major role in the royal elevation of 1002. In each instance the archbishop of Mainz held a pivotal position in the realm and both times the newly elected king was crowned in the cathedral of Mainz. Conrad II's coronation took place on 8 September 1024. This day, the feast of the birth of the Holy Virgin, held great significance for the Salian monarchs because of their special veneration of Mary. After completing the customary ritual of anointing the new king's head, chest, shoulders, and arms with holy unction, Aribo bestowed the royal crown on Conrad II. The powerful archbishops of Mainz, whose vast metropolitan domain reached from the Rhine far eastward into Thuringia and Saxony and contained fifteen suffragan bishoprics, including Chur, Constance, Strasbourg, Speyer, Worms, Würzburg, Augsburg, Eichstätt, Bamberg, Prague, Olomouc, Paderborn, Verden, Hildesheim, and Halberstadt, considered themselves the spiritual leaders of the imperial church (see fig. 3). The expansion of royal preeminence and the energetic assertion of royal authority throughout the realm depended heavily on the episcopate during this period; and the metropolitan of Mainz, who was imperial archchaplain as well, did not hesitate to take advantage of these converging interests to further his own position within the imperial polity.

Archbishop Aribo had favored Conrad II's candidacy from the very beginning; one might even say that he actually masterminded his election. The metropolitan of Mainz, more than any other prince, bore the

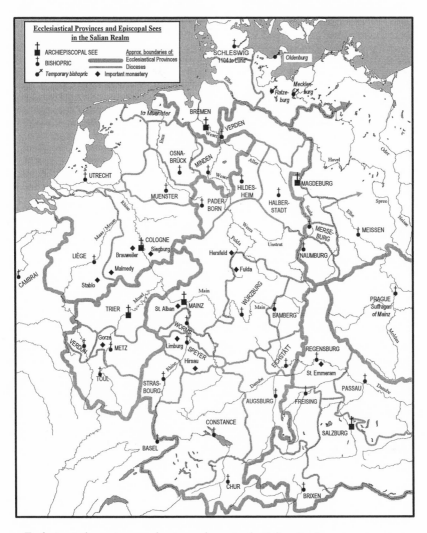

Ecclesiastical Provinces and Episcopal Sees in the Salian Realm

■ ARCHIEPISCOPAL SEE
● BISHOPRIC
✗ Temporary bishopric   ◆ Important monastery

Approx. boundaries of:
▬▬▬ Ecclesiastical Provinces
───── Dioceses

3. Ecclesiastical provinces and episcopal sees in the Salian Realm.

responsibility for preserving imperial unity that was in turn a prerequisite for peace (*pax*) and for the healthy growth of ecclesiastical life. Conrad II seemed ideally suited for these tasks in Aribo's eyes. At first, the archbishop concerned himself very little with genealogical questions. These matters became an issue, however, following Conrad's coronation, when Aribo was asked to crown the royal wife, Gisela, as well, either immediately or the next day. Unspecified charges against the queen had meanwhile been brought to the archbishop's attention. Today it is generally assumed that these allegations must have involved Gisela's marriage to Conrad II which, because of consanguinity, may have been in violation of canon law. In such matters Aribo would not compromise, as he had demonstrated by his ruthless legal action against the marriage of Count Otto of Hammerstein. Aribo, a descendant of the old Aribonen kindred from Bavaria, was an almost fanatical advocate of biblical and canonical norms. He was so convinced of his own infallibility, in fact, that Abbot Bern of Reichenau remarked in a letter with mocking praise: "Divine providence has endowed you with such riches of knowledge that it did not only guide you through the waters of the Holy Book up to your ankles or to your knees, but clear up to your waist."[4] Adhering strictly to his principles, Aribo declined to crown Gisela. If consanguinity was indeed the underlying cause for his refusal, it might indicate that originally he had not troubled himself with the extended kinship of the newly elected royal couple.

In the long run, Aribo's refusal had grave implications for the coronation privileges of the metropolitans of Mainz, particularly because his colleague and relative in Cologne, Archbishop Pilgrim (1021–1036), eagerly agreed to crown Gisela in his cathedral at Cologne on 21 September 1024. Prior to the royal elevation, Pilgrim had sided with the Salian opposition and now welcomed the opportunity to curry favor with the new king. His willingness to accommodate the new dynasty paid off, for Conrad II again selected the archbishop of Cologne for the coronation of his son, Henry III, at Easter 1028. This time the ceremony took place in the collegiate church of Saint Mary's at Aachen which, in principle, became the preferred site for all future coronations.

The election of Conrad II, as has become apparent, was accompanied by great expectations. It was hoped that an energetic kingship would provide a firm anchor for the realm's unity and security. How did the first Salian monarch approach these tasks? Initially, it was crucial for the new king to establish his royal presence throughout the realm. He accomplished this through a perambulation (*Umritt*) of his kingdoms which also provided the opportunity to obtain homage from those magnates who had not been present at Kamba (fig. 4). Even the Saxons recognized the new king *post factum*, probably on 25 December 1024, at Minden. In June 1025 he also won the support of many Italian magnates at an assembly in Constance. This type of royal perambulation did not yet have a long-standing tradition; it was first introduced at the beginning of Henry II's reign. By

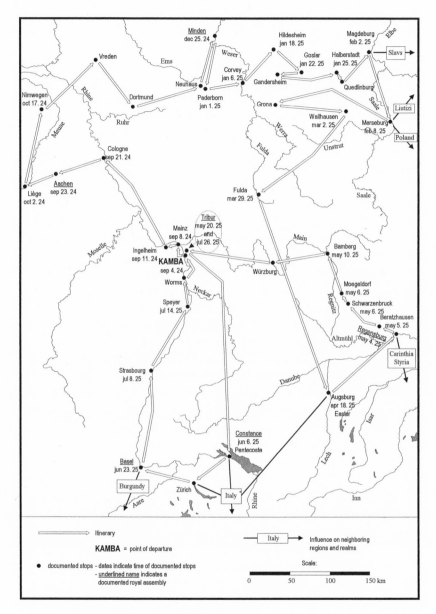

4. Perambulation of King Conrad II (adapted from H. Keller, *Zwischen regionaler Begrenzung und universalem Horizont*, 1986, p. 76).

this means, Henry wanted to demonstrate his notion of a royal authority that dominated the entire realm. In this respect, Conrad II clearly followed in the footsteps of his predecessor; and scholars have long since recognized that the first Salian monarch had a definite affinity to other aspects of Henry II's rule as well.[5] Although the Salians, as mentioned earlier, thought of themselves as an independent dynasty, devoid of any connections to the previous royal house, Conrad II nevertheless immediately grasped the significance of the principles that had determined his predecessor's policies. For instance, he retained the personnel of the royal chapel and chancery, followed Henry II's example in his relations with the Church and Italy, and pursued similar notions of empire. Last but not least, he managed to integrate the kingdom of Burgundy into the imperial polity and thus concluded a project that had been initiated by his predecessor.

One should note, however, that Conrad II saw his predecessor's kingship as a resumption of rulership practices that had long been associated primarily with Charlemagne's rule (768–814). Henry II's programmatic concept of royal leadership clearly embodied many characteristics of Charlemagne's policies, such as the energetic restructuring of the imperial polity, the forging of unity through a firm hand, the systematic reliance on the services of the imperial church (*Reichskirche*), and the splendid exaltation of the ruler by means of the imperial dignity. Henry II's motto of the *Renovatio regni francorum* (Renewal of royal dominion of the Franks) had derived undoubtedly from this conception. Following the example of Charlemagne, this program was based on the idea of a Christian sacral king whose undivided authority was recognized throughout the realm and was hierarchically superior to that of any duke, count, margrave, or bishop.[6] Shortly after his election, Conrad II demonstrated his intent to follow this very tradition. On 23 September 1024, two days after his wife, Gisela, been crowned at Cologne, Conrad entered Aachen with his court and placed himself on Charlemagne's throne. He meant to rule just like Charlemagne and his intentions were no secret to the world. "Charlemagne's stirrups are suspended from Conrad's saddle" was a common saying in those days, according to Wipo.

Conrad II's determination to emulate Charlemagne's leadership, no doubt, motivated his prompt decision to cross the Alps into Italy in order to acquire the imperial crown. At the beginning of 1026, as soon as he had managed to rein in his opponents at home, he began preparing his Italian journey. He was in such a hurry that he ordered his host to assemble at Augsburg in the wintry chill of February 1026, in a season when it was hard to secure fodder and provisions. Shortly thereafter he and his army appeared in Lombardy where he could rely on the support of Archbishop Aribert of Milan (1019–1045). This metropolitan, in the wake of Henry II's example, probably crowned Conrad II king of Italy during his stay in Milan. However, Conrad's position was still precarious since the Italian margraves had formed an alliance against the new king; and the cities did not offer a safe haven either. In Ravenna, for example, there was an uprising and the Germans, as we hear from Wipo, first had to prove their military prowess: "The Germans, however, resisted with arms and ingenuity, readied themselves for combat, surrounded the Ravennese from front and rear, cut a path toward each other with raging swords, and left those, who were caught between them, dead, wounded, or fleeing. A certain Count Eppo, a valiant warrior from Bavaria, came out of the city with a banner and overpowered those who stood upon the bridge. Most of them were hurled down from the bridge by the sole effort of this man and perished in the water."[7] This manifestation of strength subdued both land and people; the next morning the surviving Ravennese appeared in sack cloth, barefoot, and with blank swords, "as was required of defeated 'citizens' according to their laws," to pay the penalties that had been imposed.

Such a show of military prowess and superiority was crucial to establish the king's authority; for a good king had to be successful in combat. If necessary, he even had to resort to violence to enforce his rights and imperial prerogatives. German hegemony over Italy was, indeed, considered an imperial prerogative at that time. The idea, first advanced by Charlemagne's Lombard conquest and later reaffirmed by Otto the Great, had become an integral component of constitutional thinking within the imperial polity. The German kings' involvement in Italian politics had undoubtedly been motivated by a number of ever-changing political and economic realities; but its guiding principle was based on the imperial prerogatives and the kings' obligation to implement and preserve them. Such considerations show clearly why a king like Conrad II, who wanted to meet his obligations in an exemplary manner, moved to settle the "Italian question" without delay.

Attaining the imperial crown had become a fundamental right for the German kings ever since Otto the Great had established this linkage in 962, and since his successors had followed in his footsteps. In a diploma that was issued for the church of Utrecht at Cremona on 14 June 1026, Conrad II leaves no doubts about his convictions in this respect, for he calls himself "Chonradus divina favente clementia rex Francorum, Langobardorum et ad imperium designatus romanorum" (Conrad, by the grace of God, king of the Franks and the Lombards [Italians] and designated for the imperial crown of the Romans).[8] As king of the Franks (i.e., in Germany), and of the Lombards (in Italy), he was entitled to the imperial crown of the Romans. One generation later, under his son Henry III, this connection emerges as part of the royal title itself. During his first year in office, Henry III issued a diploma on 14 January 1040, where we encounter the designation *Romanorum rex*, king of the Romans, for the first time.[9] Subsequently, this title, circumscribing the imperial kingship, occurred ever more frequently and eventually became the rule under the last Salian monarch, Henry V (1106–1125).

Conceptually, such a blending of Frankish kingship with the crown of imperial Rome formed a part of Conrad II's vision from the very beginning of his rule. Pursuing this idea with unwavering zeal, he achieved his imperial coronation in Rome on Easter 1027 when both he and his wife, Gisela, were crowned by Pope John XIX (1024–1032). In the presence of such luminaries as King Cnut of Denmark, King Rudolph III of Burgundy, and Abbot Odilo of Cluny, just two years after Conrad II's elevation to the kingship, the newly emerging Salian dynasty staged a magnificent demonstration of its imperial aspirations.

Conrad II's ambitions did not stop at this point, however. Shortly after returning to Germany in June 1027, he sent an embassy to the imperial court at Byzantium which was instructed to win a bride for his young son Henry. The delegation, headed by Bishop Werner of Strasbourg (1001–1028), experienced great difficulties when King Stephen of Hungary refused passage through his lands. Subsequently, the group reached Byzantium only after a harrowing sea voyage via Venice. The envoys were given an honorable reception at the court of Basileus Constantine VIII and as a gift of recognition received a precious piece of the Holy Cross, measuring more than thirty centimeters (about twelve inches). The significance of this relic, as we shall see, would soon spark a fervent veneration of the Cross throughout the realm.

Marriageable ladies with imperial credentials, however, were in short supply in Byzantium at that time, and the death of Bishop Werner of Strasbourg must have delayed negotiations further. When the basileus felt his own end approaching soon thereafter, he ordered a Byzantine magnate by the name of Romanos Argyros to leave his current wife immediately, lest he be blinded, and to wed one of the imperial daughters in order to become his successor. Constantine VIII died on 12 November 1028. The new emperor now offered one of his own sisters to the Salian delegation; but the women in question were in all likelihood already married. Since the new head of the embassy, Count Manegold of Donauwörth, did not want to engage in such dealings, the envoys returned to Germany empty-handed early in 1029.

What was the purpose for this pursuit of a Byzantine bride? The newly crowned Salian emperor obviously was eager to have his meteoric rise recognized by an authority of equal rank through a marriage alliance. The renowned splendors of the Byzantine court and its imperial legitimation through Roman continuity must have been the driving force behind Conrad II's efforts to seek a marital union between the two houses. Supported by such familial ties, the strength and prestige of Roman legitimacy could provide an independent rationale for the permanent establishment of a Salian dynasty with imperial stature. Two imperial seals from Conrad II's reign illustrate that such ideas really played a crucial role. The first of these—attached to a royal charter issued on 23 August 1028[10]— on its reverse side shows the figure of the emperor's young son Henry, surrounded by the words *Heinricus spes imperii* (Henry, the hope of the empire) (fig. 5). At Easter of the same year, just a few months earlier, the eleven-year-old Henry had been crowned king and heir apparent of his father at Aachen. The wording on the imperial seal, however, emulating a Byzantine custom, already alluded to him as future *emperor*. A second imperial seal from this period, originating in the year 1033,[11] shows on its adverse side the pictures of Conrad II and his son Henry, again alluding to the idea of a "co-emperorship," embodied in the father-son relationship. On the reverse we find a stylized view of Rome with the inscription *Aurea Roma* (Golden city of Rome) and surrounded by the following text: *Roma caput mundi / regit orbis frena rotundi* (Rome, the head of the world, holds the reins of the globe) (fig. 6). This clearly indicates that Conrad II viewed his imperial office as a continuation of the Roman tradition; in his eyes, it had sprung from the same root as the Byzantine emperor's. Conrad II's Trojan origin (through his mother's lineage), as reported by Wipo, seems to fit into this concept as well; for the Romans, according to ancient tradition and contemporary belief, descended from the Trojans; and thus the Salian and the Byzantine imperial houses could claim the same origin.

All these initiatives, maxims, and programmatic declarations pursued by Conrad II and his inner circle revolved around one single purpose, namely, to tie the kingship and the imperial office to the Salian dynasty. The Salians' unusually energetic and targeted pursuit of patrimony long

5. Imperial seal of Conrad II of 23 August 1028 (MGH DD
K II. 129) (Posse, *Die Siegel der deutschen Kaiser und Könige*,
1, 1909, plate 13, nos. 5 and 6).

6. Imperial seal of Conrad II of 19 July 1033 (MGH DD
K II. 195) (Bayerisches Hauptstaatsarchiv, Munich, Kaiser-
selekt 337).

before they became kings and the great expectations placed in the new ruler by the election at Kamba must have been the main reasons for the remarkable dynastic consciousness that became the hallmark of the first Salian king and emperor. A famous fresco, which has recently been rediscovered and restored, reflects these ideas programmatically. Painted in the apse of the cathedral church of Aquileia around 1028, the mural depicts the imperial house of the Salian dynasty. Placed on the right side of the Virgin Mary with her child, Conrad II, Gisela, and their young son Henry III, "the hope of the Empire," appear among figures of saints (figs. 7, 8). Not the individual ruler is represented as was the custom in previous periods, but the prospective dynasty as a group, pointing toward the future. As an aside we might point out once more that Mary occupies a central position in this representation, underscoring the Salians' special relationship to the Holy Virgin.

These observations beg a fundamental question. To what extent had the idea of transpersonal kingship (a kingship that would endure as an institution and constitutional entity beyond the person of any individual king) already been incorporated in Conrad II's concept of royal lordship? We must recall that fear and unrest prevailed after the death of Henry II; the realm was threatened by disunity since the power of the kingship had expired with the king. The kingship could not be separated from the person of the king. An episode related by Wipo provides an interesting illustration of this context. During Pentecost 1025 a group of Italian nobles appeared before the ruler at an assembly in Constance to render homage. Among them were several citizens of Pavia who did not find favor with the king, however. To explain Conrad II's displeasure, Wipo offers the following explanation: the royal palace in Pavia, which "once had been magnificently built by Theoderic" and richly adorned by Otto III, had been torn down to its foundation by the Pavians following Henry II's death so that no future king would ever again consider the construction of a palace in their city. The representatives of Pavia tried to justify their actions with these arguments: "Whom did we offend after all? We served our emperor humbly and faithfully clear to the end of his life. We only destroyed the house of the king after his death when we no longer had a king. We, therefore, have done no wrong." Conrad II, however, replied: "I know that you did not destroy the house of your king since you did not have one at that time. But you cannot deny that you destroyed a royal palace. Although the king is dead, the things connected to the kingship remain, just as a ship remains whose captain has perished."[12]

7. Fresco in the apse of the cathedral of Aquileia, representing the earliest (1028) depiction of the Salian royal family, appearing among the group of saints to the right of the enthroned Virgin Mary (smaller persons next to and between the saints are Henry III, as a child, Conrad II, and his wife, Gisela). (Photo: E.-D. Hehl)

8. Earliest depiction of Emperor Conrad II with the imperial crown on the fresco
in the apse of the cathedral of Aquileia (probably 1028); detail of the illustration
in fig. 7. (Photo: E.-D. Hehl)

This slightly sophistic passage has been subject to various interpretations. But the incident seems sufficiently clear, in the eyes of Wipo at least, to show the emergence of a marked difference between Conrad II's ideas on the permanence of the kingship and previously held beliefs. Using the metaphor of a ship, the Salian ruler meant to say that the kingship (*regnum*) does not perish with the death of the king.[13] The kingship embodies transpersonal permanence; and it is for the same reason that fiscal lands pertaining to the kingship maintained their own constitutional status, independent of any individual king. Wipo, of course, did not write this account until Henry III's early reign when such ideas had become much more refined.

The transitional nature of early Salian rule also becomes apparent when we consider the new royal burial site in the cathedral at Speyer. Recent studies have shown fairly convincingly that Conrad II had designated the church of Speyer as his burial place,[14] dispelling the idea that the Salian proprietary monastery at Limburg on the Haardt had been considered for this purpose. Speyer had been Conrad II's choice from the very beginning and construction on this royal monument was started soon after his elevation, probably in 1025. Nevertheless, the extremely elegant church at Limburg on the Haardt fascinates the visitor even in its current ruined state because of its strikingly "modern" conception and its amazing size (fig. 9). Moreover, the fact that Conrad II chose to transform a strategically located fortress into a monastery underscores how much he valued Limburg and its church. But the dimensions of his newly acquired imperial status virtually excluded a monastic church as a dynastic burial site, especially one without a venerable tradition. A ruler who was aspiring to Byzantine rank and glory could not possibly have been satisfied to repose in a place like Limburg, particularly since his predecessor, Henry II, had set new standards in this respect when he built his magnificent ecclesiastical center at Bamberg. This was an example which the Salian emperor could not leave unchallenged. How early Conrad II and his wife, Gisela, focused their attention on Speyer can be illustrated by a land grant that the royal couple made to this church on 11 September 1024.[15] The diploma states that they had pledged to make this donation prior to the royal election; and now that the kingship had been attained, they were gratefully transferring these possessions to the altar of the cathedral of Speyer. According to contemporary belief, Speyer and its patron saint, the Virgin Mary, had undoubtedly played a decisive role in Conrad II's elevation to the kingship, and this divine assistance had created an indissoluble bond between this church and the Salian dynasty.

The Life of Bishop Benno II of Osnabrück (1068–1088), probably writ-

9.a. The Salian monastic church at Limburg on the Haardt River, b. reconstruction and blueprint (Manchot, *Kloster Limburg an der Haardt*, 1892, Taf. II et III).

ten by Abbot Norbert of Iburg around 1090, addressed in particular why Conrad II had chosen Speyer. This narrative states:

> That was the time when the city of Speyer on the Rhine, through the devout fervor of the emperors who now repose there, had gained new vitality and began to flourish again, as we can see today. Previously it had been reduced to insignificance, had become old and decrepit, and had almost ceased to be an episcopal city. Yet these pious emperors, lacking the means to found a new ecclesiastical see in the realm, apparently had the laudable desire to rebuild this bishopric, which had almost ceased to be one, with their own resources and to make it into a memorial site. Because of their actions, clerics from all over the realm congregated there in large numbers; for the emperor's unflagging devotion to all spheres of life had turned it [Speyer] into a flourishing center of learning.[16]

Other sources confirm that Speyer must have been a rather poor bishopric at the turn of the millennium. In a dedication to his teacher, Bishop Balderic of Speyer (970–986), the poet Walther of Speyer (later bishop of Speyer himself, 1004–1027) invokes the following image of this city: "O fortunate cowtown, distinguished by such an eminent lord." On the other hand, we have to remember that Speyer coin became the prototype for

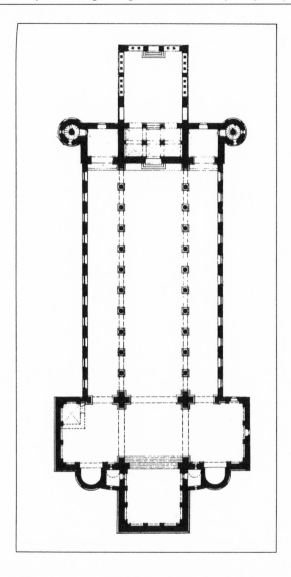

the coinage at Selz in 993;[17] this can mean only that Speyer must have had a certain importance as a mint and market place during this period. In any case, the Salian ruler had no other alternative within his patrimonial domain; Mainz was firmly in the hands of its sitting metropolitan, and Worms, whose bishops had long been hostile to Salian interests, also was out of the question (fig. 10).

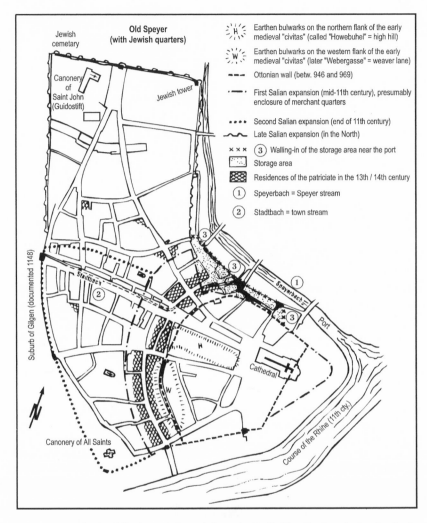

10. Speyer in the Middle Ages (adapted from A. Doll, *Zur Frühgeschichte der Stadt Speyer*, 1954, p. 172).

An even more compelling reason for Conrad II's preference for Speyer might have been connected to the iconographic significance of the Holy Virgin. Already in the tenth century the Virgin Mary began assuming the crucial role of a mediator and patron saint for the emperors in Byzantium. Shortly after the year 1000, the Hungarian kings adopted the same tradition.[18] Contemporary Byzantine representations of the coronation ceremony consistently show the Virgin Mary who, appointed through God's blessing hand, performs the crowning act. We also know that Saint Stephen, king of Hungary (1001–1038), had placed his person and his realm under the heavenly protection of the Holy Virgin. Finally, we must consider that Mary, especially if represented with the child, was perceived as the Mother of the heavenly King and as a patron saint of each and every royal house. For these reasons Peter, the patron saint of Worms, was ill suited to lend credence to the Salian kingship. Choosing the Virgin Mary as patron saint for Speyer, on the other hand, provided an excellent foundation for a royal cathedral.

In 1024 Speyer still had its old episcopal church dating from Carolingian times; it was, in all likelihood, a very modest structure whose location is obscure today. The state of insignificance and neglect that had befallen this bishopric gave Conrad II the opportunity to realize his grand visions through the construction of a splendid new cathedral church. Here he could become the "second founder" of an episcopal see, emulating his predecessor Henry II, who in 1007 had created his own bishopric in Bamberg. Although written in retrospect, *The Life of Bishop Benno II of Osnabrück* clearly shows how deeply Conrad II's concept of royal representation must have been affected by the example of Emperor Henry II.

Nevertheless, significant differences existed between the two rulers. For example, it is striking that Wipo, writing circa 1044/45, gives Conrad II credit for having "distinguished" Speyer with "large endowments" when, in fact, we only know of very few donations that the first Salian emperor had made to this episcopal see. It seems as if Conrad II had earmarked his resources for the construction project of "his" cathedral exclusively while lending little support to the church's spiritual institutions. Further one should note that Conrad II paid only one documented visit to Speyer during his reign, in contrast to at least four stays at Limburg on the Haardt. Was he perhaps trying to spare the resources of his bishopric? Likewise one finds little evidence that the city of Speyer was meant to be transformed into a "sacred landscape," surrounded by a ring of monasteries and chapter houses, as had been the case in Bamberg. Despite the foundation of St. John's canonry, the layout of Speyer was and still is completely dominated by the compelling, clear lines that converge on the towering structure of the cathedral. The whole design conveys one powerful purpose.

What exactly does the design of the Speyer cathedral reveal about Conrad II and his concept of royal dominion? Thanks to recent archaeo-

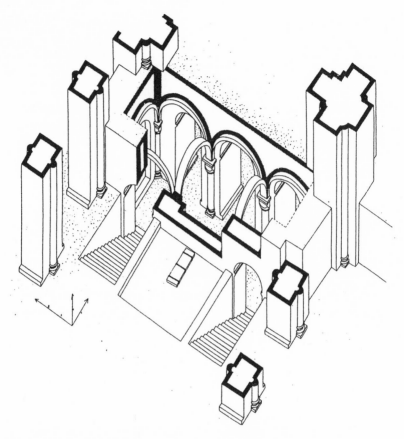

11. The burial site of Emperor Conrad II in the cathedral of Speyer (with vestibule to crypt), isometric reconstruction (R. Hussendörfer).

logical and art-historical studies, we are extremely well informed about the architectural history of this magnificent church.[19] At Conrad II's death in 1039, the vaulting of the crypt had been completed, parts of the eastern apse and the corner towers were under construction, and the foundation of the nave was in place (figs. 11, 12). We also know that the original design of the cathedral was much more modestly conceived than the structure towering before us today; its nave was supposed to be much lower and about 55 meters (about 180 feet) shorter. But the church edifice had been conceived as a "directional structure" (*Richtungsbau*) from the very beginning, as a sanctuary whose longitudinal axis directed the eyes from the entrance in the west straight toward the choir in the east. The power of this architectural simplicity, considered "modern" at that time, has a much

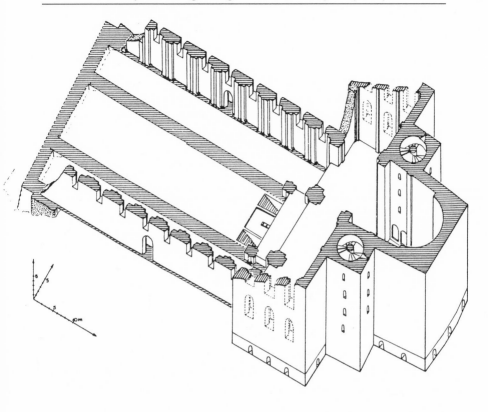

12. Conrad II's cathedral at Speyer, isometric view (D. Von Winterfeld).

more uplifting effect than the arrangement we encounter in Bamberg. No central entrance leads into the sanctuary there and the space within the cathedral is held in a balance by the presence of both an eastern and a western choir. Conrad II clearly preferred the dynamic concept, as is also evident in the design of the monastic church at Limburg on the Haardt. One can hardly escape the impression that this new style of construction somehow reflected a novel way of thinking, a take-off into a new age.

But a closer look at the burial site that Conrad II commissioned for himself in the new sanctuary is even more revealing in this context. In front of the area leading to the crypt, between two flights of descending stairs, a space of 4 by 5 meters (about 215 square feet) was prepared on the central axis of the church, exactly within the line that focuses on the altar (fig. 11). It was in this central location that the sarcophagus of the first Salian emperor was deposited in July 1039; and it has remained there, although it is now located beneath the main flooring of the church. The area immediately in front of the crossing was considered the most distinguished grave site; this sacred location was usually reserved for a rood altar which, in this case, might have been moved to the area where the crypt is entered. These observations lead to the crucial question whether Conrad II had only planned for his own founder's tomb or whether the grave sites for his wife Gisela and his son Henry III had been included in his conception from the very beginning. Ample space existed for three graves; and Gisela and Henry III, indeed, found their last resting places here next to Conrad II. Still, the question remains whether this had been the first Salian ruler's intention. Might we be witnessing the first stages of a transpersonal kingship in the design of a burial site that could accommodate a whole dynasty rather than just one ruler?

There are no easy answers. But the previous observations would allow us to account for the planning of a common grave site for Conrad II, Gisela, and Henry III, particularly in view of the first Salian's novel practice of letting both wife and son share in his imperial authority. A systematic comparison of the most important names appearing in royal diplomas together with the ruler's during the reign of Henry II and Conrad II clearly supports the idea of Salian co-rulership. Moreover, it seems to make sense that the Salians would continue their distinctly dynastic burial tradition, originally centered on Worms, once they had attained royal status. The establishment of a formal familial grave site was not just a matter of reverent care for the dead as it is today, but it served the very specific purpose of preserving the memory of a prominent kindred's origin, proving its legitimacy and powerful identity. Such a consciously designed memorial location allowed the departed members to remain ever present; and this "presence of the dead" created for a dynasty a sense of permanence both spiritually and liturgically as well as legally.[20] Thus, it should not surprise us that Conrad II showed more zeal in integrating such ideas into his kingship than his predecessor did. The fact that Henry III's first wife, the Danish princess Gunhild, was buried in the monastic church at Limburg on the Haardt rather than in Speyer does not necessarily contradict the Salians' memorial concept. Although Gunhild had given birth to a daughter, Beatrix, she had not produced a male heir. Consequently, she made no contribution to the maintenance of the dynasty and was eliminated from the inner circle of the royal house in her burial site.

It seems plausible that Conrad II had reserved the sacred space in front of the cupola crossing in the cathedral of Speyer not only for his own founder's tomb but also for all those persons within the newly established dynasty whom he had included in his rule. His view of being king, accordingly, transcended his own person, but did not yet encompass an abstract concept of kingship. These examples, as others that I have examined, clearly point toward a new way of thinking. During Conrad II's kingship, we can only recognize its beginnings, though; the actual changes and innovations did not take root until the reign of his son Henry III.

3

Royal Prerogatives and
Authority Under Conrad II

IN THE DEDICATION to his *Deeds of the Emperor Conrad II*, addressed to the latter's son Henry III, the chronicler Wipo makes the following comparison between father and son, "One"—namely Conrad—"performed a salutary incision upon the body politique, that is, the Roman Empire; the other"—namely Henry—"in his wisdom restored it to its health." The first Salian ruler's reign, which had ended seven years earlier, now appeared to Wipo as a period of decisive action and energetic planning, as a turning-point ushering in a new beginning. Conrad II's impressive size may have contributed to this image. When his sarcophagus was opened on 23 August 1900, his mummy-like body was completely intact and official measurements yielded a length of two meters (about 6.6 feet). A long beard was in evidence, perhaps resembling the one worn by the enthroned Emperor Conrad on the representative depiction of the Salian dynasty discussed in the Introduction (see frontispiece).

Conrad II's leadership was characterized by tenacity and successful assertion of authority. His actions and decisions were primarily motivated by his desire to preserve the imperial prerogatives and to meet the obligations of kingship at all times. Typical of Conrad II's energetic approach was, for example, the investigation concerning fiscal estates[1] which, following the imperial coronation, was ordered at the assembly of Regensburg in 1027. The Bavarian counts were instructed under oath to determine which holdings might have been alienated from the crown and could appropriately be reclaimed. It seems, however, that some counts who had been pressed into service executed the royal orders with exaggerated zeal. Among these was Count Poppo who, admonished by the emperor (*ab imperatore admonitus*), wrongly included the abbey of Moosburg in the inventory of alienated fiscal properties. Subsequent judicial proceedings determined unequivocally that this monastery belonged to the domain of the bishop of Freising. It is essential to note in this context that the court document that was issued in this case used the wording *ad solium sui imperii iure pertinere*, inferring that Conrad II wanted to establish which estates could "legitimately be claimed by the crown." Once again, we find the concept of transpersonal kingship suggested; the crown outlives the succession of rulers and is a metaphor for kingship.

Prerogatives of royal authority had to be safeguarded in Italy as well. A powerful coalition of Italian, Lotharingian, and Southern French magnates, which the French king Robert II (996–1031) joined and in which Duke William V of Aquitaine and Count Odo II of Champagne played a leading role, collapsed soon after Conrad II assumed the throne. The Salian monarch firmly reestablished German hegemony over Italy when he was crowned king of Italy by Archbishop Aribert in the cathedral of Milan in March 1026. Until the end of the Hohenstaufen era, the kingdom of Italy was continuously connected to the German realm. This relationship was primarily tied to the person of the king, however, and meant that the king, in a personal union, ruled both Germany and Italy. Once again, the significance of the monarch as an integrating figure becomes apparent. His unifying function and the accompanying responsibilities are underscored.

Conrad II's authority in Italy initially was largely based on a number of interests which he held in common with the bishops of the Italian realm. These prelates, mostly of German origin, were expected to take an active role in the interlinking of the two kingdoms. As the power structure in northern Italy began to change in the 1030s, however, a shift in social dynamics may be observed. After the turn of the millennium, the bishops' authority over the cities, their jurisdictional power and use of *regalia* (such as tolls, taxes, coining rights), as well as their control over the surrounding countryside, the *contado*, were increasingly challenged by the *captianei*, their chief fief holders. This military elite could rely on sizable support from many lesser nobles, called *valvassores*; these two groups together were essential for maintaining military control over imperial Italy. When the bishops tried to curb the growing power of this warrior elite and increasingly sought to reclaim the fiefs of the valvassores, they were faced with unrest and rebellion. Particularly in Milan, where Archbishop Aribert resorted to unusually harsh measures, the Milanese valvassores, reinforced by others, staged a serious uprising at the turn of 1035–36. Wipo reports the following: "Also at this same time, a great turmoil, unheard of in our times, occurred in Italy because the people rose up against their princes.

The Burgundian Legacy

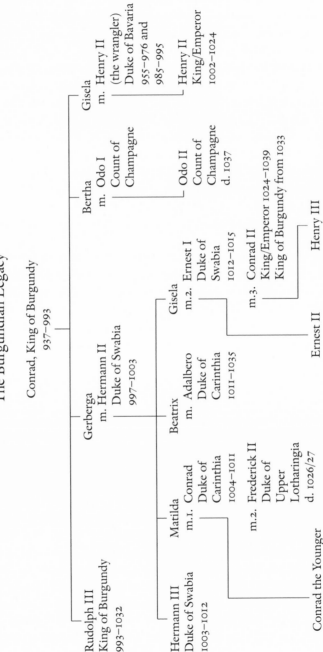

Conrad, King of Burgundy
937–993

Rudolph III
King of Burgundy
993–1032

Gerberga
m. Hermann II
Duke of Swabia
997–1003

Bertha
m. Odo I
Count of
Champagne

Gisela
m. Henry II
(the wrangler)
Duke of Bavaria
955–976 and
985–995

Henry II
King/Emperor
1002–1024

Odo II
Count of
Champagne
d. 1037

Hermann III
Duke of Swabia
1003–1012

Matilda
m.1. Conrad
Duke of
Carinthia
1004–1011

m.2. Frederick II
Duke of
Upper
Lotharingia
d. 1026/27

Beatrix
m. Adalbero
Duke of
Carinthia
1011–1035

Gisela
m.2. Ernest I
Duke of
Swabia
1012–1015

m.3. Conrad II
King/Emperor 1024–1039
King of Burgundy from 1033

Ernest II
Duke of Swabia
1015–1030

Henry III
crowned king from 1028
King of Burgundy from 1038

Conrad the Younger
Duke of Carinthia
1036–1039

All of the Italian valvassores and lesser nobility conspired against their lords, all the lesser ones against the greater [ones]. They were no longer willing to tolerate their lords' arbitrary actions toward them in total disregard of their wishes. If the emperor would not come to protect their interests, they would take the law into their own hands."[2]

Characteristically, Conrad II reacted with great determination to this crisis and without delay embarked on his second Italian campaign in 1036. While investigating the causes that had led to the events in Milan, he at once recognized that episcopal attempts to undermine the small fief holders would in effect weaken the military presence of the German kings in Italy. There was no doubt that the imperial prerogatives in this region were threatened and Conrad II, in his decisive manner, took immediate action. Archbishop Aribert was apprehended, but managed to escape when Patriarch Poppo of Aquileia (who had custody of him) switched sides.[3] Conrad II also dealt harshly with the bishops of Vercelli, Cremona, and Piacenza; he ordered their arrest and banishment "without any judicial proceedings" (*sine iudicio*), as even Wipo commented disapprovingly. Once again, the Salian monarch proved to be a man of deeds, deriving his authoritative actions from his responsibilities as protector of imperial prerogatives and from his concept of being Christ's vicar on earth (*vicarius Christi*).

The valvassores thus owed the protection of their interests to the emperor. Subsequently, when Conrad II had to rely on their assistance in his ensuing conflicts with the Milanese archbishop and during the siege of Milan, he issued the famous diploma *Constitutio de feudis* to them.[4] This document, dated 28 May 1037, regulated the terms of their fiefs. It stated that no vassal, be he a *capitan* or a lesser valvassor, could be forced to forfeit his fief without a judgment of his peers. In addition, the valvassores were granted the right to pass on their fiefs to sons and grandsons in hereditary succession. Wipo comments with good reason: "He [Conrad II] managed to win the fief holders over to his cause by stating that a descendant could not be deprived of a fief which had rightfully been passed on to him by an ancestor."[5]

The imperial prerogatives in Italy and the linkage of the German and Italian realms seemed secure. Now Conrad II's attention could be directed toward another realm, the kingdom of Burgundy, referred to as Arelat in the thirteenth century. This particular example provides an excellent illustration of the Salian emperor's views of royal rights and obligations.

In this context it must be mentioned that King Rudolph III of Bur-

gundy (993–1032), who had no legitimate heirs, had bequeathed his kingdom to the emperor Henry II, his closest relative. Rudolph's sister Gisela
was Henry II's mother; and although feudal justifications were added, the
arrangement rested chiefly on hereditary principles and was directly tied
to the person of Emperor Henry II. But when he died in 1024 before his
uncle Rudolph, prevailing legal practice rendered the original agreement
null and void. According to strict hereditary principles, Count Odo II of
Champagne (d. 1037) should now have become the closest heir in line to
the Burgundian throne. One degree further removed were the hereditary
claims of Conrad the Younger, as well as those of Henry III, Conrad II's
son. The first Salian monarch himself, however, had no hereditary rights to
Burgundy, and whatever claims he might have derived through the lineage
of his spouse Gisela (Rudolph III's niece) would have been rather weak.
His only avenue to the Burgundian legacy lay in its ties to Henry II's suzerainty.

As soon as Conrad II had been elected, he sought to advance the idea
that the German king or, more plausibly, German kingship had priority
rights to the Burgundian crown. His pretensions hinged on the argument
that his predecessor's arrangement with Rudolph III should be viewed as
an anticipated legacy to the realm, respectively to German kingship, and
that he as the new king was obligated to claim this imperial prerogative
with a firm hand. This strategy must have been transparent to all interested parties from the very beginning. Conrad II's struggle with the obsti-
nate Lotharingian opposition and his rebellious stepson Duke Ernest II of
Swabia, who in 1030 did not shy away from conspiring with Count Odo II
of Champagne, leave no doubt that the Burgundian legacy must have
played a pivotal role. Traditional hereditary law reacted against a newly
emerging constitutional prerogative.

Conrad II employed remarkable determination and tenacity in pursuing and securing this new imperial prerogative. After forcing his stepson, Duke Ernest II of Swabia, into submission, he immediately met with
Rudolph III of Burgundy at Basel in August 1027 to make arrangements
for the transfer of the Burgundian kingdom. According to Wipo, it was
the empress Gisela who ultimately negotiated an understanding (*pax*) between the two parties, an indication that she had considerable influence
at the imperial court. But even more important in our context, as evident
from Wipo's comments, is the fact "that the kingdom of Burgundy was to
be transferred to the emperor under the identical conditions (*eodem pacto*)
as had been promised to his predecessor, the emperor Henry [II]."[6] This

agreement was a perfect reflection of the Salian monarch's understanding of royal rights and privileges; the same prerogatives were due to him in his position as king as had been due to his predecessor, and it was his duty to prevail in these matters.

On 6 September 1032, Rudolph III of Burgundy died. This was an extremely inconvenient time for Conrad II since he happened to be on campaign in Poland. But when a Burgundian noble presented him with the royal insignia, the first Salian ruler's remarkable resolve manifested itself once again. He immediately called off the Polish campaign and, to the great surprise of his foes, marched his troops to Burgundy in the middle of winter 1032–33. According to Wipo, it was one of the coldest winters ever. Horses in the military encampment outside the stronghold of Murten froze to the ground during the night and had to be cut loose with picks and axes. One man reportedly even had to kill his horse and barely managed to skin the poor creature before its whole body was frozen solid and remained standing there in its icy condition. "Men too suffered considerably from the severe frost. Old and young appeared alike, as all of them were covered with hoary frost and looked white and bearded, notwithstanding that most of them were young men who did not wear beards. However, these unfavorable conditions were no reason for the emperor to give up the campaign."[7]

On 2 February 1033, Conrad II's supporters assembled at Peterlingen and elected and crowned him king of Burgundy; an additional group of Burgundian nobles recognized his royal authority at a meeting in Zurich. The Salian ruler's prompt and resolute actions, executed under such adverse circumstances, proved extremely disconcerting to Count Odo II of Champagne, who was attempting to occupy large sections of Upper Burgundy in his own right. In the summers of 1033 and 1034 two sizable campaigns against Odo II were necessary before the emperor could celebrate his acquisition of Burgundy with a demonstrative coronation ceremony in the cathedral of Geneva on 1 August 1034.

Thus began the time of the three kingdoms, the union of Germany, Italy, and Burgundy under the crown of the German king and emperor. However, both Italy's and Burgundy's bonds to the realm were primarily tied to the person of the ruler, and it must be stressed that large parts of Burgundy escaped the control of royal authority altogether. In the long run, Burgundy remained of marginal concern; and in 1057 after Henry III's death, the empress Agnes even turned its supervision over to Duke Rudolf of Swabia, who was not exactly a close ally of Salian causes. This salutary neglect also may explain why some Burgundian nobles had turned against Odo II in 1033/34; they justifiably feared that the count of Champagne, given his proximity, would demand even greater submission than the remote German emperor. The transfer of the Burgundian crown from Conrad II to his son Henry III in 1038 must be viewed in this context as well, for this act had been preceded by an election, the paying of homage, and an acclamation by the Burgundians. Recent research has shown convincingly that the sequence of these rituals demonstrated that the Burgundian crown had been passed on to the Salians according to hereditary principles and not through force.[8] Henry III was, after all, a great-nephew of Rudolph III through his mother, Gisela, and the closest legitimate heir to the Burgundian kingdom, since Odo II of Champagne, had died the previous year.

Assertion of imperial prerogatives and establishment of royal authority also characterized Conrad II's moves against Bohemia and Poland. The emperor demanded that the Bohemian duke submit to his vassalage and ordered his regular attendance at imperial assemblies, and the Polish rulers were expected to enter into a similar relationship to the German crown. Thus, when Duke Boleslaw Chobry of Poland arranged for his own coronation after Henry II's death, and when his son Mieszko II followed his father's example shortly thereafter, Conrad II must have viewed these acts as an assault on the very essence of his kingship. Campaigning unrelentingly against Mieszko II, he was not satisfied until the Polish prince sued for peace in 1033, renounced his kingship, and accepted his position as a vassal of the emperor and the German realm.

Some background sheds additional light on this situation. In 1026/27 Matilda, the mother of Conrad the Younger, sent a precious liturgical book with a truly remarkable dedication to Mieszko II. Matilda, who was also the sister of Empress Gisela, expresses effusive praise for the dignity of the Polish king. She extolls his merits, his virtues, his sense of justice, and his care for the poor. She calls him a warrior of Christ on earth and an "invincible king who had his royal diadem bestowed through the providence of God the Almighty."[9] She closes her letter by wishing him "auspicious triumph over all his enemies." This letter, addressed to Conrad II's rival and—from a Salian point of view—to the foe of imperial prerogatives, illustrates clearly that the opposition within the realm faced similar difficulties as the Polish king and that these circumstances formed the basis for a common bond. Mieszko appears as the "just king," providing a sharp contrast to Conrad II whose authoritarian style appeared "unjust." Matilda's comments are significant. As mother of Conrad the Younger and wife of

Duke Frederick of Upper Lotharingia, she was the connecting link be-tween the members of the opposition and, undoubtedly, played a pivotal role, as evidenced by an entry of this group in the memorial book at the monastery of Reichenau.[10]

Young Duke Ernest II of Swabia, a son from Empress Gisela's pre-vious marriage to Duke Ernest I of Swabia (d. 1015), also belonged to this opposition. At the age of sixteen or seventeen he was still vacillating, though, and in 1026 he sought a reconciliation with Conrad II, who then granted him the abbey of Kempten in fief. Ernest II was further charged with keeping the peace in this region, which meant in real terms that he would be forced to move against his former ally, Count Welf II, who was feuding with the bishop of Augsburg. No sooner had the Salian king embarked on his Italian campaign than young Ernest rejoined the rebels, invaded Alsace, and started building strongholds on the Burgundian fron-tier—obviously with an eye on the Burgundian legacy.

After Conrad II had returned from Italy in 1027, he summoned the conspirators to an assembly in Ulm. Once again we have a comprehen-sive report from Wipo detailing the events at court: "Here Duke Ernest appeared as well, yet hardly in a submissive stance, but trusting that the presence of the great number of his important vassals would either allow him to reach an agreement with the emperor that was to his liking or else to secure his departure by virtue of his own power." However, when Ernest reminded his followers of their oath of fidelity to him, the counts Frederick and Anselm supposedly answered for the whole group:

We are not denying that we have given you a firm promise of fidelity against all except him who has given us to you. If we were servants of our king and emperor and had been given unto your jurisdiction by him, it would not be permissible for us to separate ourselves from you. However, since we are free men and look upon the king and emperor as the foremost protector of our liberty on earth, we are apt to lose our liberty (*libertatem*) if we abandon him. And as it has been said, no good man gives up liberty except with his life.[11]

This argumentation is revealing in several respects. It makes clear, for ex-ample, that a servile man—in contrast to a free man—owed obedience to his lord, but it particularly emphasizes that the king was considered to be the foremost protector of liberty within the realm and that this func-tion was one of the major characteristics of royal authority. During the tenth century the Ottonian rulers interfered little in the southern German duchies of Swabia and Bavaria; as a consequence the counts of these regions became primarily vassals of their dukes, regardless of the fact that the comital office with its responsibility for public justice used to be conferred by the king. Duke Ernest II of Swabia obviously still relied on tenth-century practices. Personal ties of fidelity which bound the Swabian counts to his person as duke ranked much higher to his way of thinking than any loyalty they might have had to the king because of their office. The king as an institution of protective authority must have posed a serious threat to Ernest's pretensions and presumed ducal rights. Yet Wipo's report addresses exactly this novel conception of royal authority, which had been initiated by Henry II and had increasingly taken root in the consciousness of the Swabian counts under Conrad II's kingship.

One should add, of course, that the counts exploited these changes to their own advantage and that they used them as a pretext to gain a measure of independence from direct ducal control. The duke of Swabia—and this holds true for the duchy as an institution within the realm as a whole—henceforth was in danger of being squeezed from both sides, from the king on one and from the counts on the other. A process was under way that would slowly but surely undermine ducal power; although it would take more than one hundred years, it would bring about the steady decline of the traditional duchies.

By all accounts, Duke Ernest II of Swabia was stunned by the words of his counts and submitted to the emperor unconditionally. Once again, the ruler's insistence on asserting his royal authority had prevailed. Comparable to his cooperation with the Italian valvassores, Conrad II sought to establish an alliance with the lesser powers at the expense of the intermediate ducal power. In the wake of these events, the rest of the rebels who had tried to defend their rights also gave in, including such powerful nobles as Welf II and Conrad the Younger. The "good" king was now obliged to show mercy. In 1028 Conrad II granted the young Ernest II clemency and reinstated him in his duchy—but apparently under the provision that he drop his closest friend and faithful vassal, Werner of Kyburg,[12] and move against him for breaching the public peace. Once again *raisons d'état*—to use a modern expression—were to supersede personal loyalty.[13] Ernest was to prove that he had learned his lesson. This offer was extended to Ernest for the last time at the Easter assembly of 1030 at Ingelheim on the Rhine. But the sixteen- or seventeen-year-old youth spurned political expedience in favor of personal loyalty which, in his eyes, constituted a higher form of justice. Wipo summarizes as follows: "Hereupon he was declared a manifest enemy of the emperor; he lost his *ducatus* irretrievably and escaped with a small band of supporters. . . . Based on the recommendations of all the princes, the emperor ordered him and all other offenders against public law and peace excommunicated by the bishops and had their estates confiscated." The Empress Gisela, no doubt, must have experienced great pain and suffering when her son was declared an outlaw who could be hunted down with impunity; but even she submitted to the higher ideal of royal justice and authority. To quote Wipo's words: "Even she laudably abandoned her ill-advised son in favor of her spouse's wisdom and pledged publicly that, regardless of her son's fate, she would forego any attempt of satisfaction and would be no one's enemy because of this matter."[14]

The young outlaw's end approached rapidly. On 17 August 1030, Ernest II and his friend Werner, accompanied by few faithful retainers, were surrounded by their pursuers. In spite of a desperate attempt to defend themselves, the rebels had no chance against the superior numbers of their attackers and eventually were felled by fatal blows. When Conrad II was informed of his stepson's death, he supposedly said sarcastically: "Rabid dogs rarely produce offspring." Royal authority had been asserted once again. However, the emperor's actions did not meet with universal approval. When Ernest II's body was brought to Constance, the bishop there absolved him of his ban and buried him honorably in the Church of Saint Mary's; in an entry in the necrology of the famous imperial monastery of Saint Gall we find the following words under his name: "Duke and adornment of Swabia." Equally revealing, on the other hand, is that, except for his name, bards and poets integrated few elements of his tragic life into their legend of Duke Ernest. This ballad had its roots in the fate of the unfortunate Luidolf, the rebellious son of Otto the Great, which may explain why the essential *leitmotiv* of Ernest's story, namely personal loyalty and friendship, did not become part of it.

The shifting dynamics of power between ruler and dukes also becomes apparent in connection with a vacancy in the Bavarian duchy. At the end of February 1026, Duke Henry V had died there, but Conrad II made no provisions for a successor until he returned from his imperial coronation in Rome. At the assembly of Regensburg in June 1027, he finally conferred the duchy on his son Henry III after the Bavarian nobles had confirmed his choice. Most scholars view this political move as a prelude to the eventual "institutionalizing of the prerogative of royal selection."[15] Although the emperor would still consider hereditary principles in the bestowal of ducal honors, he would include many individuals in the pool of possible candidates so that he could easily choose the person of his preference. In the case of Bavaria, he clearly ignored several contenders whose hereditary claims were far more legitimate than those of Henry III, and he obviously employed the "election" of the magnates to justify their elimination.

The basic principle of Conrad II's approach to the filling of ducal vacancies becomes evident when we consider that his son Henry III further assumed ducal power over Swabia in 1038 and also took over the Carinthian duchy a year later. The three southern German duchies were now united in the hands of the future king; and after his accession to the throne in 1039 they came directly under royal authority. This is a remarkable development and another palpable example of Conrad II's systematic implementation of policies designed to concentrate governing powers in royal hands. As mentioned previously, Henry II had conceived and partly put into practice a similar program at the beginning of the eleventh century; but there is no doubt that the first two Salian rulers stepped up their efforts to translate these ideas into a tightly structured governmental system totally subordinate to royal authority. The Salian handling of ducal politics differs fundamentally from the one practiced by Otto the Great. This ruler regularly attempted to confer available ducal offices on members of his family—brother, son, brother-in-law—and thus used the duchies as a sort of substitute realms (*regna*) to provide close relatives with an opportunity to share in imperial governance. Although the idea of establishing familial ties between the duchies and the crown may have played a role, the decisive factor was definitely the concept of compensation, since the realm was no longer divided among all those with hereditary claims, as had been the custom during Carolingian times. The duchies thus assumed the function of substitute kingdoms (*regna*) and in this respect promoted the decentralization of royal power. Only a comparison of Ottonian practices with the policies of Henry II and Conrad II makes the radical shift of direction transparent. These emperors were no longer concerned with compensation, but consciously sought to concentrate power in the ruler's hands, to retrieve the royal prerogatives into the safety of the king's house, so to speak.

Conrad II's growing propensity toward absolute authority and royal monopoly may be illustrated by yet another example. From a report by a cleric from Worms we learn that, at the emperor's instigation, Duke Adalbero of Carinthia was indicted at an assembly in Mainz in 1035.[16] But when Conrad II urged the magnates who were assembled for the judicial proceeding to render a judgment against Adalbero and to deprive him of his duchy, they hesitated and requested the presence of young king Henry III. The emperor now summoned his son and insisted that *he* render the judgment. Yet to his father's greatest consternation, Henry III declared that he could not comply with his wishes in this case, in spite of his desire to be an obedient son, because of a previous agreement (*pactum*) with Adalbero. Conrad II now sought to persuade the prince with admonitions, pleas, and threats, but Henry resisted steadfastly until the emperor, exasperated by his son's refusal, lost his power of speech and collapsed. Having recovered his senses, Conrad summoned the magnates once again and publicly fell to his knees before his son. Under bitter tears the emperor implored Henry to yield to his wishes, reminding him that protracted opposition would bring great glee and exultation to his father's enemies while causing shame and disgrace to king and realm. After this demonstration, the young king submitted to his father and confessed that, advised by his teacher Bishop Egilbert of Freising (1005–1039), he had sworn an oath to Adalbero. When the bishop of Freising was asked to account for his behavior, his justifications left no doubt that the two princes had sworn an oath of mutual fidelity. Conrad II supposedly did not comment on Egilbert's excuses, but immediately flew into another rage and expelled the bishop from the court. Finally, the emperor, his son, and the assembled magnates resumed the judicial proceedings and a judgment was rendered which deprived Adalbero of the Carinthian duchy and its marches.

Yet what was Adalbero's crime? According to recent research,[17] it is very probable that Adalbero pursued his own, independent plans in Carinthia. Supported by the bishop of Freising, but contrary to imperial policies, he seems to have worked toward a truce and eventual peace treaty with Hungary. Although the Austrian marches would be subject to substantial losses in the process, permanent security for the southeastern frontier regions seemed possible at last. The exchange of oaths between Adalbero and Henry III in his capacity as duke of Bavaria apparently was meant to expand the circle of interested parties and, particularly, to hamper any rigorous countermeasures that the emperor might take.

Considering Conrad II's concept of kingship and imperial leadership, it is not surprising that he must have perceived such actions as an ominous threat to his main objectives and royal authority. Imperial lands and prerogatives were to be forfeited against his will, which was a monstrous offense against a ruler who saw his main mission and obligation in preserving the imperial polity in its entirety. "Shame and disgrace for realm and king," as the cleric from Worms states so aptly, were in Conrad II's eyes, indeed, the inevitable consequences. In addition, the disregard of royal authority even manifested itself in a perfidious attempt to pit it against the

virtues of personal fidelity. There is a striking parallel between this situation and the case of Ernest II of Swabia where the dichotomy between
royal authority and personal loyalty was also a crucial element. Adalbero,
however, had gone much further than Ernest II by using an oath to challenge the king in his own house, so to speak. The audacity of this move
must have been extremely alarming to Conrad II, and it may explain why
he went to such extremes to eliminate Adalbero: falling to his knees before
his son. The king's self-imposed humiliation indicated that he was willing
to sacrifice his personal dignity for the preservation of kingship and realm.
He played for the highest stakes to make his son accept the principle of
royal authority and to cope with the momentous crisis that had befallen
the budding Salian kingship. Conrad II prevailed once more, in sharp contrast to his future grandson, Henry IV, who was forced to renounce the
crown by his own son, Henry V, and who could not regain clemency even
by falling to his knees.

The main supporter of this kind of exalted royal authority was the
Church. The idea of a Christian ruler and the concept of the divine rights
of kings allowed the monarch to assume an extremely elevated position
and to legitimate the implementation of an hierarchical order. The Church,
furthermore, played a decisive role in the direct administration of royal
affairs. Imperial abbeys and episcopal sees rendered an extensive array of
dues and services to the king and his court, commonly referred to as *servitium regis*. The sacral nature of kingship also enabled rulers to install
bishops in their office and even to invest them with their spiritual symbols,
the ring and the staff.[18] Although canon law prescribed that a new bishop
must be chosen by the clergy and the people, the selection was frequently
made at court or by the king personally and the election process was replaced by a subsequent request for the respective clergy's consent. In this
manner the kings made sure that the imperial bishops shared their idea of
kingship and pledged undivided loyalty.

It has generally been assumed that the idea of an imperial Church
(*Reichskirche*) had already been highly developed in the tenth century under
the Ottonian rulers and that it had actually become the backbone of the
imperial administration. Scholars have coined the term "Imperial Church
System" (*Reichskirchensystem*) for this concept. However, a much more dif-
ferentiated picture is currently emerging.[19] Careful analyses have shown
that the alleged Ottonian "system" was rather rudimentary in its nature
and that the prototype of the ideal Ottonian bishop, Archbishop Brun
of Cologne (953–965), and his vision of the episcopal office represented a

rather defensive position. There is no evidence of systematic royal control over imperial bishoprics until the reign of Henry II. This ruler definitely employed this principle as an administrative tool and so did his successor, Conrad II. In 1025, for example, shortly after assuming his kingship, the first Salian ruler appointed Azecho to be the new bishop of Worms. This was an extremely presumptuous act in the eyes of Archbishop Aribo of Mainz, who expressed his dismay in a letter to the clergy, vassals, and ministerials of the church of Worms. The metropolitan of Mainz complained bitterly that his spiritual authority had been totally ignored: "If we had not received this information from you personally and truthfully, I could not in good faith have believed the messengers or letters reporting that our lord, the king, meant to violate our rights in our absence, rights that are due to us and that have been exercised by our predecessors already, and that he actually invested the bishop, who should have been elected and consecrated by us, without our advice and consent."[20]

The bishoprics, on the other hand, became the beneficiaries of generous royal endowments as the rulers transferred to them extensive properties and powers of governance (*staatliche Hoheitsrechte*), which then were commonly removed as immunities from the jurisdiction of the designated public officials, the counts. Around the turn of the millennium entire counties were conferred on episcopal sees; and this process accelerated under Henry II and was continued by Conrad II and his successors. By the reign of Henry IV a total of fifty-four counties had presumably been passed on to episcopal lordships.[21] The bishops thus were held to shoulder former comital functions although their clerical status would not allow them to perform personally such important tasks as the administration of justice. Moreover, the substantial revenues accruing to the bishoprics benefitted the rulers indirectly in form of the *servitium regis* (the services that were due to the king). Having a stake in the realm's destiny must have heightened the bishops' sense of responsibility and may have provided the impetus for the unifying forces emanating from the Church. A sense of episcopal responsibility must already have been present at Conrad II's election in 1024,[22] playing a much more prominent role than in previous royal elevations. Most crucial, though, was the fact that the involvement of the Church provided the imperial polity with impulses toward an inner stability that paralleled the integrating power of the king. This development is an essential hallmark of the Salian ruler's royal lordship and will require further scrutiny in the course of this book.

The cooperation between king and bishops has long been interpreted as a device to rein in the power of secular princes and nobles. This view may still apply in individual cases. However, recent studies point out that the bishops, who were themselves of noble birth, as a rule maintained close ties to their families.[23] Noble property was regularly transferred to episcopal sees and close relatives frequently assumed the advocacy and other protective functions for the respective churches. Bishop Egilbert of Freising, mentioned earlier in this chapter, typically illustrates this situation, as he assumed the role of an integrative figure among an extended circle of Bavarian magnates. The king thus had access to large segments of the influential aristocracy through his bishops and could use these channels to attain the elite's recognition of his authority. Only if we consider this whole nexus of forces can we understand how much the imperial church accomplished on behalf of German kingship, especially under Henry II and Conrad II, as long as the king's status as God's anointed servant (*Christus domini*) and as Christ's representative on earth (*vicarius Christi*) remained uncontested.

If we pay close attention to this context, the previously mentioned acquisition of particles of the Holy Cross, which Conrad II's delegation had brought back from Byzantium, assumes special significance. While the Holy Lance—also known as Mauritius Lance or Longinus Lance— had been the most venerated symbol under Henry II, it was now rapidly replaced by the imperial cross which served as a reliquary for the newly acquired particles of the Cross. It can be easily shown how quickly the veneration of the Holy Cross was disseminated within the Salian dynasty and among those churches and nobles who had close ties to the royal house.[24] Many abbeys and chapter houses were furnished with minute particles of the new relic and subsequently quite often adopted the Holy Cross as their patron saint, as for example, Limburg on the Haardt, the Salian family monastery. The cult of the Cross was actively promoted by such nobles as the counts of Egisheim, also known as the Manegolds of Donauwörth, who were closely connected to the Salians, as well as by the counts of Metz, who were relatives of Conrad II's mother, Adelheid. Pope Leo IX, who was a member of the comital family of Egisheim and became bishop Bruno of Toul in 1026, eventually expanded the veneration of the Holy Cross into a systematic program for the nascent reform papacy.

These liturgical aspects cannot be ignored if one wants to gain an understanding of the unique interaction between Church, nobility, and king; for they illustrate the intensity of the religious forces that were at work in this nexus of power. But the Cross as a holy relic must likewise be seen as a vital source of liturgical support for the kingship since it sym-

13. Imperial (German) crown (Kunsthistorisches Museum, Vienna).

bolized the ruler's *imitatio Christi* in an exemplary manner. The veneration of the Cross, representing Christ's suffering, meant that the king, being Christ's vicar on earth, could claim the authority of the exalted Christ as his own. The cult of the Cross was vigorously promoted by Conrad II and his entourage and spread throughout the realm. It even motivated Bishop Heribert of Eichstätt (1022–1042) to praise the Holy Cross (*Salve crux sancta*) in a liturgical hymn which was presented to the court and gained considerable popularity. This linkage between the Cross and the kingship greatly enhanced the acceptance of the ruler's authority; it not only legitimized his royal elevation—as in the idea of divine right of kings—but also lent credence to his actions, his decisions, and his claim to leadership altogether. The religious and liturgical significance of the Cross and its crucial role in Conrad II's heightened sense of authority and divine mission are further underscored by the fact that the imperial cross, which had been crafted as a reliquary for the new relics from Byzantium, soon became the most distinguished of all imperial insignia. The first Salian emperor also had the imperial crown adorned with a precious cross, a crown that possibly originated from his reign (fig. 13).[25] More than any of his predecessors, he placed himself and his kingship under the sign of Christ as a source of strength and legitimacy for his extremely energetic and hierarchical royal lordship.

4

Realm and Society
in Transition

AN UNPRECEDENTED AWAKENING AND ECONOMIC upswing were not
the only hallmarks of an emerging dynasty; for as the Salian era progressed,
a dynamic process set in and percolated throughout all levels of the social
and political order. While signs of these changes were already noticeable
around the turn of the millennium, other developments did not become
palpable until the middle of the eleventh century. By the end of the Salian
century, however, popular perceptions had been substantially transformed
and a new world view had taken root.

After the nascent realm had survived its gravest perils in the tenth century, notably the Hungarian incursions with their ominous threat to life
and property, and when the world had not come to an end at the turn of the
millennium, as widely anticipated,[1] energies and resources were channeled
in new directions. Steady, rather than erratic, population growth[2] and considerable economic investment played an important role in this process.
But intellectual and religious life underwent momentous changes as well.
The Burgundian monk Rodulfus Glaber (Rudolph the Bald) provided an
excellent description of this awakening. In his work *Five Books of History*,
written shortly before the middle of the eleventh century, he commented:

Almost everywhere churches were made anew. Although most of them [existing
churches] were pleasing and well-built so that there would have been no need to
replace them, each Christian community attempted to outdo its neighbor by boast-
ing of an even more beautiful sanctuary. It was as if the whole world were shaking
off the old age by donning a shining new cloak that was studded with churches. In
those times, the believers enlarged and richly adorned most churches in their episcopal sees, as well as many monasteries and smaller village sanctuaries.[3]

The Salian era witnessed a spectacular building boom in Germany. Although harbingers of this development can be traced to the end of the

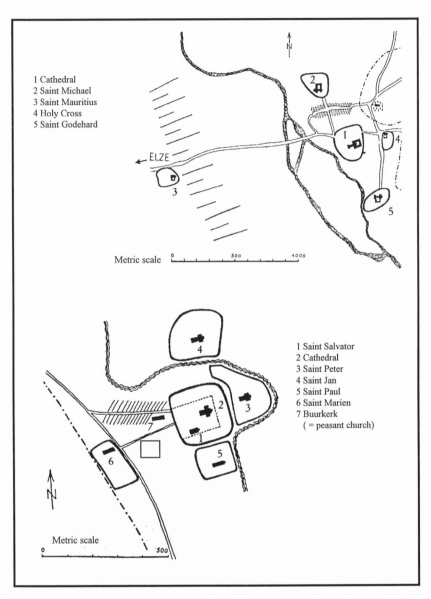

1 Cathedral
2 Saint Michael
3 Saint Mauritius
4 Holy Cross
5 Saint Godehard

ELZE

Metric scale

1 Saint Salvator
2 Cathedral
3 Saint Peter
4 Saint Jan
5 Saint Paul
6 Saint Marien
7 Buurkerk
(= peasant church)

Metric scale

14. (*top*) Hildesheim in the eleventh century (E. Herzog, *Die ottonische Stadt*, 1964, p. 241).

15. (*bottom*) Utrecht in the eleventh century (E. Herzog, *Die ottonische Stadt*, 1964, p. 253).

tenth century, it did not reach its full extent until the beginning of the new millennium.[4] Only a few Carolingian buildings survived the middle of the eleventh century. Archbishops and bishops invested unprecedented resources and energies in the erection of magnificent administrative and ecclesiastical centers. Cathedrals of breath-taking proportions and splendid episcopal palaces arose at their bidding. Everywhere, whether in Mainz or Worms, in Strasbourg, Würzburg, Eichstätt, Hildesheim, or Hamburg, monumental architectural complexes heralded a new age. Additional ecclesiastical foundations and monasteries, growing up in the vicinity of cathedrals and episcopal palaces, were often laid out according to certain theological principles. For example, they were designed to convey the blueprint of a cross—as in Hildesheim, Utrecht, Minden, and Trier—or to imitate the architectural constellation of Rome. As a consequence, many episcopal cities began to assume the character of "sacred landscapes" (figs. 14, 15).[5]

A typical example of such an episcopal building patron was Meinwerk of Paderborn (1009–1036).[6] Motivated by his own noble birth and family wealth, he did not tire to increase the possessions and privileges of his church; and he further performed more services for his king than the ruler could have expected. Meinwerk's biographer jocularly mentions that this engagement for the church might have prevented him from keeping up with his Latin.[7] When Emperor Henry II celebrated Christmas at Paderborn in 1022, he supposedly obtained the missal on Christmas eve and secretly changed the wording of a prayer of supplication. By allegedly erasing the respective "fa's" which occur in the phrase *pro defunctis famulis et famulabus* (for the deceased male and female servants), he made the passage read *pro defunctis mulis et mulabus* (for the deceased male and female mules). The next day the bishop reportedly read this edited text aloud during the Christmas service. Whether true or invented, this anecdote was probably designed to illustrate the intimate relationship between king and bishop rather than to denigrate the cleric. For Meinwerk, from all accounts, was truly dedicated to the furtherance of proper liturgical practices and ecclesiastical discipline.

When Meinwerk assumed the bishopric of Paderborn, he found the cathedral, then under construction, lacking in grandeur. Within three days of his arrival, he gave orders to have everything torn down and to commence a more glamorous building project. At his death in 1036, the most magnificent monument ever constructed in Paderborn stood completed. In addition, a large imperial palace adorned with an exquisite Saint Bartholomew chapel of Greek craftsmanship arose to the north of the cathe-

dral. On the south side a new episcopal palace was built; it had unusually
high towers and its walls were made of stone. To the west of the imperial
residence, the large Abdinghof monastery was laid out; and to the East
emerged the ecclesiastical foundation of Busdorf. During the planning
stages of this canonry, the bishop sent its abbot, Wino of Helmarshausen,
on a special mission to Jerusalem to measure the Holy Sepulcher so that its
exact replica could be incorporated into the new Busdorf sanctuary. Since
the church of Abdinghof was built according to Roman patterns (*more
Romano*) and since the whole complex of sacred edifices was arranged in
the shape of a cross, it is clear that Paderborn was designed to reflect
the characteristics of an universal center. Both Jerusalem and Rome were
conceptually incorporated, and the four ends of the cross pointed toward
the four cardinal directions, indicating the inclusion of the whole world.
Simultaneously, commercial quarters grew up adjacent to the episcopal
complex and craftsmen settled to cater to the needs of the various ecclesiastical foundations. This substantial building program radically transformed
the appearance of Paderborn. Adorned with monasteries and magnificent churches, the old episcopal castle evolved into a beautifully designed
bishop's seat, an episcopal residence of princely proportions.

Paderborn is but one example among many. Similar building pro-
grams can be identified in most other episcopal cities. Attempts to emulate the city of Rome appear already in the tenth century, for example in
Constance, Cologne, and Eichstätt.[8] The adoption of patron saints from
Rome's patriarchal churches and the emulation of the Roman topography
became widespread. In the case of Mainz, these ideas were directly related
to the archbishop's claim to preeminence within the imperial church system (the so-called *Reichskirchensystem*) and manifested themselves in the
city's appellation, *Aurea Moguntia*, the "golden city of Mainz," in analogy
to the golden city of Rome.[9]

Spreading like a tidal wave, these building projects put tremendous
strains on the resources of eleventh-century society. The labor force consisted predominantly of serfs (*Grundholden*) from the building patron's manorial estates, and these workers, it seems, were expected to be involved in
heavy construction in addition to their customary obligations. Thanks to
an anonymous chronicler from Eichstätt, known as Anonymus Haserensis
(1075/1078), we are well informed about the unprecedented construction
craze under Bishop Heribert of Eichstätt (1022–1042) and his successors:

For the first time, a bishop in our town initiated the destruction of old buildings
and the erection of new ones. His predecessors had been contented with structures

of modest proportions and had concentrated on embellishing their interiors with elaborate decorations. In contrast, this bishop and all of his successors sought to erect either new churches or new palaces or even fortifications; and, by constantly pursuing these projects, they drove the people who were forced to serve them into poverty and utter exhaustion. The majority of the time that used to be devoted to fertilizing, plowing, and caring for the fields, was now utilized to fit together stones; and all the while the customary services and dues were still being ruthlessly extracted. Thus, the previous state of prosperity deteriorated into dire want, and the zest for life, so prevalent under the preceding bishops, was replaced by bitter distress.[10]

Similar woes were reported by Adam of Bremen in his contemporary *Ecclesiastical History of Hamburg* and in the biography of Bishop Benno II of Osnabrück. Archbishop Adalbert of Hamburg-Bremen (1043–1072) supposedly exploited his workers relentlessly for the construction of his monumental cathedral, as well as for the building of walls and castles, and did not shy away from putting "new grievous demands on land and people." Generally speaking, we are told, he treated "his parish children with great harshness, instead of showing loving care for them as would a shepherd for his sheep." Bishop Benno II of Osnabrück (1068–1088), who in the 1080s assumed the chief responsibility for the expansion and reconstruction of the cathedral in Speyer, supposedly "drove his peasants into compliance through beatings" and rounded up large numbers of people to labor on his construction sites.

These and similar examples demonstrate how the bishops of this era began to attribute a novel significance to their authority. They not only created ecclesiastical centers, but also invested in episcopal residences that were designed for a prince whose power and influence was clearly superior to that of the nobility at large. More and more episcopal parchments, coins, and seals as well as the entire management of the bishop's household assumed forms and proportions that used to be reserved for the king and his court. A special hallmark of this new assertiveness was the programmatic image of the enthroned bishop (fig. 16); especially toward the end of the eleventh century the adoption of episcopal seals bearing the likeness of a bishop sitting on the throne became very common.[11] This throne motive, designed to underscore the ruler's majesty, had first been introduced on *royal* seals a hundred years earlier during the reign of Otto III (983–1002). Such subtle changes foreshadowed, no doubt, the rise of full-fledged ecclesiastical principalities. But one needs to take into account that neither the bishops' changed perception of their office nor their conspicuous manifestation of authority was initially directed against the king. On

16. Archbishop Bruno of Trier (1101–1124) enthroned, illuminated initial, early twelfth century (Gotha, Forschungsbibliothek, Hs. Memb. I 70, fol. 100).

the contrary, the strength and splendor of an individual episcopal center was considered to be an asset for the realm and the king, and administrative prowess allowed the bishops to provide effective leadership and to fulfill their functions and responsibilities vis-à-vis the realm. Toward the end of the Salian era, however, a definite shift can be observed; pursuing their own, ever more aggressive territorial policies, bishops often disregarded royal interests.

On the surface it may look as if the recasting of the episcopal office had been motivated mainly by secular greed or had occurred only because of the bishops' increased involvement in affairs of the realm. There is an interconnection, to be sure, but such a superficial assessment would not do justice to the bishops' genuine concerns. What mattered most to them was the creation of a system that would allow a more efficient implementation of episcopal functions and official duties. Therein lay the main reason for reorganizing the bishoprics into discrete archdeaconates and deaneries. Traditionally, ordained auxiliary bishops, so-called *chorepiscopi*, were assigned to specific regions within a diocese to perform all episcopal functions with little guidance. During the eleventh century these chorepiscopi were replaced by archdeacons who, as mere officials without episcopal consecration, were strictly subordinate to the authority of the diocesan bishop. Thus another step was taken toward the systematic organization of a hierarchical church order headed by the bishop. Previously, monastic foundations often held the right to collect tithes in certain parishes; now the bishops hotly contested these privileges in many cases. Nonetheless, these developments should not be interpreted as mere power politics but rather as a determined effort to provide administrative leadership designed to enhance the episcopal authority.

Toward the end of the Salian period, some bishops sought to increase their authority on the basis of the *auctoritas sancti Petri*; in other words, they looked at their office as a direct extension of the papal mission. By mentioning this stage of development I am rushing ahead, however; this type of reasoning could be employed only after the pope had been formally recognized as the supreme authority in all ecclesiastical matters. I will address this issue in Chapter 7. A further source of episcopal empowerment derived from the monastic and, above all, the clerical reform of the late eleventh and early twelfth centuries. This movement was particularly concerned with the proper administration of the sacraments and postulated that only personally unblemished priests could perform these holy rites if the salvation of the faithful was to be ensured.[12] Inspired by these

ideas, certain bishoprics, such as Halberstadt, Passau, and Salzburg, initiated the training of special clerical elites. Members of this new confraternity of clerics, known as regular canons, lived exemplary lives, renounced
all worldly possessions, adhered to monastic virtues, and assumed pastoral
duties either in parishes or from their base in reformed abbeys. Spiritually
and canonically they answered directly to the diocesan bishop and upheld
his authority throughout the see.

The Salian period witnessed radical changes in the ways bishops administered their dominion. As a tightly controlled, hierarchical structure
emerged, the prestige and power of the episcopal office became the bishops' primary concern. They now emphasized their churches' traditions
more zealously than previously and relied on them to support the legitimacy of their pretensions. Mainz, for example, derived its many prerogatives, including its claim to preeminence within the German church system,
emphatically from the traditions of Saint Boniface. Generally speaking, the
bishops did not consider their increasing power in terms of enhanced personal authority, but saw their person linked to the chain of their predecessors and to the obligations that they owed to the church. The luxuriously
crafted bishops' book of Eichstätt (*Pontifikale Gundekarianum*) (1071/72)
emphasized this concept by depicting all of the see's bishops in sequen-
tially arranged portraits, starting with its founder, Willibald. Through
vivid images, it illustrated the canonical and spiritual roots of this church
(fig. 17). These developments within the German episcopate point toward
the growing importance of institutional thinking. I will scrutinize this
phenomenon even further when I consider Henry III's idea of kingship.

To summarize: the outward symbols of episcopal power and identity were clearly aimed at emphasizing the bishops' hierarchical position.
What already had become a trend in the royal domain, now also manifested itself at the level of the bishoprics. Functions, obligations, and tasks
connected to the bishop's office were being centralized and simultaneously
transposed into an activist episcopal agenda.

Many characteristics of the episcopal reorganization paralleled developments in the secular sphere. In fact, we must assume that an even
greater driving force behind political and social change emanated from the
nobility. Under Salian rule momentous transformations took place in the
lower strata of the elite when nobles began pursuing innovative approaches
to concentrate power. Strategies to create dynastic centers, so successfully
employed by the early Salians, appealed to ever wider circles of aristocrats
in the eleventh and twelfth centuries. The practice of combining allodial

17. The bishop's book of Eichstätt (*Pontifikale Gundekarianum*) of 1071/72, depicting the founder of the bishopric, Willibald (upper row, center), and his successors (Diözensanarchiv Eichstätt, Cod. B, fol. 17).

wealth with accumulations of advocacies, counties, and clearing privileges became widespread. Such schemes of concentrating power were generally accompanied by the building of a substantial castle, which then assumed the function of a territorial power center (*Sitzkonzentration*). A new type of noble lordship was emerging whose hallmarks were fortified residences perched on lofty promontories and mountain tops (*Höhenburgen*). The landlord loosened his ties to the manorial estate (*Fronhof, Salhof*) and moved to his towering castle, which henceforth constituted the center of his territorial dominion. The self-confidence of powerful secular leaders is reflected in the seal of Duke Henry VII of Bavaria (fig. 18) dating from the mid-eleventh century.

The formation of secular lordships, though intensely pursued, did not evolve as systematically as the restructuring of the bishoprics; greater regional discrepancies occurred in this process.[13] Secular lordships faced the constant threat of discontinuity since the male lineage of a family could become extinct at almost any time. As a consequence they were greatly disadvantaged vis-à-vis the episcopal lordships which were firmly established and secure through the permanence of the episcopal office. The demise of several powerful families around the middle of the eleventh century, such as the Ebersbergers in Bavaria, the Conradines in the Wetterau, and the Ezzos in the lower Rhine region, led to a radical redistribution of power and privileges and prompted the rise of new aristocratic dominions. Toward the end of the eleventh and the beginning of the twelfth century, this process was further accelerated by a close association between certain segments of the nobility and the monastic reform movement, especially in Swabia. Recent research has shown convincingly that the so-called reform aristocracy managed to enhance the independence and permanence of its dominions through the assistance of the reformed monasteries of Hirsau and Saint Blaise.[14] While nobles in this group renounced any and all proprietary claims vis-à-vis these foundations, they received in return advocacies, which granted them jurisdictional and administrative rights. Through guaranteed protection and the administration of justice, the noble advocate managed the monastery's secular affairs. An advocacy, generally tied to a specific noble family by hereditary right, was not subject to the customary division of inherited wealth. Consequently, such arrangements could aid in concentrating power in the hands of a particular lineage, providing the foundation for a secure future. If a magnate succeeded in acquiring advocacies from several monastic foundations, he could substantially expand his dominion. Many noble families who eventually rose to great promi-

18. Seal of Duke Henry VII of Bavaria (1045) (Bayerisches Hauptstaatsarchiv, Munich, U III).

nence established themselves during this period. Among them were the Scheyern-Wittelsbach, who in the waning years of Salian rule used such schemes to create a territorial power base and to position themselves for their meteoric rise within the Bavarian duchy.[15]

Seemingly countless references in the sources indicate that the eleventh century witnessed a first thrust toward tightly structured territorial dominions that drew their strength from hierarchical stratification. The source materials, furthermore, frequently associate the progressive restructuring of church and nobility with a novel practice of harshness and a related decline of mercy and compassion, especially in the second half of the eleventh century. We thus learn from the *Church History of Hamburg* that Archbishop Adalbert of Hamburg-Bremen would have been happy to give his people a sound thrashing every day. His colleague Archbishop Anno II of Cologne (1056–1075) supposedly treated the people of his city with such severity that they rose up against his arrogance and harshness (*insolentia* and *austeritas*).[16] We shall hear more about Anno's conflicts with the townspeople of Cologne later in this chapter. Around 1080 when the bishop of Bamberg threatened one of their brothers with harsh punishment the canons of the Alte Kapelle in Regensburg countered with a biblical quote: "Whoever does not know any pity deserves a judgment without pity himself."[17] And in the *Episcopal History of Eichstätt* (1075/1078), Pope Leo IX (1048/49–1054), reminds church reformers, who demanded severe punishment for any and all offenders, to bear the following in mind: "Brothers, it should not displease you if I, a sinner, show indulgence toward sinners. It should rather displease you that I would punish any sinner more harshly than the one who never sinned and whose lips never let an evil word escape. Nowhere in the entire gospel will you find a passage where our Lord Jesus disciplined anyone with fasting and beating; to those who repented, he would say instead: 'Go in peace and sin no more!' "[18]

Many more such examples could be cited. Each represents a vivid illustration of the slow changes that also began to affect the legal system by altering its focus from judicial compensation to judicial punishment. The idea of providing the injured party with adequate compensation increasingly lost ground to the demand of inflicting just punishment on the offender. The "Truce of God" and the "Peace of God," a movement that spread into the German realm from Burgundy around 1080 and embraced the concept of public peace (*Landesfriedenidee*), lent additional support to these developments, for this movement was primarily concerned with a centralized and uniform administration of criminal justice. In particular, the conduct of feuds as lawful means for settling disputes among aristocrats was to be curbed—an idea that met with little success initially. In this context it should be mentioned that at the very end of the Salian era, rudimentary forms of inquisitorial proceedings began to appear, a phenomenon that reflects the growing obsession with the discovery of absolute truth. Only unequivocal proof of guilt would allow for proper punishment. Viktor Achter summed it up aptly when he entitled his book on these matters *The Birth of Punishment*.[19]

Magnates and office holders alike adopted the concept of obedience as a legal norm for their actions. In 1065 King Henry IV deposed Abbot Udalrich of Lorsch "because of disobedience" (*propter inobedientiam*).[20]

In the same year a jurisdictional dispute between Archbishop Anno II of Cologne and the monastery of Malmedy led to a serious confrontation. When the monks refused to submit to the metropolitan's authority, he worded a summons to the four representatives of Malmedy as follows: "I give you this order in the name of holy obedience that you owe" (*per sanctam obedientiam precipio*).²¹ Eventually the duty of obedience was elevated to the level of a hallowed law when the great reform pope, Gregory VII (1073–1085), demanded unconditional obedience in all matters and from all mortals. He wrote to King Henry IV as early as 1075, that he would only greet him "if he would obey the Pope as was befitting to a Christian king" (*si tamen apostolice sedi, ut Christianum decet regem, oboedierit*).²²

These innovative lordships and hierarchical structures also required managers. Trustworthy dependents emerging from the strata of servile peasants, men who could easily be directed, seemed ideally suited to take on such responsibilities. Of course, there had always been servants who, based on outstanding ability and talent, were employed for special assignments by their lords. These were rarely the same individuals who were responsible for cultivating the land (*Hufenbauern*) or who had managed to secure special privileges within the manorial system by replacing their service obligations with payments in coin or kind (e.g., *Wachszinser*, individuals who owed wax for candles). Servants chosen for extraordinary services most likely came from the ranks of dependents living on the manor in close proximity to their lords. Under Salian rule powerful magnates increasingly relied on these personal servants (*servi properii*) to fulfill administrative functions and to provide military security for their newly created dominions. The designation *ministerials* for this group of trained warriors seems to have originated in the episcopal lordships. Men who fulfilled the same or similar functions at the royal court, in contrast, were commonly referred to as *servientes* until the end of the Salian era.²³

These changes occurred over an extended period of time, of course. But already in the 1060s we encounter a document which describes the rights of the ministerials of Bamberg (*iusticia ministerialium Babenbergensium*, 1061/62). It clearly shows that a group with special legal status had emerged, separate and distinct from the rest of the peasantry. Here we find the remarkable sentences:

The son of a ministerial is entitled to his father's fief. If there is no son, the closest arm-bearing relative (*Schwertmage*) shall turn over the dead kin's armor and a horse—the best that he had owned—to his lord; the fief of the deceased, however, he may keep for himself. If a ministerial participates in a campaign, he shall join his lord's host at his own expense. After that, he shall be maintained by the lord. If the campaign goes to Italy, the lord shall contribute a horse and three pounds for each of his armored knights (*Panzerreiter*). If the campaign goes elsewhere, two ministerials shall bear the expense of a third.[24]

The ministerials of Bamberg were obviously provided with a special support system for their services; they were given service fiefs (*Dienstlehen*) which, according to the provisions, were inheritable. The special privileges that the lord granted to his ministerials became permanent entitlements for the beneficiaries' family. The wording "he [the ministerial] shall join his lord's host at his own expense" further shows that these functionaries (*Dienstleute*) had long since ceased to live as personal servants (*Eigenknechte*) in close proximity to their lords. They now dwelt on their own ministerial estates.

Another provision in the *iusticia ministerialium Babenbergensium* is noteworthy: ministerials were supposedly exempt from the judicial authority of the advocate. Such a privilege seems truly extraordinary since serfs (*Grundholden*) who were dependents of a church, a bishopric, or a monastic foundation were almost universally subject to the jurisdiction of the advocate who, for a fee, administered justice. Earlier than their counterparts in other bishoprics, the ministerials of Bamberg had apparently succeeded in attaining a separate legal status vis-à-vis the judicial court of their episcopal lord. Questions of jurisdiction often led to bitter disputes between advocates and ministerials or, occasionally, even between advocates and bishops. Diocesan advocates (*Hochstiftsvögte*) regularly attempted to use their jurisdictional power to bring episcopal ministerials under their direct authority in order to draw them into their own ministerialage. All of these phenomena bear witness to the rapid rise of the ministerials as a new estate and show how energetically this group sought to expand and safeguard its special military and legal status.

The size of this rising warrior class is hard to estimate. We do know, though, that the number of ministerials steadily increased under Salian rule. Around 1100 their ranks had become so powerful that, on occasion, they even posed a threat to the established nobility. Such a situation arose when Count Sighard of Burghausen, a determined foe of ministerial aspirations, was murdered at Regensburg in 1104. Archaeological evidence convincingly conveys that a network of fortified ministerial residences (*Ministerialensitze*) was forming throughout episcopal and secular lordships in the second half of the eleventh century. Within these ministerial centers a new type of courtly lifestyle first began to evolve. Next to military exercises, board games must have enjoyed great popularity, as evidenced by the large number of chess, morris (*Mühle*), and backgammon boards that have recently been retrieved from archaeological sites at eleventh-century castles. This new warrior elite composed of ministerials must have been fairly well established by the end of the Salian period, for the author of *The Life of Henry IV* demanded in 1106: "Return the people, who have been taken away for military service, to work the fields, and your barns will once again be full!"[25] This appeal fell on deaf ears, however; there was no stopping of the forces that had been unleashed.

Because of its pivotal role in assisting with the formation of new episcopal and secular lordships, the emerging ministerial class gradually attained a more favorable legal status than other groups of "unfree" people. Two factors are crucial within this context: social advancement through special function and the ascent into a warrior elite designed to support the expanding territorial lordships. These observations are important because the growing emphasis on "functional values," as opposed to "redemptive values," became a hallmark of the Salian era. Typical were the efforts of the secular clergy to gain preeminence over the members of monastic orders; the clerics based their claim on the premise that they were actively engaged in the saving of their fellow men's souls while the monks were only concerned with their own salvation. As a consequence the cleric became functionally "more important to the Church" than the monk whose occupation had only personal redemptive value.[26] "Rising in the service of the lord" is another phenomenon that deserves close scrutiny, especially since research traditionally has dealt with the Salian period as if the whole society had been on the move, as if vertical and horizontal mobility had given all people broad opportunities for social improvement and had made it easy to escape traditional bonds. Such trends did exist, of course, particularly in and around the Rhenish and Lotharingian cities; however, the common man never enjoyed the type of social mobility that we associate with modern times. Ministerials and city dwellers, moreover, comprised only a very small segment of the servile population. Overall the large mass of serfs and other dependents became subject to more rather than less seigniorial pressure, as has been shown in connection with the construction boom and the implementation of increased severity in the newly constituted dominions.

It is hard to uncover how rural populations were affected by these extra burdens or how the whole scenario played itself out in detail. However, the question remains whether or not this new social order was paral-

19. Building the tower of Babel, symbolizing the widespread construction activities in the second quarter of the eleventh century (London, British Museum, Cotton MS Claudius B IV, fol. 19).

leled by more intensive methods of production in agriculture and craftsmanship, which in turn provided a basis for enhanced achievements. The
enormous accomplishments in the field of construction in the course of
the eleventh century (fig. 19), whether in cities, churches, or fortifications,
can only be explained on the basis of corresponding changes in work
efficiency. As trade and commerce kept gaining momentum through the
expansion of cities, new markets developed and stimulated economic initiatives and innovations. It is known, furthermore, that a trend toward the
dissolution of the manorial system set in during this period, and that to a
degree compulsory labor services could be replaced by regular payments
of dues and tithes. This situation provided many people with opportunities to turn their work potential into a personal advantage, thus creating
greater incentives to improve individual performance levels. Within the
confines of such a general framework, which is loosely defined and subject
to great regional variations, crucial shifts began stirring up the lower strata
of society as well. Increased seigneurial pressure, as graphically portrayed
in the *Episcopal History of Eichstätt*, could therefore be interpreted as a con-
scious attempt to exploit the options of a more productive work force.

Both lords and dependents were, in principle, participants in these
changes and had a stake in them. For these reasons a constant finetuning
of the equilibrium between the demands of the lord and the performance
of the serfs was indispensable. The serfs, undoubtedly, had the option of
appealing to their customary rights when their lords' demands wrought
hardships or when arbitrary orders were given.[27] The rendering of dues and
services was basically determined by justifiable procedures and parameters
embedded in customary law. Despite this fact dependents unobtrusively
sought ways to reduce their workloads while landlords, conversely, tended
to demand increased productivity. For example, it is well known that the
ministerials, whom King Henry IV had assigned to garrison the castles
in the Harz Mountains, considered it their unequivocal right to requisi-
tion supplies and provisions from the local peasantry at will. The agents of
the new ruler did not feel constrained by the traditional rights of the afflicted parties and never looked upon their actions as contrary to the law.
Nevertheless, the ambivalence of such situations was clearly understood,
as demonstrated by a document issued under Conrad II for the monastery
of Limburg on the Haardt River on 7 January 1035. The reasons for issuing
this diploma is spelled out as follows: "In order to prevent future abbots
from demanding more from their dependents than permissible and to prevent dependents from forgetting their customary obligations in the course

of time, from becoming haughty towards their abbot, and from neglecting to fulfill their duties toward the monastery, it was deemed necessary to write down everything that the abbot—if needs be—may demand and that the dependents must render."[28]

The intricate web of interlocking bonds between manorial lords and their dependents was gradually transformed into a polar relationship between autocratic noble masters and their subjects. Simultaneously, the old system was slowly torn asunder by the enormous expansion of urban life. Paralleling the ascent of the ministrials, urban growth was primarily promoted by those who ruled over the cities, particularly the bishops. Beginning in the tenth and more intensively in the eleventh century, the episcopal lords invested great energy in the development of their urban centers. They secured royal trade privileges and obtained market and mint rights to enhance the economic potential of their cities. The fact that the bishops viewed their seats increasingly as economic centers was clearly indicated by their coinage. Although most bishops had been authorized to issue their own currency since the tenth century, they continued the tradition of minting coins with the image of the secular ruler. Then, in the middle of the eleventh century, a crucial shift occurred: the episcopal lords began the production of actual bishop's coins that were imprinted with their own image as a symbol of economic patronage.

During the Salian period cities experienced unprecedented growth, increasing their original area tenfold in some cases, as in Speyer for example.[29] Entire new quarters cropped up and innovative building techniques, frame construction instead of post and lintel, facilitated the erection of structures with several stories. A ring of fortifications, often the first stone constructions of their kind, surrounded the newly established centers, protecting the recent settlements of merchants and crafts people.

The urban lords needed people to support the expansion of their cities and their commerce. The search for an appropriate workforce was, therefore, often accompanied by special incentives, such as the promise of improved legal status. A document issued to the city of Speyer in 1025 under Conrad II may serve as a typical illustration.[30] Bishop Walther of Speyer offered eleven children, born into marriages contracted between a servile man and a free woman, the opportunity to enter into the *censuality*, that is, into the most favorable legal status available to a servile individual. In the aforementioned document, Conrad II confirmed the measures initiated by the bishop. Consequently, these children were no longer required to render compulsory labor services. They were now in a position to dispose

20. The oldest seal of the city of Cologne (1114/19) (Historisches Archiv of the city of Cologne, HUA 1/269b).

more freely over their own labor, whether in city services or in commercial ventures. The close connection between the privileges of *censuality* and the legal status of townspeople in early urban centers (*urbana lex*) is particularly compelling in the case of Regensburg.[31] Recent research has shown, moreover, that leading townspeople in many developing cities, such as Worms, were predominantly ministerials in the service of the bishop.[32] These men often held important offices, such as heading the mint or customs. They also had property in town, owned houses, and accumulated wealth.

The unprecedented urban development setting in during the Salian period, however, showed great variation from region to region and from city to city. Regensburg, Worms, and Mainz, without any question, were at the cutting edge of these changes. But no urban center was further advanced than Cologne whose city seal hails from the waning days of Salian rule (fig. 20). This urban community provides an excellent case study of the evolving social dynamics. Here the *Richerzeche* (literally the guild of the rich), a body of influential townspeople, was already firmly ensconced at the close of the Salian era;[33] and it can be observed how a wealthy, self-assured "bourgeoisie" early on began to challenge the domineering aspirations of its metropolitan overlord. In 1074 Archbishop Anno II of Cologne unceremoniously requisitioned the commercial vessel of a Cologne merchant for the conveyance of a visitor. There seemed no doubt in the archbishop's mind that he had acted within his rights, within his canonical rights so to speak, as became evident during subsequent judicial proceedings against the insurgent townspeople. The merchants and other inhabitants of Cologne, in contrast, viewed the seizure of the boat as an act of arrogance and tyrannical harshness against the people and felt compelled to voice their opposition.

This incident resulted in a popular uprising that posed a serious threat to Anno II's life. He was saved only by a fortuitous coincidence. Shortly before these events, a cathedral canon had commissioned the construction of a private passage that led from his residence through the adjoining city wall beyond the urban enclosure (fig. 21). This arrangement allowed the archbishop to escape from the cathedral which was being assaulted by an angry mob. He reached the secret back door through the dormitory of the chapter house, the atrium, and the canon's house, and got away on horseback under cover of darkness. When Anno II and his supporters regained control of the city a few days later, a harsh judgment was imposed. It was designed to suppress the flagrant disregard of archiepiscopal

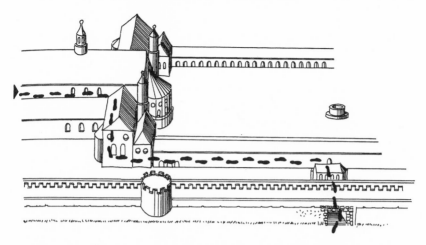

21. Route of escape taken by Archbishop Anno II of Cologne 1074 (Diederich, Ausstellungskatalog "Monumenta Annonis," 1975, S. 31).

authority. The merchants' houses and homes were pillaged, resisting individuals were killed or bound in chains, the ringleaders were blinded, and others were whipped and shorn. Lampert of Hersfeld, a contemporary chronicler, reported that all participants were heavily fined and lost many of their assets. Lampert added: "Thus, the city that until recently had been the most populous and, next to Mainz, the most important and preeminent among Rhenish cities, suddenly had become desolate. Where streets used to teem with pedestrian crowds, hardly a human soul can be seen, and an eerie silence prevails among places where pleasure and enjoyment used to dwell."[34]

The archbishop prevailed and proper order was restored. Once again it must be emphasized, though, that Anno never doubted the legitimacy of his claims and actions, a fact that is underscored by his subsequent demands for canonically prescribed penances. To mete out punishment based on power alone would have been alien to the medieval concept of justice, however. The very principle of determining justice through the assembled court required a high approval rate for every decision. Consequently, we must presume that the Salian era, in a more general way, gave rise to ideas and models that envisioned a social order which was compatible with and supportive of hierarchical structures and seignorial claims.

In the early Middle Ages the prevailing view divided society into three distinct orders (*tria genera hominum*) — laypeople, clerics, and monks. This division was based on the interpretation of certain biblical passages, such as Augustine's reference to Jesus' discourse on the end of times: At the end of the world it will be as in Noah's days, and two will be found in the field, two working in the mill, and two resting on their beds.[35] Augustine saw the workers in the field as leaders of the church (workers in the vineyard), the people at the mill as laymen (the mill as the world), and those on their beds as monks. The monks were inward looking and frail, attended to prayer, had neither house nor family, and did not participate in the work of the church. Such interpretations were designed to explain the entire world within a spiritual framework of biblical truth. Each group of people was assessed according to its way of life and was biblically ranked in terms of its redemptive value.

Toward the end of the tenth century and in the course of the eleventh, this societal view was slowly superseded by a novel, almost revolutionary model. The new concept was based on a *functional* interpretation of social groupings. No longer were the social divisions determined by biblical or redemptive principles, but rather by secular functions. Accordingly, there was an order that prayed, an order that fought, and an order that worked: praying men, warriors, and workers (*oratores, bellatores, laboratores/agricultores*). Secular clergy and monks were merged into one group, lay people, on the other hand, were divided into two (fig. 22). The most remarkable factor was, however, that these new classifications lacked any biblical foundation whatsoever.

In the 1020s Bishop Adalbero of Laon (977–1033), in his *Song to King Robert*, further developed some of the themes that had been vaguely sketched by earlier authors. In his text we find the following clarification: "The House of God is divided into three parts: some pray, others fight, the third work. There are only these three groups, and there is no further division. The duties of one group enable the other groups to fulfill their tasks, and through their respective duties all are served."[36] Each order, accordingly, had to share in designated responsibilities in order to allow the others to fulfill their functions. All orders were mutually interdependent and, therefore, had to accept their lot without complaint.

Clerics were not allowed to participate in any type of worldly activity according to the *lex divina* (the divine law); their tasks consisted of prayer, spreading the gospel, and administering the sacraments. The life of laymen was determined by the *lex humana* (the human law) which distinguishes between two orders, noblemen (*nobiles*) and servants (*servi*). All members of the first lay group, emperor, kings, and noblemen, essentially

22. Knights and peasants, tympanon from the defunct church of Saint Ursin in Bourges, end of eleventh century (Le Goff, *Kultur des europäischen Mittelalters*, 1970, p. 454, illustration 114).

had the same obligation: they were to serve as warriors and protectors of the church and to stand up for those who were defenseless. They were supposed to be the *bellatores* or *pugnatores*. The king, in particular, was responsible for keeping the peace and for curbing the magnates' propensity for violence.

Adalbero used the term *servi* to describe those people whose lot within the tripartite functional nexus (*Funktionsverbund*) was defined by work. Their lot seemed truly deplorable to him: "These down-trodden people have nothing except their work. Who can describe their duties, their toil, and their efforts, their incredible burden? They provide cloth and food for all, and no nobleman can survive without his workers. . . . Thus, the lord is fed by the servant and not the other way round, as the nobleman would have it. But the tears and lamentations of the workers are without bounds." The servile status of the laborer, thus, became an indispensable prerequisite for the functioning of society; the ancient Christian view of freedom as the natural state of all men and of the servile condition only as a consequence of sin was thrust aside.

Historians have long debated whether the emergence of this new societal model was due to the influence of Greek philosophers or to a particular developmental stage in society itself.[37] Both possibilities deserve consideration, but the decisive factor was, undoubtedly, the need of this age to find a model that would provide a plausible explanation for social change. New ideas had been spreading eastward from Lotharingia and Burgundy and, once they had reached the regions north and east of the Rhine, merged in with the new seignorial aspirations of the secular and ecclesiastical elite. Because of their functional bonds and their earthly lot, the laborers (increasingly referred to as the "peasant estate") were obligated to provide the services that the other two orders needed and demanded. This fateful twist furnished the conceptual foundation and justification for the harsher treatment that the serfs now experienced at the hands of their lords.

Another aspect of this model is noteworthy; it basically no longer provided a slot for an exalted ruler who dwelt in splendid isolation as God's representative on earth. Within functional parameters, king and nobility were essentially assigned the same tasks. This fact, on the one hand, underscored the idea that the distance between ruler and magnates could not possibly be very significant and, on the other hand, that both bore an equal responsibility for the realm and for keeping the peace. Whether such theoretical considerations actually affected the thoughts and actions of the elite is hard to determine. However, it is remarkable that the conceptual model and the political development seemed to be converging. From this perspective, it was hardly accidental that Henry III's autocratic and arrogant rulership with its blatant disregard for social realities was facing increased criticism.

5

Henry III: The Emperor of Peace and His Critics

THE EMPEROR CONRAD II DIED IN 1039. Having been afflicted with gout for a long time, he was stricken by unbearable pain on 3 June while celebrating Pentecost in Utrecht. The next day he felt that his end had come. "He summoned his bishops and had the body and blood of Christ, a holy cross, and holy relics brought to him. Shedding fervent tears, he pulled himself upright and with true humility received communion with the saints and absolution of his sins after sincere confession and prayer. With friendly admonitions, he took leave of the empress and his son King Henry [III] and departed from this life on Monday, 4 June."[1] The emperor's entrails were buried in the Cathedral of Utrecht; but the splendidly veiled body in its coffin was transferred to Speyer. Accompanied by Gisela, her son Henry, and the royal retinue, as well as many of the imperial princes, the emperor's body was first brought to Cologne and from there to Mainz and Worms, then to its final destination. Thirty days after his demise, Conrad II was given a magnificent burial in "his" cathedral at Speyer on 3 July 1039.

Conrad II's death must have come unexpectedly, even though he had not been well for a while. However, his passing did not jeopardize the continuity of the realm and the kingship since the royal succession had been more meticulously prepared than ever before. Henry III had been a crowned head since 1028 and was, so to speak, a monarch-in-waiting. His father had taken great care to provide him with an outstanding education at the court of Bishop Bruno of Augsburg (1006–1029), who happened to be the brother of Emperor Henry II. For this reason, he was particularly well-suited to impart regal concepts and imperial traditions. Considering this tutelage, it should not be surprising that Henry III's rulership in many respects bore a close resemblance to that of Henry II's. Conrad II

23. Henry III presents the Virgin Mary, patron of the cathedral of Speyer (note architectural features in background), with the precious evangelary. To the right the royal wife Agnes bows. The four medallions represent the four cardinal virtues. Dedicatory image in the Golden Evangelary of Henry III, end of 1045 or first half of 1046 (made in the monastery of Echternach; now located in the Escorial in Madrid, Cod. Vitrinas 17, fol. 3).

had personally introduced his young son to the intricacies of royal governance. Furthermore, the Salian's acquisition of the three southern German duchies provided Henry III with a powerbase which exceeded that of any individual duke. At this point it must be emphasized once again that Conrad II had fulfilled his electors' expectations: he had secured the continuity of the kingship, the uninterrupted existence of royal authority, and hence the preservation of peace and unity.

Henry III, born on 28 October 1017, not only assumed the rulership and continued his father's preconceived course, but further exalted this monarch's prestige. This process is mirrored in the early history of the royal cathedral at Speyer. In 1043 Henry III buried his mother, Gisela, there; and around the same time he began to bestow special favors on this episcopal see. Almost every year he spent time in Speyer, his "beloved place." Toward the end of 1045 at the earliest, but probably shortly before departing for his imperial coronation in Rome, he donated a richly adorned evangelary, the *Codex Aureus*, to Saint Mary's church. This precious manuscript, currently kept in the Esquorial in Madrid, contains the sentence: "Speyer shall shine in splendor through the favors and gifts of King Henry" (*Spira fit insignis Heinrici munere regis*) (fig. 23). Speyer and its cathedral were to be expanded on a magnificent scale and the fame of its school was to spread throughout the realm. During Henry III's reign the original structure was substantially enlarged and its length extended by fully one third. The royal cathedral at Speyer with its gigantic proportions and a length of almost 134 meters (about 500 feet) emerged as the largest sacred edifice north of the Alps and found no equal in Western Christendom: Saint Mary's towered above all other churches (fig. 24).

Most remarkable, though, were the alterations undertaken at the Salian grave site. The two openings leading to the atrium in the crypt, located next to the graves of Conrad II and Gisela, were filled in and replaced by new flights of stairs descending directly to the main crypt from the lateral aisles. These measures freed the entire width of the middle aisle for the burial site. But that was not all: about one third of the nave, a huge expanse of nine by twenty-one meters (about 2,200 square feet), was set apart for royal graves, providing enough space to bury kings and queens for centuries to come (fig. 25). These alterations comprise the essence of the second Salian ruler's royal consciousness: his dynasty's kingship had been established to include all future generations and was expected to be tied to the cathedral of Speyer forever. Such dynastic aspirations rested not only on the Salians' hereditary claims, but were also nourished by an insti-

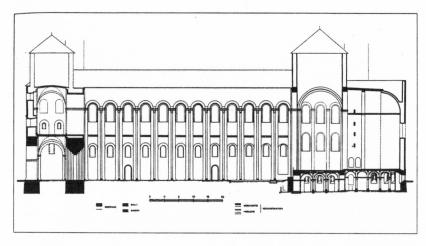

24. Henry III's cathedral at Speyer, longitudinal cross-section reconstruction (Fenner/Von Winterfeld).

tutional ideology, that is, the transpersonal legitimacy. Just as the kingship could never perish, there was no end to the royal dynasty. What had been vague notions under Conrad II emerged as a set of well-defined ideas during the reign of his son.

Why was the concept of a transpersonal kingship pursued with such intensity? The answer to this question must be sought in ecclesiastical and religious forces that were at work during this period. As pointed out earlier, institutional thinking became more and more important in the episcopate of the eleventh century; as the idea of continuity, expressed through orderly succession, became firmly established in the episcopal consciousness, each bishop saw himself as a link connected to the chain of his predecessors, responsible for carrying on their mission. In many places old church traditions were revived with renewed fervor, as, for example, in Mainz, Hamburg, or Cologne, in Paderborn or Eichstätt.[2] The idea of looking at the king as Christ's representative on earth was now apparently shaped by the changing mentality within the church and, increasingly, became part of an institutional pattern. Moreover, Henry III's marriage in 1043 to the extremely devout Agnes of Poitou from Burgundy undoubtedly strengthened his own confirmed piety and must have augmented the influx of ecclesiastical currents into the conception of kingship. These arguments show clearly that it does not suffice to focus on the fact that the bishops furthered their status through the acquisition of regalia and

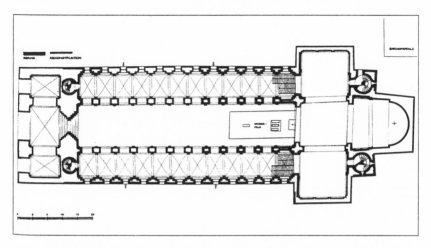

25. Blueprint of the cathedral at Speyer with expanded burial site (1056) (Richter/ Von Winterfeld).

crown lands and through the emulation of royal practices. Equally important are the ways in which the king employed the forces emanating from
the church to support the idea of a transpersonal kingship. Once again, we
encounter a constellation of forces that can visibly be grasped in the impressive design of the Salian cathedral and burial site at Speyer.

As frequently indicated in contemporary sources, Christian and ecclesiastical ideals determined Henry III's concept of royal authority in other
respects as well. Abbot Bern of Reichenau and other authors compared
him to King David, for example.[3] Such comparisons were not new, of
course; they had appeared already in Merovingian and Carolingian sources
and were also applied to Henry II and Conrad II; yet their increased
frequency in reference to Henry III is striking.[4] Showing the ruler in a
favorable light through his association with David's name served multiple
purposes, among them the reference to a king who combined a desirable
personality with a firm grip on his reign (*desiderabilis et manufortis*). This
nexus of ideas is significant because it suggests that David had brought
about a Golden Age which now, under Henry III, would be revived.
David's kingship associated the ruler with the royal house of Christ, and
just as David in his person had preceded Christ, Henry now appeared as a
postfiguration, as an "imitatio" of Christ.

Such allusions became even more obvious when Henry III ended the
papal schism during his stay at Rome in 1046. His intervention in the dis-

pute among rival claimants to the papacy gave him the stature of a purifier and savior of the Church and likened him to Christ who had cleansed the Temple in Jerusalem. In the autumn of 1044, Pope Benedict IX (1032–1045), a member of the Tusculani family, had been driven out of Rome because of rivalries among the Roman patriciate. In his place Bishop John of Sabina from the house of Crescenti was elected at the beginning of 1045; he assumed the name of Sylvester III. Yet in March of the same year, Benedict IX managed to regain the papal throne. For unexplained reasons, on 1 May 1045 he sold his office for a considerable sum of money to the Archpriest John Gratianus of Saint John's at the Porta Latina; this pope adopted the name Gregory VI. The Salian court initially did not suspect any irregularities in this papal elevation; and even Peter Damian, the prior of the congregation of eremites at Fonte Avellana and later cardinal-bishop of Ostia (1057–1072), one of the great ecclesiastical reformers of his time, welcomed Pope Gregory VI enthusiastically. Damian, paradoxically, urged the new pope to champion the fight against simony—the common practice of buying and selling ecclesiastical offices.

These are not the only reports relating to the circumstances surrounding the Roman Church in 1045. For example, there is a contemporary poem that pleads with the king to resolve the scandalous situation of having three competing "popes" and to find *one* pontiff worthy of the apostolic office.[5] According to recent research,[6] though, Henry III traveled to Rome in the summer of 1046 not to end the papal schism, but for the sole purpose of securing the imperial crown. Just as his father, Conrad II, he believed that he was entitled to the imperial crown through his kingship. Wipo, a court insider, characteristically addressed Henry III as *pius rex caesaresque futurus* (pious king and future emperor) as early as Christmas 1041. Preliminary negotiations with Pope Gregory VI presumably went smoothly, and both king and pontiff had their names entered in a prayer confraternity at the church of Piacenza in northern Italy. Yet soon thereafter, long before the coronation scheduled for Christmas 1046, Henry III heard rumors that, in fact, Gregory VI had purchased his papal office. In great haste, the king proceeded to convene a synod at Sutri north of Rome for 20 December. For now closer scrutiny of the pontiff's legitimacy had become a matter of great urgency. Henry had to be absolutely certain that the integrity of the pope who was to crown him emperor was beyond reproach. No spectacular transformation of established Roman practices and certainly no radical Church reforms were being contemplated. At this point, the Salian monarch worried only about the future incontestability of his imperial coronation.

Nevertheless, these events bear witness to the amazing self-assurance with which the Salian rulers claimed the authority to examine the Church at its highest level and to take corrective action if it seemed warranted. Even if Henry III did not personally preside over the synod, as recent scholarship presumes, and if Pope Gregory VI, after fruitless justifications, gave up his papacy without being formally deposed, a point still hotly debated, it is evident that the whole scenario surrounding this imperial coronation was dominated and determined by the authority of the Salian king.

The compelling force behind this authority was nourished by the conviction of the king and his court that royal rule was firmly rooted in ecclesiastical norms and canon law. Based on this view, the ruler could consider himself the primary guarantor of the proper observance of Church teachings. Henry III fought the practice of simony with great persistence. Despite most bishops' opposition to strict enforcement of canon law, the *Episcopal History of Eichstätt* reports for the year 1042 that no son of a priest could hope to be appointed to an episcopal office by the king. Thanks to the response of Bishop Wazo of Liège (1042–1048) and the anonymous author of the tract *De ordinando pontifice* (Concerning the Elevation of a Pope), composed in 1047, we have reliable documentation concerning contemporary reactions to the events at Sutri. Both critics relate Gregory VI's resignation and his subsequent imprisonment at Cologne directly to Henry III's authoritative actions. They accused the king of usurping rights that were the prerogative of priests, bishops, and popes who, by the very virtue of their office, were set over all lay people. Clerics were ordained to help men obtain eternal life; the king, on the other hand, was consecrated for war and, therefore, for men's death. Wazo supposedly said: "As high as life is placed above death, as high the priest is placed above the king!"[7] And the anonymous author of *De ordinando pontifice* even poses the question: "Where is it written [in the scriptures] that emperors are Christ's representatives [on earth]? . . . This depraved emperor did not hesitate to depose the one whom he was not even entitled to elect." Such critical voices still had little impact; however, they did not remain isolated, as we shall see shortly.

Yet another synod was called for 24 December 1046, designed to elevate a new pope. It is not known who presided over this synod, but there is no doubt that it was dominated by the authoritative presence of the king. He had hoped—as we learn from Adam of Bremen's *Ecclesiastical History of Hamburg*—that Adalbert, the archbishop of Hamburg-Bremen, would become the next pope. However, the latter supposedly declined the honor and recommended his friend, Bishop Suidger of Bamberg, for the

26. Christ, enthroned on the orb, is crowning Henry III and his royal wife, Agnes. Image of coronation in the Codex Caesareus of 1050 or shortly thereafter (made in the monastery of Echternach; now located in Uppsala, Sweden, Universitetsbiblioteket, Ms. C93, fol. 3).

papal office. Lacking other candidates, Bishop Suidger was eventually approved and enthroned as Clement II on 25 December 1046. Immediately after this event, the new pope crowned Henry III and his spouse Agnes as emperor and empress. It is apparent, however, that the pontiff served only as a tool of the divine will in the whole process, as is symbolically expressed in the coronation image of the *Codex Caesareus*.[8] This valuable manuscript was a gift from the emperor to the newly consecrated foundation of Saints Simon and Jude in Goslar (1050). The miniature depicting the coronation shows the following inscription above the figure of Christ who, surrounded by the mandorla, is enthroned on the globe of the earth: "Henry and Agnes rule through me, they shall live" (*per me regnantes, vivant Heinricus et Agnes*). Christ stretches out his hands to both sides and bestows the crowns on the emperor and the empress (fig. 26).

Henry III's "act of purification" at Sutri and Rome—apparently motivated by concrete circumstances rather than ideology—ushered in a new phase in which the Church provided the mortar to bind the disparate entities of the realm together. Not only the fact that Clement II was the first of a series of "German" popes is noteworthy, but also that he and his successors were all imperial bishops who did not give up their German bishoprics after their elevation to the papacy. Combining the papal dignity with an episcopal office (*papa qui et episcopus*) was perhaps an attempt to satisfy the canonical requirement that a bishop never abandon his flock once it has been entrusted to him. This reasoning makes even more sense if we remember that Henry III meticulously observed canon law. In addition, such a configuration opened up new avenues for the incorporation of the Roman Church into the overall framework of the German imperial church system.[9] In any case, in subsequent papal elevations this principle was consistently observed: Clement II was followed by Bishop Poppo of Brixen[10] as Pope Damasus II (1047/48). His successor, in turn, was Bishop Bruno of Toul as Pope Leo IX (1048/49), and after the latter's death Bishop Gebhard of Eichstätt ascended to the pontifical throne as Pope Victor II (1054/55). Through an enduring personal union between pope and German imperial bishop, the head of Western Christendom would be closely tied to the secular ruler who, in turn, could insist on his loyalty. This principle offered the ideal solution: the universality of the apostolic office, needed to support claims to imperial power, was left intact, while at the same time the pontiff remained a member of the imperial church system, which was oriented toward the king as its highest authority.

Attuned to the emperor's ideals, these popes pursued the purification of the Church with great energy: the fight against clerical abuses reached its first climax under Pope Leo IX (1048/49–1054). During his five-year tenure, he convened and personally conducted twelve synods in Germany, France, and Italy, each dealing with clerical reform. All of these assemblies focused on questions of simony and priestly marriages (Nicolaitism). Going further than any of his predecessors, Leo IX pleaded for the invalidation of any and all consecrations that had been performed by simoniacs. However, he failed to prevail in this matter at the synod of Vercelli in 1050. He also assumed an unyielding position regarding priestly marriages: at his first Roman synod in April 1049 already, he argued that all women married to priests should become the property of the Lateran Church [in Rome] without delay. It was Leo's explicit goal to achieve radical renewal and purification of the Church in accordance with the norms of canon law.

In this context, it is noteworthy that the "German" popes, especially since Leo IX, pushed vigorously for an institutionalization of the supreme power of the papacy. The new approach to synodal politics allowed the pontiffs to expand their influence beyond the regional confines of Rome and central Italy. Just as the kings had sought to control their realm more thoroughly since Henry II and Conrad II, the popes now increasingly undertook extensive visitation journeys throughout the entire Church, using their physical presence to underscore their supreme authority (fig. 27). The synod, under the direction of the papacy, now purported to be the one and only body that was representative of the whole of Christendom. Changes in the composition of the curia and the college of cardinals further allowed the pope to pursue the reform of the priesthood without interference from the Roman patriciate. Efforts to centralize and reorganize the entire Church hierarchically under the firm grip of the papacy definitely accelerated during the tenure of Leo IX. Although several more steps were required before the process could culminate in the great reform papacy of Gregory VII, the seeds for his claim to universality had definitely been sown. Convinced of his preeminent position within Christendom, Leo IX, as early as 1054, dared order the patriarch of Constantinople, Michael Kerullarios (1043–1058), to submit to the authority of Rome; when the Byzantine metropolitan refused to comply, he condemned him and his followers as recalcitrant heretics. In Peter Damian's words: "Whoever does not agree with the Roman Church is branded a heretic by the holy canons." This definition of a heretic clearly captures the intellectual and theological background that led to the schism.[11]

Only within the framework of these early reform efforts and the in-

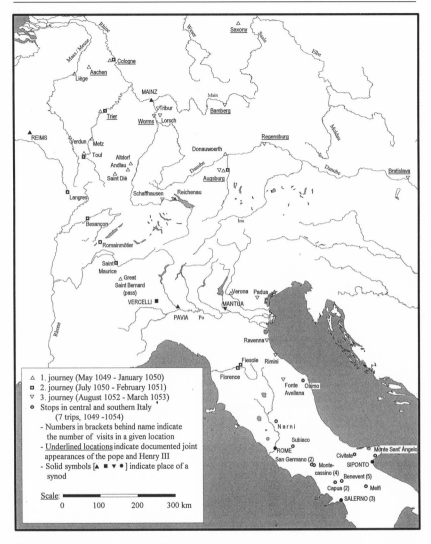

27. Journeys of "the traveling Pope," Leo IX (1048/49–1054) (adapted from H. Keller, *Zwischen regionaler Begrenzung und universalem Horizont*, 1986, p. 108).

cipient hierarchical restructuring of the Church does the scope of the interaction between Church and ruler become intelligible. The emperor had succeeded in playing a crucial role in the papal election; and by crowning himself "patricius," that is, lord over the city of Rome, he had secured his position against all possible challenges. Moreover, he had managed to integrate the pope, who was an imperial bishop as well, into the "Imperial Church System" under the leadership of the king. Under these circumstances, royal authority was actually enhanced through the centralizing tendencies of the papal reform; for in Henry III's view the papal efforts were an extension of the highest secular power, of the imperial office itself.

The Church's focus on the authority of the "central power" also affected the ranks of close clerical confidants at court, in other words, the royal chapel (*Hofkapelle*). Since 965 the archbishop of Mainz had continually held the office of archchaplain. As archchaplain he was also archchancellor of Germany; however, he only used the more distinguished title *archicapellanus* on the recognition line of royal diplomas. This practice underwent crucial changes during the reign of Henry III. Beginning in 1040, Bardo, who was archbishop of Mainz at that time (1031–1051), appears ever more frequently under the designation "archchancellor" on royal documents. Around the same time, it can be observed that the head of the royal chapel now often came from the ranks of leading clerics at court. The first of these was Theodoric, the chancellor and provost of the canonry at Saint Mary's in Aachen (1044–1046) who later became bishop of Constance (1047–1051). Eventually the title *archicapellanus* disappeared altogether and was replaced by the new title *capellarius*.

What was the purpose of this radical reshuffling of the top offices in the royal chapel? One important reason may have been the desire to disassociate the royal clergy from the jurisdictional power of the archbishop of Mainz.[12] Inevitably, any *capellarius* residing at court was more directly subjected to the ruler's authority and could execute his duties more efficiently. The old honorary office, held by the archbishop of Mainz, had thus been converted into a functionally defined institution directly subordinated to royal power.

A further aspect needs to be considered, however: through the demise of the archchaplain's office, the archchancellorship became the most prestigious of all the ecclesiastical offices at court. For instance, the archchancellor had the privilege of sitting next to the emperor (*primatus sedendi*), and was thus able to demonstrate his preeminence vis-à-vis the rest of the nobility. The archchancellor for Germany, as noted earlier, was the archbishop of Mainz. Italy had its own archchancellorship which King Conrad II had conferred on Archbishop Pilgrim of Cologne (1021–1036); and his successor, Hermann II (1036–1056), continued in this office under Henry III. Archbishop Hermann II was a descendant of the powerful Ezzonen family that for several generations held the office of count palatine on the Rhine and could boast of a royal blood line. He attained great prominence at the court of Henry III and was his closest confidant next to Bishop Gebhard of Eichstätt (1042–1057), the later Pope Victor II (1054/55–1057). As a trusted counselor, Hermann II accompanied the king to Italy and on the campaign against the Hungarians; he further supported him in his struggle with Godfrey the Bearded of Upper Lotharingia (see below). Hermann II's rank and position were so widely recognized that Pope Leo IX endowed him with the chancellorship of the Roman Church and hence with an honor that allowed him direct access to the Holy See. Hermann is another outstanding example of an imperial bishop who, in the service of Church and ruler, acted as a stabilizing force on behalf of the realm and the royal lordship. Eventually, in 1042/43, Henry III created a third chancellorship for Burgundy to parallel those for Germany and Italy. Deferring to the power structure in Burgundy, he conferred it on Archbishop Hugo of Besançon, who proved to be the perfect intermediary for this realm. This case illustrates vividly how Henry III employed the office of archchancellor to forge political alliances with high ecclesiastical dignitaries, who were expected to represent the ruler directly and to use their office to institutionalize the authority of the ruler.

If we take another look at the royal chapel overall, we notice that under Henry III more than half of the new bishops came from the ranks of the chaplains and that the royal chapel had actually become an elite institution for the training of future bishops. The palace at Goslar, with its royal canonry of Saints Simon and Jude (fig. 28), now played a leading role within the royal chapel and emerged as a significant educational center. These chaplain-bishops, almost as a matter of course, established very close ties between their episcopal sees and the royal court. In the process they helped intensify the trend toward a central regal authority, on one hand; on the other, they became the guardians of royal interests throughout the realm. Those chaplains in charge of the imperial relics or engaged in administrative and legal tasks achieved a remarkable level of sophistication in the field of public documentation; the quality of royal diplomas of this era remains unsurpassed (fig. 29).

We further learn that Henry III often joined the clergy at court in reading the scriptures or in pursuing learned discussions. Generally speaking, an unprecedented fervor aimed at improving the efficiency of the royal chapel can be observed. According to the *Augsburger Annals*, the ruler's enthusiasm for learning and active promotion of the arts and sciences led to a flourishing intellectual life. For example, at the emperor's suggestion

28. The palace of Henry III at Goslar, reconstruction (U. Hoelscher).

Master Ebbo of Worms, a member of the royal chapel, assembled a collection of songs which apparently were designed for recitation at court. These songs—as has been determined—constituted the core of the famous *Carmina Cantabrigiensa* (Songs of Cambridge). The scholarly and spiritual interests that bonded the king to his chaplains and other men in his following had a far-reaching impact and were instrumental in transforming the court into *the* intellectual center of the realm. In 1041 the royal chaplain Wipo even urged the king to issue an edict for all German lands, requiring the nobility to send their children to school to assure their familiarity with and knowledge of the written law.[13] Significant poetic works from this period reflect close connections to the royal court as they deal with such topics as court life and lordship, theology and church reform, and especially the ideology of peace. The epic *Ruodlieb*, though of somewhat later origin, exemplifies the concerns typically addressed in this literature.[14]

The intricate religious, political, and organizational linkages between ruler and Church during Henry III's reign created a unique situation. Only when we combine the various strands of royal ideology and authoritative leadership do we penetrate to the essence of Henry's kingship: the idea of universal peace.[15] The best introduction to the programmatic nature of this concept can be found in the *Tetralogus*, a treatise written by Wipo, Conrad II's biographer, in which *lex* (law) and *gratia* (grace) team up with

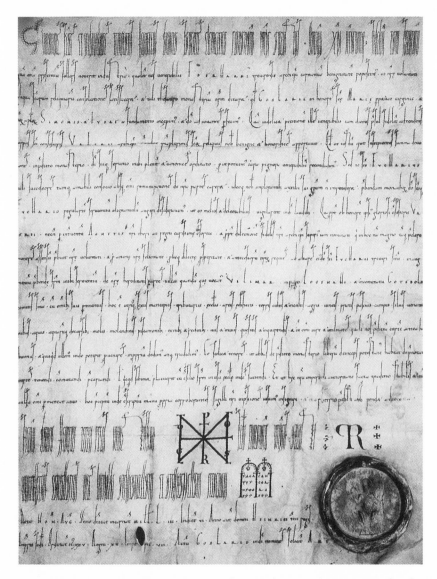

29. Charter of Emperor Henry III, issued in Goslar on 5 August 1053, for the monastery of Saint Eucharius in Trier (MGH DD H III. 309; Landeshauptarchiv Koblenz, Bestand 210, no. 20).

the author and the Muses to hold a four-way discourse in praise and encouragement of King Henry. Wipo, intermittently, had been one of this ruler's teachers, and as early as 1028 had authored a small tract with basic tenets of wisdom (*proverbia*) for the young prince's edification. No doubt, Wipo was intimately acquainted with the prevalent ideas at court; and his *Tetralogus* was not only a didactic tract, but a mirror image of the intellectual world that circumscribed Henry III's self-perception. The author presented the twenty-four-year-old king with the *Tetralogus* on Christmas Day 1042.

Five years prior to his imperial coronation, this treatise urged Henry III to devote his energies to the imperial task of maintaining order. It encouraged the young king to lead all mankind (*totus orbis*) into an age of all-encompassing peace (*pax*) according to God's will and pleasure. The Muses postulate that Henry's love for peace would preserve his memory through the ages if only he granted peace, in other words, if he insisted on it. But universal peace could only be achieved if law and mercy were observed. Higher justice, in this case royal justice, must be nourished by mercy: just as God in heaven mitigates punishment by mercy and grace and just as the Law of the Old Covenant was followed by the grace of the New Covenant through Christ. Within this framework, the ruler's person was projected as the closest approximation to Christ himself, and this concept of the king as peacemaker lent energy and legitimacy to his role as the sole representative of Christ's lordship on earth. Consequently, neither the universal Church nor the Pope were mentioned; the implementation of this ideology of peace rested strictly on a theocratic concept that placed the ruler at the pinnacle of the world order.

Wipo was not the only one to disseminate such ideas, however. Abbot Bern of Reichenau elaborated on similar themes in a letter to Henry III around the turn of 1044 to 1045:[16] God sent the bishops (*apostoli*) into this world to guide the king, being filled with divine mercy and justice, in his endeavor to achieve peace throughout the realm. The same ideas were discussed once again in Wipo's preface to the "Deeds of the Emperor Conrad II," dedicated to Henry III in 1046. His comments imply that Henry's program of *nova gratia* (new grace) was bound to have a healing effect on the realm. Just as Christ, through his redemptive death, had mediated God's mercy (*misericordia*) to this world, Henry's mission consisted in practicing divine mercy in his own right to prepare the world for universal peace.

Henry III's frequent acts of penitence and mercy show that his whole program was clearly in keeping with the way he perceived himself and his mission. We also learn from the abbot Bern of Reichenau[17] that, at the funeral of his mother Gisela, the king put his magnificent royal attire aside, and wearing only a penitent's sackcloth, threw himself prostrate on the ground in front of the assembled people. Making a public display of his penitence, he performed this act barefooted and with out-stretched arms, simulating the shape of a cross, and wetted the ground with many tears. At the synod of Constance in October 1043, shortly after his successful Hungarian campaign, the king stepped up to the altar and, according to the *Annals of Saint Gall*, preached a sermon admonishing the people to keep the peace. At the conclusion of the synod, according to Hermann of Reichenau, he issued a royal edict mandating "a peace such as had not been seen in many centuries." He also granted a general amnesty to his opponents in Swabia and urged them to follow his example. Such public displays occurred repeatedly during this period; in each case it was apparent that religious motives were intertwined with notions of the king's supreme authority: he had the power to will the peace. The ruler's mandates were binding by their very nature. However, in a society where civil peace and justice lay mainly in the hands of collectively organized judicial assemblies, such peace mandates from above were not well received. They "had been unknown in previous centuries" and ran against the grain of tradition.

It is difficult to pinpoint the propelling forces behind this ideology of peace. Did it derive its momentum from internal dynamics evoked by the image of a strong Christian ruler? Or was it based on impulses emanating from southern France and Burgundy where the Peace of God movement (*pax Dei* and *treuga Dei*, that is, peace of God and truce of God) had taken root? This movement, spearheaded by a coalition of bishops and princes, sought to extend special protection to certain groups of people and to certain religious holidays and hallowed times. Henry III's special attention to Burgundy and his marriage to Agnes, the devout daughter of Duke William V of Aquitaine, seem to support the notion of southwestern influences.[18] Nevertheless, I am personally inclined to assign greater significance to the impact of the powerful concept of the king as Christ's representative on earth and as post-figuration or *imitatio Christi*. These were religious and ideological concepts that had already been fostered by Conrad II, particularly through his veneration of the cross. They had also played a major role in the kingship of Henry II, who in many ways served as a role model for Henry III. In sharp contrast to the Peace of God movement, the peace that Henry III envisioned was not to be achieved through a coalition of princes, but rather through royal mandates issued from above, from the solitary pinnacle of the sacral ruler. The actual implementation of these ideas might, in fact, have provided the crucial ingredient in the shift toward a functional interpretation of the social order. According to these views, the king, in his capacity as a role model and inspirational force for the nobility and the warrior class, was to guarantee justice and peace in the secular world: therein consisted *his* function and obligation.

Let us recall the substantial changes that occurred in the character of the episcopal office around the middle of the century; increasingly, the bishops functioned as an integrating force within the realm and bore at least partial responsibility for its well-being. Yet parallel to these far-reaching developments, the idea of Henry III as a Christ-like king and an emperor of universal peace kept gaining its own momentum. For these reasons, the rise of serious tensions within the nexus of the "constitutional" structure must have become inevitable. In the aforementioned letter Bern of Reichenau hardly suppressed his criticism of Henry III's autocratic rulership; he urged the king to accept the bishops as guiding lights in his pursuit of peace.

Much more pointed, however, were the charges made in an epistle from abbot Siegfried of Gorze (1031–1055) to abbot Poppo of Stablo (1025–1048). The primary purpose of this letter consisted in proving that the king was too closely related to Agnes of Poitou and that the prospective marriage would be violating canon law. The abbot, furthermore, expressed his concern about the "conspicuous consumption" that was cropping up everywhere, but particularly at the royal court. He objected to the sumptuous displays of luxurious clothing, fancy hairdos, and expensive armor and horses, all practices that he blamed on the corrupting influence of the West Frankish neighbors (*francisci*). Especially grievous, however, were his scathing remarks about the peace program promoted by the court; for his criticism was directed at the very essence of Henry III's concept of kingship. Siegfried charged that the royal counselors had led the king to believe that his marriage to Agnes would bring about a splendid peace (*magna pax*) through the joining of realms. Yet such a peace was in reality false and pernicious (*pax perniciosa*) because it had come to pass in violation of canon law and therefore in violation of divine law which unequivocally forbade such a marriage. Siegfried further charged that the court's endeavors were based on secular considerations alone, on a concept of peace that did not have anything in common with the true peace of

God. He then continued that this earth could not possibly generate a true peace (*pax vera*), but that the righteous and devout could attain it if they obeyed the divine commandments and, with the assistance of the angels, rushed toward the eternal peace (*pax eterna*) of the heavenly kingdom. Although Siegfried avoided explicit criticism directed at the person of the ruler, he hastened to point out the limits of a peace concept that was based on the overwrought pretensions of a secular prince.[19]

But Henry III's idea of kingship not only raised theological issues. Otloh, a monk at Saint Emmeram in Regensburg who died shortly after 1067, related the following incident in his *Book of Visions*, written between 1063 and 1065. In 1056 a Roman nobleman was on his way to see Henry III. Shortly before he reached the locality where Henry stayed, the traveler lay down for a nap around noon. In his sleep he saw the emperor on his throne surrounded by a host of nobles. Unexpectedly, a poor man appeared before the ruler, pleading with his majesty to show mercy and to grant him an audience. The emperor, however, was annoyed and said: "Wait, you numbskull, until I find time to listen to you." Yet the poor man replied: "How could I possibly wait any longer, o emperor, since I have already been waiting for so long and have used up all I ever owned while doing so." In spite of his protestations, the pauper was sent away; the same thing happened to a second and a third supplicant. As the third man was leaving, he turned to God with his plea. And suddenly a voice resounded in the heavens: "Remove this leader and subject him to lengthy punishment that shall teach him what type of justice poor people can expect. Whatever he has given, he shall receive himself, and he shall suffer the agony of indefinite postponement" (*Auferte istum rectorem et facite eum inter penarum moras discere, quomodo pauperes valeant iudicia sua expectare. Que dedit, accipiat, que sit dilatio, discat*).[20] As soon as these words had been uttered, the emperor magically vanished from the assembly. When the Roman nobleman awoke, he received a message that the emperor had just died. Thus it was self-evident, God himself had punished the emperor by death because he had violated a ruler's principal virtue: helping the poor and listening to their plights. This anecdote shows clearly that discontent among the people was widespread or, at least, that certain circles found the imperious demeanor of Henry III repulsive. The rift between him and his people kept widening. The emperor of peace with his lofty program of mercy and compassion had lost sight of the concrete hardships and daily concerns of the common man. Rather than lending a sympathetic ear, he increased his splendid isolation and made it known throughout the realm that any one who dared to defy him (*contemptor imperator*) was prone to suffer the death penalty.[21] This was the first time that a ruler had issued such a decree in the German Middle Ages.

Dissatisfaction with Henry III's kingship also festered among the powerful magnates who had been developing their own lordly aspirations. The chronicler Hermann of Reichenau (d. 1054), renowned for his reliability, wrote in the year 1053: "Around this time the influential magnates of the realm along with less powerful nobles more and more frequently grumbled about the emperor. They complained that he had long since strayed from his initial stance of justice, love of peace, piety, fear of God, and various other virtues wherein he should have been making daily progress; instead he had steadily been slipping into selfishness and neglect of duties, and soon he would be much worse than he used to be."[22] When the emperor in the same year 1053, at the palace of Trebur,[23] asked to have his three-year-old son Henry IV elected as his successor to the kingship, the electors expressed unprecedented reservations, indicating that they would accept the young monarch's leadership only if he turned out to be a just and compassionate ruler (*si rector iustus futurus esset*). In view of Henry III's autocratic rule, they apparently felt that royal justice could no longer be taken for granted in the future.

The princes' reservations were well founded. Particularly the settlement of the ducal succession in Lotharingia had led to serious confrontations.[24] Duke Gozelo I of the house of Ardenne-Verdun had held power in both Lower and Upper Lotharingia since 1033. When he died on 19 April 1044, his son Godfrey the Bearded, who had shared authority with his father and was already in charge of Upper Lotharingia, expected to be invested with both Lotharinigan duchies (fig. 30). Henry III, however, took advantage of the temporary power vacuum and granted Lower Lotharingia to Gozelo II, Godfrey's younger brother, who was deemed to be cowardly (*ignavus*) and incompetent by most contemporaries. This move posed a serious threat to the power base of the ducal house of Ardennes-Verdun. Godfrey, for his part, viewed it as a blatant violation of his rights, an arbitrary act of the king, and a grave misjudgment of Lotharingia's special position within the constitutional framework of the realm.[25] Because of the early rise of mighty noble families in this region, ducal authority could be sustained only if it were supported by an extraordinary constellation of power. Yet Godfrey faced a situation where his ducal prerogatives and obligations, so essential for the maintenance of peace in Lotharingia, were totally undermined.

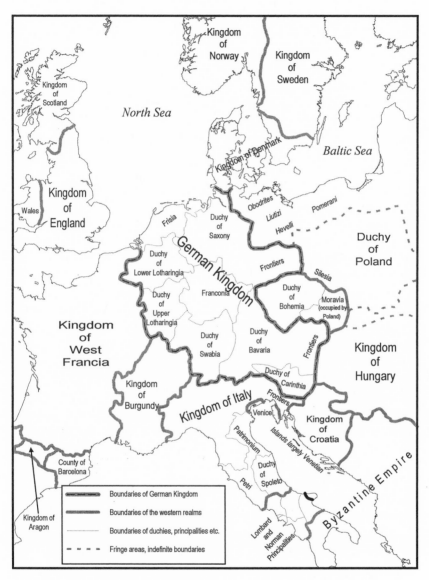

Kingdom
of
Norway

Kingdom
of
Sweden

Kingdom
of
Scotland

North Sea

Baltic Sea

Kingdom of Denmark

Wales

Kingdom
of
England

Frisia

Obodrites

Liutizi

Pomerani

Hevelli

Duchy
of
Saxony

German Kingdom

Frontiers

Silesia

Duchy
of
Poland

Duchy
of
Lower Lotharingia

Franconia

Duchy
of
Upper
Lotharingia

Duchy
of
Bohemia

Moravia
(occupied by
Poland)

Kingdom
of
West
Francia

Duchy
of
Swabia

Duchy
of
Bavaria

Frontiers

Kingdom
of
Hungary

Duchy of
Carinthia

Kingdom
of
Burgundy

Kingdom of Italy

Frontiers

Venice

Kingdom
of
Croatia

Patrimonium

Islands largely Venetian

County of
Barcelona

Petri

Duchy
of
Spoleto

Byzantine Empire

Kingdom of
Aragon

	Boundaries of German Kingdom
	Boundaries of the western realms
	Boundaries of duchies, principalities etc.
	Fringe areas, indefinite boundaries

Lombard
and
Norman
Principalities

30. The German realm and its neighbors circa 1050 (adapted from H. Keller, *Zwischen regionaler Begrenzung und universalem Horizont*, 1986, p. 19).

When Henry III, in spite of Godfrey's protestations of loyalty and submission, did not show any inclination of giving in, the Lotharingian noble resorted to the only means that, in his eyes, could rectify the situation: he chose the feud. It is important to note that according to prevailing customary law, Godfrey was practically forced to pursue this course since it was his duty to preserve the integrity of his family's power base and to pass it on to his descendants; therein lay the foundation of his family's status, prominence, and honor. In the emperor's eyes, however, Godfrey's actions smacked of rebellion, particularly if we consider Henry III's claims to hierarchical rulership. As a ruler, he looked on the duchy simply as an office which he could bestow at his own discretion, as long as the beneficiary came from a spectrum of nobles who were interrelated by inheritance rights. Henry III thus continued a practice that had been initiated by his father Conrad II.

The rebellion of Godfrey the Bearded was put down in 1044–45 and 1047–49; and when Pope Leo IX excommunicated him in addition, he had no choice but to submit to the mercy of the emperor at an encounter in Aachen. Although many princes (*principes*) pleaded his cause, Godfrey was forced to give up his duchy. In this context it was of little consolation that Pope Leo IX elevated his brother Frederick to the papal chancellorship. However, Godfrey soon found ways to establish a new power base. In 1054 he married Beatrice of Tuscany, whose husband, Margrave Boniface (1032–1052), had been murdered two years earlier. Hermann of Reichenau commented disapprovingly that Godfrey had secretly sneaked away to Italy, confronting the emperor with a done deal.

Henry III was furious and fiercely determined to nip in the bud the Lotharingian's attempt to create a new power base. He led an army into Italy to challenge the defiant noble, but Godfrey managed to escape. Beatrice and her daughter Matilda, however, were apprehended and brought north of the Alps as captives of the emperor. Even Godfrey's brother, the cardinal presbyter Frederick, who had never openly taken sides in this conflict, became subject to the Salian ruler's wrath. The emperor demanded that Pope Victor II, who had succeeded Leo IX in 1054/55, surrender Frederick without delay. The Lotharingian cleric barely escaped by entering the monastery of Monte Cassino. Clearly, Henry III had made a great display of his power and his implacable toughness. But if we cast a glance at the following years, it becomes evident that his posture lacked a solid foundation and would hardly be sustainable in the long run. Frederick of Lotharingia became abbot of Monte Cassino and, succeeding

Victor II in 1057, he even attained the papal dignity as Stephen IX. Eventually, twenty-two years after her capture by Henry III in 1055, Matilda was vindicated. From her castle in Canossa with Pope Gregory VII at her side, she witnessed the ultimate humiliation of her late opponent's son: Henry IV's act of submission to papal authority.

Superficially, Henry III had achieved his goal: the break-up of a powerful duchy. However, the long-term effect of his action was not advantageous to the crown. The weakening of ducal authority in Lotharingia made it progressively harder to rein in the influential families of the region. This in turn brought about an increasing fragmentation of the frontier area to the west. One of the mighty beneficiaries of these circumstances was Count Balduin V of Flanders, who unceremoniously occupied the lands adjoining his county to the east. At an assembly in Cologne in December 1056 while he and his son paid homage to the six-year-old king Henry IV, Balduin demanded that his overlordship over the annexed territory be officially confirmed. He further demanded recognition of his son Balduin VI's authority over the county of Hainault which had been acquired through marriage. Another potential threat arose from the French king Henry I (1031–1060), who sought to exploit the power vacuum created by the deposition of Godfrey the Bearded. He might even have harbored plans to incorporate Lotharingia into his kingdom—an assumption that has been challenged.[26] According to the episcopal history of Liège, it was Bishop Wazo of Liège who ultimately persuaded the French king to abandon such endeavors. Although a friendship treaty was concluded in 1048, the relationship between the two realms kept deteriorating and reached a critical stage in 1054 when Count Theobald III of Blois paid homage to the German emperor. An attempt to clarify the respective positions of the two rulers through a meeting at Ivois after Pentecost 1056 ended in failure. The French king charged Henry III with breach of contract and left the scene prematurely. The notion that he was trying to avoid a duel, supposedly proposed by the Salian ruler, must be relegated to the realm of mythology.

The rift with France and the internal turmoil in Lotharingia ultimately forced the emperor to seek a reconciliation with Godfrey the Bearded. Shortly before his death, Henry III actually held out the prospect of restoring one of the Lotharingian duchies to him. This gesture might have contributed to Godfrey's emergence as a wise and circumspect moderator of Lotharingian affairs after Henry III's demise on 5 October 1056. Taking charge, he initiated negotiations at Andernach where he met with the region's most influential men, such as Archbishop Anno of Cologne (1056–

1075), Archbishop Eberhard of Trier (1047–1066), the Rhenish count palatine Henry (1045–1061), and others. His defense of the realm's interest in
its western territories is not devoid of irony if we consider that he had been
a victim of the Salian ruler's vengeful persecution for more than a decade.
This paradox shows that it is unwarranted to view Godfrey the Bearded
as a rebel and troublemaker. The steadfast defense of his ancestral rights
was, in his eyes, by no means directed against the realm's interests; on the
contrary, it was proof that he possessed a keen sense of responsibility for
the realm's destiny. Henry III, however, at the pinnacle of his imperial
power chose to disregard former traditions of cooperation and solidarity.
Thus his image as an emperor of peace slowly changed to that of an unjust king (*rex iniquus*)—a perception that was confirmed by the accounts
of Hermann of Reichenau.

But not only the western fringes of the realm had grown restless;
trouble was brewing in Saxony as well. An incident at Lesum in 1047
clearly shows that a latent opposition had grown up under a seemingly
calm surface. During a stay at this royal palace, the emperor barely escaped
an assassination attempt, attributed to count Theotmar. The would-be as-
sassin was an offspring of the powerful Billung dynasty and a brother of
the Saxon duke, Bernard II. Due to Theotmar's subsequent trial and his
death in a judicially mandated duel, the relationship between the Billungs
and the royal house deteriorated rapidly.[27]

Saxon opposition was by no means confined to the ducal house;
it was based on multifaceted grievances and had deep roots. The Salian
ruler's tightly administered management and extensive development of
fiscal lands in the Harz region drew severe criticism when it became apparent that the Saxons were bearing a disproportionate share of maintaining
the royal court. A chronicler in southern Germany, quite appropriately,
called Saxony *coquina imperatoris*, the emperor's kitchen.[28] In any event,
Henry III transformed the budding town of Goslar into a major center
of royal power through the building of a splendid new palace—the most
magnificent secular edifice of its time—and an adjoining royal canonry,
dedicated to Saints Simon and Jude (fig. 28). The crown also intensively
exploited the silver resources of this area. The rift with the ducal house of
Saxony worsened even further when the king appointed a certain Adalbert to the metropolitan see of Hamburg-Bremen in 1043; this archbishop,
in due time, became one of the Billungs' most embittered enemies. The
bad blood between the Saxons and the crown reached its climax, however, shortly before Henry III's death, when a Saxon contingent which

had gone into battle without royal assistance suffered a devastating defeat against the Slavs. As a consequence of this disastrous encounter at the mouth of the Havel in September 1056, the Saxons began contemplating the overthrow and assassination of the still minor king, Henry IV. Lampert of Hersfeld reported in his *Annals* of the year 1057:

Meeting frequently, the Saxon princes debated the injustices they had suffered at the hands of the emperor, and they believed that there would be no better vindication for their grievances than wrenching the imperial rule away from his minor son as long as the latter's extreme youth provided an opportunity for such a violent act. After all, it was not unreasonable to assume that the son's character and lifestyle would follow his father's patterns, as one is wont to say. . . . They decided to kill the king wherever there might be an opportunity.[29]

In the southern German duchies of Bavaria, Swabia, and Carinthia, Henry III had kept the ducal authority in his own hands and had shut out any indigenous dukes for a long time. In 1045 he finally transferred Swabia to an offspring of the Ezzonen family, Otto II (1045–1047), who was then followed in office by Otto III of Schweinfurt (1048–1058). Welf III was endowed with the duchy of Carinthia (d. 1055) in 1047. Bavaria had been bestowed on Henry VII of Luxembourg as early as 1042, and at the latter's death, Conrad I, another of the Ezzonen kindred, became his successor. All of these appointments had either been motivated by external threats, as in the case of Bavaria and Carinthia, or were intended to bring disgruntled magnates back into the fold. In spite of these changes, the rise of opposing forces could not be stemmed. Toward the end of 1052 the voices of discontent were growing and developing into a full-fledged conspiracy by 1055.[30] It was probably triggered by Henry III's political posturing toward Hungary. Notwithstanding his unsuccessful Hungarian campaign of 1052, the emperor refused to consider a reasonable settlement, ignoring the wishes of those Bavarian and Carinthian nobles who were directly affected by his frontier policies. Henry III was in no mood to compromise and moved ruthlessly against his opposition. At the assembly of Merseburg in 1053, he had the Ezzonen duke Conrad I removed from office and then entrusted the Bavarian duchy to Bishop Gebhard of Eichstätt (1042–1057), the later Pope Victor II (1054/55–1057). This move motivated the leaders of the opposition to plot the emperor's assassination and to consider as his replacement Duke Conrad I, the very duke that had been deposed by him. The fact that the coup did not happen in 1055 may be attributed to the coincidental and unexpected deaths of both Welf III and

Conrad I. Nonetheless, the emperor showed no inclination to take these political shifts into consideration. Had he been sensitive to the prevailing climate, he would hardly have transferred the Bavarian duchy to his wife Agnes in 1055. Lampert of Hersfeld commented in his Annals of 1056: "The emperor bestowed the duchy on the empress according to private right (*privato iure*) and for an unlimited time"—an unveiled criticism of this unprecedented action.[31] A ducal office was being treated as a private prerogative of the royal house, so to speak as a dower for the empress.

These events and developments show clearly that Henry III's over-wrought concept of kingship and royal authority often led to precarious situations, especially at the fringes of the realm, and that the emperor's arrogance unnecessarily provoked or escalated hostilities. This conclusion of recent scholarship contrasts sharply with older views that perceived Henry III as a man of vision who had stabilized the frontiers through the creation of marcher lordships.[32] The marches of Cham, Nabburg, and Bohemia, as well as the so-called Neumark facing Hungary, were attributed to the Salian ruler's "creative initiative and farsighted design." Yet these assumptions can no longer be defended in the light of recent findings; it now appears that Henry's establishment of marcher lordships was a sheer construct of scholarly imagination. The true protectors of the eastern frontiers must be sought among the powerful nobles of this region, the Diepoldingers, the Babenbergers, and other aspiring dynasties, who created an organizational and seigniorial infrastructure in the eastern frontiers. These new insights offer a plausible rationale regarding the nobility's vehement opposition to the emperor's rigid posture vis-à-vis the Hungarians. If the development of frontier lordships was to be successful, flexibility and a willingness to compromise with the eastern neighbors were indispensable.

Criticism of the ruler grew progressively more contentious after the middle of the century. The realm's powerful magnates no longer perceived the emperor as their advocate and felt that their concerns were being ignored or neglected. Henry III had chosen to distance himself from the high nobility in a way that was bound to increase tensions. Then, on 5 October 1056, Henry III unexpectedly died at age thirty-nine while hunting at his palace at Bodfeld in the Harz mountains. For a long time historians interpreted his premature death as a catastrophe posing a serious threat to the stability of the realm. But in reality Henry III's reign had lasted longer than that of his father and his death seems to have forestalled a further escalation of the smoldering crisis that was on the verge of erupting into an unmitigated disaster. The subsequent regency of Empress

Agnes helped diffuse the tense atmosphere within a relatively short time by granting the powerful nobles ample consideration and giving them opportunities to participate in the governance of the realm. However, competitive jockeying for powerful positions would in time cause new problems. Henry III left his son and successor a troubled legacy indeed.

How easily pent-up antagonisms were dispersed after the emperor's death can be illustrated by a controversy involving the Salian grave site at Speyer. In connection with the Easter celebration of 1052 there are reports of serious altercations between Henry III and Bishop Sigebod of Speyer (1039–1054). This dispute was apparently related to the emperor's intent to sequester an entire third of the church's central nave as a royal burial site, a project that in the eyes of the bishop seriously impaired the cathedral's function as an episcopal church. At the time of Henry III's death in 1056, the structural changes for the accommodation of the enlarged grave site had been completed; it was here that the emperor found his last resting place. After his heart and entrails had been buried in the royal canonry at Goslar according to his wishes, a spectacular funeral procession brought his body to Speyer. On 28 October, the day of Saints Simon and Jude which was also his birthday, more than three weeks after his demise, Henry III was entombed next to his father, Conrad II, in the cathedral of Speyer. Pope Victor II, Empress Agnes, King Henry IV (still a minor), and many princes of the realm attended this solemn occasion. However, soon after the funeral, drastic measures were taken to reduce the size of the royal burial space and to confine it to the area that contained the existing Salian graves. Subsequently, these were enclosed by an eighty-centimeter-high wall, covered with flooring, and shielded by a base molding toward the west. The expediency of this incisive action dashed Henry III's ambitious dream of establishing a monumental burial place to celebrate Salian royalty into the indefinite future. The size of the grave site was cut down to dimensions that were acceptable to Bishop Conrad of Speyer (1056–1060) who, no doubt, had been the prime mover in executing these changes. In any case, the alterations had already been concluded when the new Speyer cathedral, the mightiest church of Latin Christendom, was finally near completion and was consecrated by Bishop Gundekar II of Eichstätt (1057–1075) on 4 October 1061.

6

The Coup: The Princes' Concern for the Realm

WHEN EMPEROR HENRY III DIED in 1056, his son, Henry IV, born on 11 November 1050, was barely six years old.[1] Although he had been consecrated as future king on 17 July 1054, it was by no means certain that the kingship of the royal child would find universal acceptance, particularly in light of the great tensions that had developed between the princes and his father, Henry III. Indeed, the opposition in Saxony was not only prepared to resist but even to assassinate the young king, as we have seen previously. However, the powerful elite steered a different course, as documented in a passage by the chronicler Lampert of Hersfeld: "All those who had the future of the realm at heart worked diligently to stop these unsettling activities." In the interest of stability and general peace, support for the Salian succession seemed crucial at this point.

These circumstances may account for the fact that Pope Victor II, who took charge of the realm's affairs after Henry III's death, succeeded in securing Henry IV's recognition without major delays. Immediately after the emperor's demise at Bodfeld, the pope sought to obtain the consent of persons and regional interest groups who had previously voiced opposition.[2] Following Henry III's burial at Speyer, Victor II traveled straight to Aachen with the royal boy to place him on Charlemagne's throne to document the beginning of a new reign. In December 1056, after skillful negotiations and a prearranged agreement with Godfrey the Bearded, he reached a reconciliation with the Lotharingian magnates at an assembly in Cologne; a few weeks later, at the Christmas conclave of magnates in Regensburg, he managed to conclude an accord with Bavarian rebels. Henry III's widow, Empress Agnes, had won a wise and powerful advocate and a distinguished mentor in Victor II; and the imperial elite was obviously willing to cooperate. When the pope departed for Italy in Feb-

ruary 1057, he must have been confident that both the affairs of the realm
and the royal succession were set up for a smooth transition.

Empress Agnes now assumed the regency for her minor son. How
willingly the princes cooperated with the crown under these exceptional
circumstances can be illustrated by the fact that the empress was allowed
to keep the Bavarian duchy—presumably as endowment for her regency.
Conrad III, a scion of the Rhenish Ezzonen kindred, took on the duchy of
Carinthia and the protection of the realm's southeastern frontiers (1056–
1061). Highly unusual were the additional concessions that were granted
to Agnes at this time. The princes promised under oath that she would
have the right to designate a successor to the throne if a vacancy should
occur, in other words, if young King Henry should die prematurely as did
his younger brother Conrad in 1055. Accordingly, she would be allowed to
make a binding nomination, and the new king could not be elevated without her consent. This pledge, made under oath (*iuramentum*) later caused
the princes considerable anguish when they wanted to put up an anti-king
against Henry IV who had been excommunicated by a papal bull. Pope
Gregory VII, in his manifesto of 3 September 1076,[3] first had to persuade
the princes that the apostolic authority was superior to any secular bond
and that he, therefore, had the power to relieve them of their oath. This
incident shows clearly that the realm's leading men had made a serious
commitment when, twenty years earlier, they had promised to leave the
Salian dynasty unchallenged while the empress Agnes was alive. It was a
most remarkable agreement, indeed, a compact, which, for the last time,
curbed the German princes' election privileges at the expense of an idea
that placed the unity of the kingship above all other considerations.

Agnes had won the princes' approval as the head of the Salian house
and the guardian of the kingship, and was thus recognized to be fully
competent to rule. The beginning of her regency looked propitious, notwithstanding the loss of her valuable advisor, Pope Victor II, who died in
1057. In September 1058 a peace settlement with King Andreas I of Hungary was concluded and, subsequently, sealed with the betrothal of Judith,
Henry IV's sister, to the Hungarian crown prince Salomon. But this re-
spite came to a sudden end when Salomon's uncle, Bela, attempted to
seize power in Hungary in 1060, forcing his nephew to seek refuge in the
German realm. These events inevitably precipitated a campaign against the
Hungarians; the southeastern frontier region was once again destabilized.
Because of these contingencies, Empress Agnes was compelled to transfer
the responsibilities for the Bavarian duchy to Otto of Northeim in 1061.

This wealthy count from Saxony approached his new task with great determination, and using Bavaria as his base, he immediately assumed the leadership in the Hungarian conflict.

A change occurred in Swabia as well, which clearly reveals that the empress must have acted under political duress in awarding the ducal office there. Although Henry III supposedly had promised the succession in Swabia to count Berthold of Zähringen, events took a different twist when Count Rudolf of Rheinfelden abducted the Salian princess Matilda—with her consent or through a ruse—and exchanged marriage vows with her. "For her daughter's sake," as we read in Frutolf of Michelsberg's chronicle, he compelled the empress to transfer Swabia to him in 1057. When Berthold of Zähringen protested vigorously against this action, Agnes had to compensate him with the duchy of Carinthia which became vacant in 1061.

These events foreshadowed difficult times. Initial optimism and high hopes for a smooth regency under Agnes were soon dashed when, due to political circumstances and individual power plays, the empress encountered a steady erosion of her authority and hence became severely limited in her ability to make decisions. Not even the court could overlook her feeble leadership as the annals of the monastery of Niederalteich state poignantly: "This was the beginning of the troubles. The king was still a boy; the mother, though, as is often the case with women, was easily swayed by advice from all sorts of people. The rest, who held influential positions at the royal court, were driven by greed, and no one could expect to find justice there without bribery; and, thus, justice and injustice became blended."[4]

During this period the servile ministerials began to augment their influence at the royal court. The ministerial Kuno was in charge of the young king's education; and other ministerials also assumed a high profile. Among these was Otnand, who had already been active under Henry III and who systematically defended royal interests against episcopal and ecclesiastical claims. Because of his activities, the canons of Bamberg called him *orcus ille Othnandus*, the "Otnand from hell."[5] The ministerials' energetic engagement on behalf of the crown increasingly incurred the wrath of the high aristocracy. Particularly the fact that Henry IV was brought up under the tutelage of such men and the prospect that his world view might be formed by their opinions and attitudes must have kindled deep suspicion among both secular and ecclesiastical princes.

Agnes attempted to steer a firm course by favoring Bishop Henry of

Augsburg (1047–1063) as her personal adviser, but in doing so, she increasingly ignored other powerful men, such as Archbishop Anno II of Cologne (1056–1075) and Archbishop Siegfried I of Mainz (1060–1084). Several donations to the see of Augsburg in 1061 and 1062 attest to her gratitude to Bishop Henry.[6] However, this association became the source of unanticipated problems since "she [Agnes] almost immediately was suspected of an illicit love relationship, as rumors spread that such intimacy could not possibly have grown outside a sexual bond."[7] These developments and allegations embittered the empress and apparently added a harsh note to her demeanor. Bishop Gunther of Bamberg (1057–1065) complained in a letter toward the end of 1061: "Her majesty, the empress, has treated me in an unusually cold and unfriendly manner—if not to say with disdain—and whenever I was absent, she attempted to badmouth and belittle me, especially in front of the preeminent members of the nobility, as if I had wronged her in some fashion."[8] Shortly thereafter Hermann, the provost of the Bamberg cathedral chapter, confirmed his bishop's contentions; he wrote to his superior during a stay at court: "The whole court was waiting for you, but when you did not appear, some started making taunting remarks. They claimed that you would only wield weapons and sow the seeds of war and that you had no other thought nor goal but to blow away this raging fury, or, to say it in their words, to humiliate the best of all empresses in the most demeaning fashion."[9] The climate at court was extremely tense at the beginning of the 1060s as animosities, taunts, and jealousies became common among royal advisers; and when Agnes reacted increasingly more surily and intemperately to these intrigues, she lost the respect of both ecclesiastical and secular princes and was called a "raging fury."

At the end of 1061 a further problem arose which added insult to injury and had a devastating effect on the empress. Agnes was by all accounts a genuinely devout woman who, just as her husband Henry III, was receptive to the goals of the ecclesiastical reform and sought to further them whenever there was an opportunity. However, Pope Victor II's death in Arezzo on 23 July 1057 interrupted her direct connection to the reformers; before long the empress came to the bitter realization that the reform movement had taken a different turn. Agnes' stepdaughter Beatrix was abbess of the wealthy convent of Gandersheim, a circumstance which should have bolstered the Salian presence in Saxony. However, the canonesses of Gandersheim, who came mainly from the Saxon aristocracy, accused their Salian abbess of giving away chapter property to ministerials and of endangering their livelihood by doing so. Beatrix and her stepmother Agnes turned to the pope in their predicament and apparently obtained a special privilege in their favor from Victor II. But after his death, Hildebrand, the representative of pope Stephen IX, reexamined the disputed case of Gandersheim; in contrast to the previous decision, the new legate honored the complaint of the canonesses and ordered the restitution of the respective properties. Beatrix thus had to yield to the will of her subordinates, the daughters of powerful Saxon nobles; but even worse, this matter constituted a humiliating defeat for the empress; a harsh new "wind blew in her face." [10]

This was just the beginning of Agnes' troubles. When Pope Stephen IX died prematurely on 29 March 1058, the reform party, with the sponsorship of Godfrey the Bearded who still wielded considerable influence, chose Bishop Gerhard of Florence to succeed him. Upon his elevation to the Holy See on 24 January 1059, the new pope assumed the name Nicholas II. He convened the famous Lateran Synod at Easter 1059, where many theological and pastoral issues were discussed, including the heresy of Berengar of Tours (d. 1088), simony, nicolaitism (the ban of clerical marriages), and canonical reform. Efforts were made, moreover, to establish better procedures for the election of the pope since recent elevations had revealed the vagueness of the criteria that had been employed. Lengthy negotiations and deliberations resulted in the famous papal election decree that assigned the main responsibility for papal elections to the episcopal cardinals in conjunction with other cardinal clerics. In principle, this fundamental decision has remained in force over eight centuries to the present day. Nevertheless, the rights (*honor*) of the king and future emperor Henry IV continued to be observed; and in this respect, at least, the customary law underlying the concept of theocratic kingship was taken into consideration. The crucial innovation, though, consisted in the fact that papal elections, by virtue of the synodal decree, were heretofore subject to a higher ecclesiastical authority, superseding all royal prerogatives. [11] No longer did the secular ruler make the rules but rather the pope and the Church council. The leading reformers continued to gain confidence, and a perception began to evolve within the Church that Rome and the papacy stood at the center of the universal Church.

Still, the threats posed by the Roman nobility remained. To counteract this constant menace, Pope Nicholas II took the extraordinary step of making common cause with the Normans who previously had been the Holy See's declared enemies. In August 1059, the pope enfeoffed the Norman princes Richard of Capua (1058–1078) and Robert Guiscard (1058–

1085) with the territories they had conquered in southern Italy and thereby granted them formal recognition by the highest ecclesiastical authority. The head of Christendom had joined forces with the strongest military power of that era. Simultaneously, the reform papacy gained suzerainty over all of southern Italy and ecclesiastical jurisdiction over those Arabic and Byzantine territories that had previously been assigned to the Eastern church.

The German crown was not privy to any of these decisions; yet the effect of the papacy's newly acquired position of strength soon made its mark. When Agnes requested the pallium, the symbol of archiepiscopal dignity, for Archbishop Siegfried I of Mainz, who had been installed in 1060, the pope refused the favor. The empress was told that the archbishop was to come to Rome in person in order to receive the pallium. Bishops everywhere became embittered, and the altercations reached the point where an imperial synod declared all of Nicholas II's decrees null and void and excommunicated and deposed the pope. Before any of these actions could have an impact, however, Nicholas II died on 20 July 1061.

The Roman patriciate immediately saw an opportunity to renew its influence on the papacy. It dispatched a delegation to the German court to present the young king Henry IV with the insignia of the *Patricius*, the protector of the city of Rome, and to petition for the nomination of a new pope. The Lombard bishops likewise joined this embassy since they wanted to protect themselves against the excesses of Roman centralism. The reformer's envoys, in contrast, were not received at the German court. This situation brought about a papal schism. On 30 September 1061, the reformers elected Bishop Anselm I of Lucca as pope; he assumed the name Alexander II. Four weeks later, on 28 October 1061, the court, through the eleven-year-old Henry IV, nominated Bishop Cadalus of Parma at a royal assembly in Basel; he called himself Honorius II.

These developments precipitated a complete reversal of the conditions that prevailed during Henry III's reign. The German crown under the stewardship of the devout Empress Agnes suddenly had become the enemy of ecclesiastical reform and bore the blame for the schism that tore the Church asunder. Agnes had been deeply humiliated by the arrogance of the reformers. Nevertheless, the paradoxical turn of events was alien to her spirit and was not in any way representative of her religious views. Apparently, however, she had never succeeded in steering the course of affairs according to her vision; the rudder of imperial rule had slipped from her hands. The results of this failure were so devastating to her that she withdrew from the world to enter a life of asceticism and piety. Political matters were left to drift and fell into disarray.

In spite of the unsettled situation the princes of the realm never considered getting along without a king, indeed quite the opposite. The absence of a strong ruler who could maintain peace and justice was sorely missed. However, at this stage of the evolving realm the need for a king lay less in the monarch's integrating power than in his function as an uncontested leader and a just arbitrator on behalf of the Church and the people. There was a longing for the "ideal king."

During this period of uncertainty a scandalous incident occurred, generally referred to as the coup of Kaiserswerth. The *Annals of Niederalteich* report: "The king was reaching adolescence, but the leading people at court were preoccupied with their own affairs, and no one taught the young king what was good and just. For these reasons many things had fallen into disarray in the realm. Due to these circumstances Archbishop Anno [II] of Cologne, the dukes, and many influential magnates met in frequent conferences and deliberated anxiously what could be done." [12] These men convened out of concern for the realm and the kingship. In addition to Archbishop Anno of Cologne the following nobles are documented as members of this circle: Count Ekbert I of Brunswick (d. 1068), Duke Otto of Bavaria (1061–1070), Archbishop Siegfried I of Mainz (1060–1084), and Godfrey the Bearded. But it is highly probable that Bishop Gunther of Bamberg (1057–1065), Margrave Dedi of Niederlausitz (1046–1075), and many others were also privy to these secret talks. The driving force, however, was Archbishop Anno II of Cologne.

At the beginning of April 1062 a group of imperial magnates met up with the young king at the royal palace in Kaiserswerth, located on an island in the Rhine (near Düsseldorf). Lampert of Hersfeld reports:

One day, when he [the king] was particularly cheerful after a festive meal, the archbishop of Cologne urged him to inspect a ship which had been splendidly decked out for this purpose. The unsuspecting boy was easily persuaded. No sooner than had he set foot on the boat, however, he was surrounded by the archbishop's hired accomplices; they hoisted the oars, started rowing with all their might, and steered the vessel as quick as lightning into the middle of the stream. The king, perplexed by the unexpected twist of events, had only one thought, namely that an act of violence was being perpetrated against him and that he would be murdered. In despair, he threw himself headlong into the river. In all likelihood he would have drowned in the swift current if Count Ekbert of Brunswick had not jumped after him, disregarding the great danger to his own life. He barely rescued him from the treacherous waters and brought him back on board. He [the king] now was consoled with calming words and brought to Cologne. A large crowd followed the convoy along the bank of the river, and many alleged that the royal majesty [of the king] had been violated and deprived of its self-determination. The archbishop sought to appease the ill feelings caused by this incident and to dispel the impression that he had acted out of personal ambition rather than because of his concern for the common good. He particularly directed each bishop, in whose diocese the king was expected to stay, to take care that the interests of the realm were not damaged in any way and that matters which were brought before the king were properly addressed.[13]

No doubt, the forcible abduction of the eleven-year-old Henry IV was a monstrous deed, and even in most recent scholarly studies the archbishop has not escaped charges of being obsessed with power. One analysis even attempts to rank the various motives mentioned in the sources according to their frequency in order to underscore Archbishop Anno's true motivation, namely his lust for power.[14] Still, regardless of Anno's domineering personality, such an analysis can hardly do justice to the complex circumstances that precipitated the events of Kaiserswerth. If we recall the climate at court and throughout the realm in the years 1060/61 and the fact that the kidnapping of the young king was a cooperative effort of many influential princes, it becomes sufficiently clear that additional factors must be considered. Finally, the term "coup" hardly captures the sense of genuine responsibility and obligation that the princes exhibited for the welfare of the realm.

Anno II was actually an exponent of the ecclesiastical reform and stood in high esteem as a devout, almost saintly bishop. Shortly after his death, between 1077 and 1081, he was eulogized in a poem, the famous *Anno Song*, which was written in Middle High German.[15] Its first part consists of a fast-paced summary of the history of human salvation, ranging from the creation of the world to the fall of man, from the atonement through Christ to the spread of Christianity, and further to the church of Cologne with its saints; finally it deals with Anno's tenure as archbishop. This section is followed by a description of the secular history, including the consecutive existence of four empires. The last of these was the Roman empire, which lives on in the German realm, where Cologne was founded as its most distinguished city. After the stanzas that deal with the birth of Christ, the author switches to the missionary history and through this context swings back to Anno. The third part of the poem is dedicated exclusively to Anno; it chronicles his secular and spiritual activities, his afflictions and visions, his death as a saint, and the wonders that occurred after his demise. The glorification of this archbishop was larger than life: all the threads of secular and spiritual history intersected in his person; his services to the realm and on behalf of the Church were determined by

God's will; his episcopal call was fulfilled in his exemplary demeanor. In chapter 34 we read:

> When Emperor Henry III,
> Put his trust into this lord
> And God's will was done,
> He was surrounded by large crowds of people
> When he entered Cologne for his honorable reception:
> Just as the sun in the skies,
> that moves between earth and heaven
> and casts its light in both directions,
> thus Bishop Anno strode
> in front of God and men.
> His influence at the royal court was such
> That all the other princes had their seats below him;
> And he conducted himself in his service to God
> As if he were an angel.
> On both sides he stood in high esteem,
> therefore he was counted among the truly great rulers.

And later in chapter 37:

> The realm was in a state of happiness (was fortunate)
> When the devout prince held the reins of power,
> When he brought up young Henry for his regal duties.
> His renown as ruler (regent)
> Spread far and wide in those days.
> The kings of Greece and England
> Sent him presents
> And gifts arrived from Denmark,
> Flanders and Russia.
> He acquired great wealth for Cologne.
> He adorned the churches everywhere
> And to promote the glory of Our Lord,
> He personally founded four monasteries;
> The fifth is Siegburg, his favorite abode.
> His tomb is now erected up there.[16]

This text, composed in the monastery of Siegburg, purports that Anno had found the ideal mode of combining his service to God and Church with his service to the realm. As a panegyric, the song was undoubtedly designed for recitation in front of sizable, courtly audiences, most likely at various princely residences; this may indicate that its purpose was to counteract emerging criticism of Cologne's powerful archbishop. Such an interpretation gains even more credence when we consider the divergent perspective of *The Ecclesiastical History of Hamburg*. This work was authored by Adam of Bremen around 1075 and relates the events as follows: Anno and Archbishop Adalbert of Hamburg-Bremen assumed responsibility for the realm's affairs after the "coup" of Kaiserswerth, but only the metropolitan of Bremen fulfilled his obligations with true loyalty to the young king and with the appropriate compassion. "In contrast, the archbishop of Cologne, a man of somber disposition, was accused of disloyalty toward the king. He further was the mover and shaker of all the conspiracies during this period."[17] Additional allegations follow: "The bishop of Cologne, who was accused of greed, employed anything he could grab at home and at court to embellish his church. Although it had been sizable already, he [Anno] now made it so prominent that it defied comparison with any other church in the realm. In addition, he favored his relatives, friends, and chaplains and showered all of them with the highest honors and ranks."[18]

The contemporaries' divergent opinions of Archbishop Anno II show clearly that there were conflicting interests at work: while his supporters did not perceive the targeted expansion of Cologne's episcopal power base as counteracting the welfare of the realm, his rivals viewed his aspirations with great suspicion. But these dynamics cannot properly be assessed without considering the fact that the greatest concentration of power within the Rhenish portion of Cologne's diocese had been in the hands of the family of the Rhenish counts palatine since the turn of the millennium.[19] We refer to this lineage as the *Ezzonen*, based on the name Ezzo, a short form of Erenfried. Around 991 Ezzo (d. 1034) had married Matilda (d. 1025), the sister of Otto III, and through this union had risen to the very highest ranks of the princely elite. The office of the Rhenish count palatine with its original center in the royal palace at Aachen endowed its holder with great power, especially in the lower Rhine region. The Ezzonen held a large number of counties within a wide radius around Cologne, including the Bonngau, Auelgau, Ruhrgau, and Keldachgau. They were also documented as counts in the Eifelgau and Zülpichgau. They were further responsible for the supervision of fiscal lands, vast forests, and important roadways which were located in the vicinity of their fortified strongholds Brauweiler, Tomburg, and Siegburg. In addition, they held the advocacies of the royal monasteries and canonries in Essen, Vilich, Kornelimünster, and Maastricht.

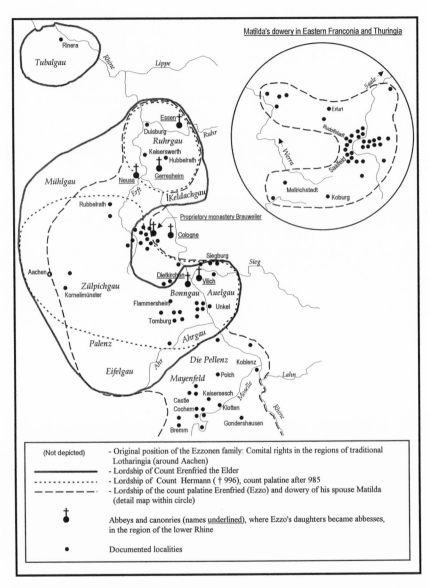

Matilda's dowery in Eastern Franconia and Thuringia

Rinera

Tubalgau

Rhine

Lippe

Essen

Duisburg

Ruhrgau

Kaiserswerth

Hubbelrath

Ruhr

Saale

Erfurt

Rudolfstadt

Werra

Mühlgau

Neuss

Gerresheim

Erft

Keldachgau

Mellrichstadt

Koburg

Saalfeld

Rubbelrath

Proprietory monastery Brauweiler

Cologne

Siegburg

Siegfried

Aachen

Dietkirchen

Vilich

Zülpichgau

Kornelimünster

Bonngau *Auelgau*

Flammersheim

Unkel

Tomburg

Palenz

Ahrgau

Ahr

Die Pellenz

Koblenz

Eifelgau

Mayenfeld

Polch

Lahn

Kaisersesch

Castle

Cochem

Klotten

Moselle

Rhine

Bremm

Gondershausen

(Not depicted) | - Original position of the Ezzonen family: Comital rights in the regions of traditional Lotharingia (around Aachen)

────────── - Lordship of Count Erenfried the Elder

·············· - Lordship of Count Hermann († 996), count palatine after 985

— — — — — . - Lordship of the count palatine Erenfried (Ezzo) and dowery of his spouse Matilda (detail map within circle)

† / ● Abbeys and canonries (names underlined), where Ezzo's daughters became abbesses, in the region of the lower Rhine

● Documented localities

31. The lordship of the Ezzonen family in the first half of the eleventh century (F. Steinbach, *Die Ezzonen*, 1964, p. 860).

The Ezzonen family dominated the entire southern tier of the archdiocese of Cologne (fig. 31). When Ezzo's son Hermann was elected archbishop of Cologne in 1036, this lineage had reached the pinnacle of its
power, especially since the archbishop's sisters were simultaneously presiding over such important convents and canonries as Essen and Gerresheim,
Nivelles, Gandersheim, possibly Altmünster in Mainz, Neuss, Dietkirchen
near Bonn, Vilich, and Saint Mary's in the Capitol in Cologne. However, serious tensions arose within the Ezzonen family when Hermann's
cousin Henry (1045–1061) assumed the office of count palatine around the
middle of the eleventh century. Increasingly the cousins worked against
each other, leading Archbishop Hermann to confer the family monastery of Brauweiler (west of Cologne) to Saint Peter, the patron saint of
Cologne's cathedral church, and to bring other important family holdings under his episcopal authority. This also included the Tomburg which
played an essential role in controlling the military road between Aachen
and Frankfurt. Slowly, but surely, the archdiocese of Cologne began to
encroach on the domain of the Rhenish counts palatine.[20]

Thus was the state of affairs when Anno II assumed the archiepiscopal office of Cologne in 1056. He had received an excellent education at
Bamberg, had been accepted as a member of the royal chapel, and had even
risen to the post of provost in the palace canonry of Saints Simon and Jude
at Goslar (1054–1056). However, as offspring of a lesser Swabian lineage,
he was considered a foreigner in Cologne and did not enjoy the protection
of the region's powerful elite. After Henry III's death, he could hardly
count on the patronage of Empress Agnes' regency; he consequently had
to rely on his own resources to establish himself in his office and in his
metropolitan see. These circumstances may explain why he took such drastic measures at times and why he was perceived as ruthless by many contemporaries. When count palatine Henry attempted to exploit this new
situation in order to retrieve the Ezzonen family's powerful position on
the lower Rhine, a bitter struggle between him and the archbishop became inevitable. In 1060, according to an account in the *Vita Annonis*, the
count palatine moved robbing and burning through the countryside clear
to the walls of Cologne, but due to the Anno's forceful response eventually retreated to the Moselle region. Here archiepiscopal forces surrounded
Henry in his castle at Cochem where, in a fit of insanity, he had his wife be-
headed. Subsequently, he was overpowered and brought to the monastery
of Echternach in shackles. His son, still a minor, came under the tutelage
of the archbishop and heretofore held his fiefs from the see of Cologne.

The power base of the counts palatine on the lower Rhine was shattered forever; they were pushed out into the Moselle and middle Rhine regions.

Anno II moved to fill the resulting power vacuum with a new type of suzerainty headed by the metropolitan of Cologne. By cleverly granting ecclesiastical fiefs and advocacies, he managed to bring the regional nobility into a dependent relationship to the archiepiscopal authority. A second important instrument consisted of the Cologne college of priors that was first documented in 1061. The provosts of the canonries in Cologne and its vicinity were united in the archbishop's most distinguished advisory council, named the college of priors; since vacancies for these provost offices were filled exclusively with members from the surrounding Rhenish aristocracy, the nobility became subservient to the archbishop's political ambitions on this level as well. A third component of his episcopal authority only came to fruition toward the end of his tenure when he founded a reform monastery on the Siegberg. Established in 1064 and replacing the Siegburg, a former Ezzonen stronghold, this new ecclesiastical center was settled in 1070 with monks from Fruttuaria, a reform monastery in northern Italy.[21] Fruttuaria, founded by the great reformer William of Dijon (990–1031), adhered to a more austere version of the Cluniac reform. Just as in Fruttuaria, lay brothers were not admitted at Siegburg; but the reform-minded forces of this new monastic community were primarily utilized for the dissemination and enforcement of episcopal policies. Aided by additional support points at Saalfeld in Thuringia (1070/71), the monastery of Grafschaft in Westfalia (1072), Saint Pantaleon in Cologne (1070/74), and perhaps even Brauweiler, a network of reform centers was established throughout the archdiocese.

This "modern" and eventually very effective system of episcopal politics strengthened the position of the archbishop at every level; all secular and spiritual forces were focused on his very person. The fact that the decisive breakthrough toward the consolidation of his power had been achieved in 1061 and that the foundation for a future expansion of Cologne's episcopal authority was thus secure may explain why Anno chose this time to become more involved in the affairs of the realm. Once again it becomes apparent that a bishop could only exercise political influence in those days if his episcopal authority was unchallenged; only if his position was firmly rooted would he be able to employ his resources on behalf of the realm. This context may explain why Anno II, seeking to impose his authority on the young king and the regency council, had a diploma issued on 14 July 1063 which decreed that fully one-ninth of all imperial and royal revenues should fall to the see of Cologne.[22] Such action had been taken, so we read in the justification, "to benefit the king and the order of the realm" (*pro incolumnitate nostra regnique nostri statu*). The church of Cologne, in other words, asked to be compensated for the considerable expenses that its archbishop incurred through his engagement for the realm. Precisely these incredibly generous, if not to say excessive, benefits for his church, enhanced by additional privileges, contributed to Anno's image as the power-greedy and despotic ecclesiastic whom we encounter in the description by Adam of Bremen.

There is no question, though, that Archbishop Anno took decisive steps to reestablish order in the realm after the coup of Kaiserswerth. As we have learned from Lampert of Hersfeld, the archbishop sought to raise the imperial bishops' sense of responsibility for the realm by requiring each bishop to preside over the royal council whenever the court was residing in his bishopric. Although we do not know whether the bishops adhered to this order, the fact that such a concept could even be developed is more important in our context. It not only illustrates the earnest search for an objectively defined, collegial obligation that was unencumbered by greed and personal ambition, but it also represents a new phase in the inner consolidation of the realm. The crisis affected the whole imperial polity, and the bishops were therefore called upon to assist in surmounting the current difficulties. In fact, the royal diplomas from this period frequently refer to bishops or magnates who had been instrumental in drawing up the respective documents; this was done by formulas, such as "based on the advocacy of the honorable Archbishops Siegfried of Mainz and Anno of Cologne and the rest of the faithful bishops, abbots, dukes, counts," or by naming the actual persons.[23] In a joint effort, ecclesiastical and secular leaders sought to reverse unpopular decisions dating from Henry III's reign. Examples of such controversial royal actions were, for instance, the transfer of market privileges at Fürth—actually owned by the cathedral canons of Bamberg—to the city of Nuremberg and the alienation of the monastery of Seligenstadt from the see of Mainz.[24]

Anno II was a tough and uncompromising advocate for ecclesiastical norms and interests. These qualities served him well when he sought to improve the relationship with the forces of the Church reform. After a brief period of negotiations, the bishops consented to recognize Pope Alexander II at a synod in Augsburg in 1062, at least until the underlying reasons for the schism could be clarified. Bishop Burchard II of Halberstadt (1059–1088), a nephew of Anno's, was dispatched to Rome to investigate the circumstances of the papal election. As anticipated, he decided in favor of Alexander II and against Honorius II who had won the support of the crown a year earlier. Thanks to Anno's leadership, communications between the royal court and the reform movement could be reestablished before it was too late, although it was not possible to heal the breach completely. Against this scenario, the archbishop of Cologne acted as a man who understood the signs of his time and recognized that someone had to assume the leadership in the realm. His insights and actions helped postpone the great showdown between the crown and the reform papacy for a few more years.

However, the archbishop of Cologne soon learned that his authority did not suffice to prevent tensions in the regency council. In 1063 Archbishop Adalbert of Hamburg-Bremen (1043–1072) joined this circle and almost immediately he became Anno's greatest rival. As related in Adam of Bremen's *Ecclesiastical History of Hamburg*, Adalbert himself "indicated that he became involved in the realm's affairs because he could not stand by idly when the people dragged his lord and king around like a prisoner." The narration then continues: "And soon he stood on the highest rung, had pushed his adversaries aside, and sat alone in the 'governing capitol,' not uncontested, of course, for such are the consequences of glory. Our archbishop, in his exalted position, now wanted to renew the 'Golden Age' and intended to eradicate all those from the heavenly kingdom who had violated the [customary] law or had dared to raise their hand against the king or blatantly robbed churches." [25]

Adalbert and the young king soon developed a very close relationship; and the archbishop particularly cultivated a climate of personal loyalty. "He taught that one must keep faith with one's lord and king till death," Adam of Bremen reports.[26] According to another contemporary source, Bruno's *Book of the Saxon War*, Adalbert supposedly boasted that, although he did not bear the name of Saint Peter, his power was equal to that of the apostle, in fact, even greater, for, unlike Peter, he had never disavowed his lord, the king.[27] Such statements make clear that Archbishop Adalbert's views fundamentally differed from those of Anno II of Cologne in regard to the principles governing position and rank within the imperial order. A glance at Adalbert's diocesan politics may enlighten us further.

Adalbert's tenure as metropolitan of Hamburg-Bremen was characterized by a long-standing struggle with the powerful dukes of Saxony, the Billungs. The archbishop supposedly sought to gain control over all ducal, comital, and judicial powers within his bishopric in an attempt to create his own episcopal duchy. The Billungs, on their part, were also striving to extend the structural and spatial dimensions of their power base; Bernard II (1011–1059), in fact, succeeded in "shaping the Billung lordship into a nearly solid complex," reaching from Westfalia to the Bardengau south of Hamburg.[28] To confront such a formidable opponent seemed a hopeless cause, at least as long as the archbishop lacked the foundation to wield power. To remedy this situation, Adalbert turned to the king who, as early as October 1063, granted him two counties between Hamburg and Bremen, as well as extensive forest lands.[29] Through the construction of castles and other strategic strongholds, he initiated steps toward establishing a coastal episcopal dominion between Hamburg and Bremen.[30]

But Adalbert's ambitions went even further. He hoped to bring all of Scandinavia, clear to the northernmost fringes of the world, under the ecclesiastical jurisdiction of Hamburg's episcopal church; and he had his claim to these mission territories confirmed by Leo IX in a papal privilege of 6 January 1053. The metropolitan's pastoral authority was not only to reach the Transelban Slavs, the Swedes, and the Danes, but was to extend as far as Norway, Iceland, and Greenland; in short, it was to include all the peoples of the north. To support him in these endeavors, Adalbert was appointed papal legate and curate to these peoples. This was an ambitious program, indeed, and would have augmented the rank and power of the church of Hamburg-Bremen in an unprecedented way. How intensely Adalbert and his inner circle were preoccupied with such ideas becomes evident when we turn to the fourth book of Adam of Bremen's *Ecclesiastical History*. There, based on hearsay or scraps of information, he attempted to describe the world and the peoples of the north. In his account we find fantastic tales, such as the one stipulating a women's land (*terra feminarum*) on the shores of the Baltic Sea where the female inhabitants conceive children by ingesting a sip of water. Their male children are born with dog's heads attached to their chests; all females, in contrast, are beautiful maidens. In Greenland, the people are supposedly pale green, matching the color of the sea, and that is where this island's name originates. There are many other stories of this genre. The whole description seems to be an attempt to adjust to a new world, so to speak (fig. 32).

Besides eyeing the northern fringes of the western world, Adalbert developed a second scheme to bolster his episcopal authority, a scheme that would actually have elevated him above the rank of archbishop. When there was talk of creating a separate ecclesiastical province in Denmark, Adalbert sought to become its patriarch and was actively promoted in his endeavor

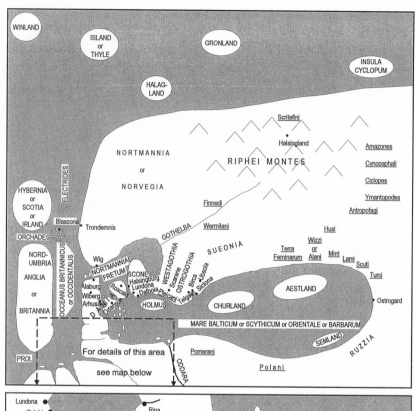

32. The Nordic world adapted from the accounts of Adam of Bremen (adapted from Möller in W. Lammers, *Das Hochmittelalter bis zur Schlacht von Bornhöved*, 1981, p. 220).

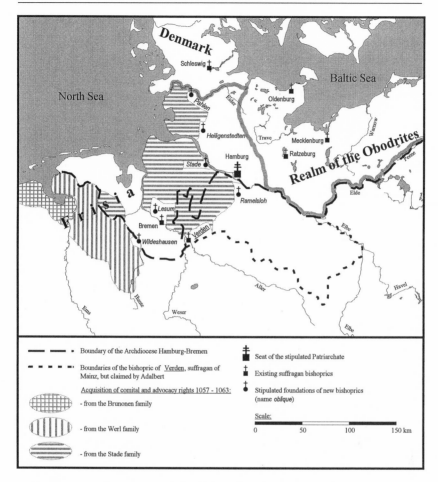

33. Acquisition of counties and the "Plan of twelve bishoprics" as stipulated by Archbishop Adalbert of Hamburg-Bremen (adapted from H. Keller, *Zwischen regionaler Begrenzung und universalem Horizont*, 1986, p. 139).

by Emperor Henry III and Pope Leo IX. But when all of these projects failed, he directed his energies toward a metropolitan structure that was to comprise twelve suffragan bishoprics (*Zwölfbistumsplan*) (fig. 33), even though some of the prospective episcopal sees would have been located in the tiniest settlements and could not possibly have met canonical requirements. This last futile effort, which occupied the closing years of Adalbert's life, once again sheds light on his unrealistic expectations. Ultimately, all of his grandiose plans came to nothing. A Wendish uprising in 1066 caused the collapse of the ecclesiastical organization in the Obodrite realm to the east, and the bishoprics of Oldenburg, Ratzenburg, and Mecklenburg, which would have become part of Adalbert's metropolitan superstructure, were now beyond the reach of the Church for a long time to come.

Adalbert's far-flung and overly ambitious projects, no doubt, depended heavily on the cooperation by the king and the pope; without their support, based on a close bond and common goals, the archbishop could not hope to be successful. Adalbert reportedly boasted that he had only two overlords, the pope and the king;[31] and, we might add that he would have needed the assistance of both to realize his ambitions. His political concept was hardly concerned with the overall welfare of the realm, but focused almost exclusively on the royal power that sustained him. Adalbert could easily win the young king's favor with this attitude since it boosted Henry IV's self-confidence and stood in sharp contrast to Anno II of Cologne's demeanor whom the royal youth detested. Compared to Anno's concept of the princes' collective responsibility for the welfare of the realm, Adalbert's explicit emphasis on a personal bond with the king seems considerably more archaic. Inevitably, the princes accused the archbishop of Hamburg of selfish and high-handed behavior. Eventually, they were so infuriated with him that in January 1066, in a surprise move and contrary to the king's will, they joined forces and expelled the arrogant outsider from the royal court. This unexpected blow also served as a warning to the young king that his personal interests and sympathies were not to be satisfied at the expense of the common good, the welfare of the realm.

7

Henry IV: King, Tyrant,
or Antichrist

A SOLEMN KNIGHTING CEREMONY at Worms on 29 March 1065, the
Tuesday after Easter, marked Henry IV's initiation to adulthood (at age
fifteen). Godfrey the Bearded, who in the same year became duke of Lower
Lotharingia, participated in the rite as shield-bearer. Despite the fact that
he had been furiously persecuted by Henry III over a period of many
years, Godfrey had never shunned his responsibilities toward the realm
and its welfare while simultaneously maintaining close ties to the reform
papacy. Now at this crucial juncture he reached out to the young king
to inaugurate a new beginning. However, Henry IV had long since developed his own idea of royal authority, an idea that was molded by the
Salian dynasty's special tradition of kingship. Young Henry, furthermore,
was even more prone to impulsive actions than his predecessors, as an account by Lampert of Hersfeld indicates. No sooner had he been invested
with his knightly armor than he is allegedly purported to move against
Archbishop Anno II of Cologne who, after Kaiserswerth, had taken him
under his tutelage and had subjected him to a compulsory education in the
virtues of being a good and just king (*bonum iustumque*).[1] "Half-cocked he
would have moved against him, had the empress' timely intervention not
placated the looming storm."[2]

Henry IV won such wildly divergent appraisals from his contemporaries that it is difficult to grasp his personality even today.[3] The grand
expansion and reconstruction of the cathedral of Speyer between 1080 and
1102/1106 show clearly that he was in tune with the intellectual and artis-
tic currents of his time. We further learn from the *Vita* of Bishop Otto
of Bamberg (1102–1139) that Henry IV could read, write, and understand
as well as interpret Latin texts: "The emperor was so well versed in the
written word that he could read and understand documents without assis-

tance, no matter from whom they had come to him."[4] In the description
of Henry IV's life, written around 1106 — probably by Bishop Erlung of
Würzburg (1105–1121) — we find the following account:

He possessed great intellectual powers and insights, and when the princes wavered
in their judgment concerning legal matters or an imperial policy, he himself swiftly
untangled the knot and explained to them, as if he were drawing from a secret well
of wisdom, which approach was more just and useful. Attentively he listened to
the voices around him while saying little himself. He did not burst out with his
own opinion prematurely, but wanted to hear what others had to say. When his
eyes looked piercingly into someone's face, he detected that man's innermost feelings and saw, as if he were looking with the eyes of a lynx, whether this person
bore hatred or love in his heart. It also seems praiseworthy to me that he was the
tallest in the circle of princes.

But the *Vita* also states: "Whoever rose up against him and his authority
willfully was so cruelly struck down that traces of his royal punishment
are visible among the offender's descendants to this very day. Thus, he preserved his own power as well as the future welfare of the realm; for men
should learn to abstain from disturbing the peace and from devastating the
realm with armed violence."[5]

Henry IV's opponents, of course, painted a different picture. Bruno's
Book of the Saxon War, which probably originated shortly after 1081 and
was possibly written by the chancellor of the anti-king Hermann of Salm
(1081–1088), reported that Henry IV, as a young boy, already had puffed
himself up with royal conceit. The account then continues that he had
abandoned the path of virtue as an adolescent and had listened to the advice of Archbishop Adalbert of Hamburg-Bremen who, himself "bloated
with pride," encouraged him to do "whatever his heart desired."[6] Henry
supposedly had two or three women at the time; he had beautiful young
maidens forcefully brought to him, only to pass them on to his ministerials. When he wanted to get rid of his wife Bertha of Savoy, three years after
their marriage in 1066, he induced an associate to tempt her with adultery.
But Bertha caught on to the foul scheme and gave her husband, lurking in
the background, such a thrashing with chair legs and sticks that he had to
stay in bed for almost a month.[7] In 1094 Henry ordered his second wife,
the Russian princess Praxedis, whom he had wed in 1088, incarcerated in
Verona after she had become involved in serious intrigues against him.
Following her liberation by Matilda of Tuscany, Praxedis spread the wild-
est accusations about her imperial husband in the camp of Pope Urban II
(1088–1099). These allegations must be taken with a grain of salt, however,

since they were launched at a time when Henry IV's detractors already perceived him as the incarnation of all evil and as the personification of the Antichrist. Godless acts and unnatural deeds were the very essence of evil men; they belonged to a general topology of evil.[8]

While many of the preceding comments are unquestionably partisan in nature, it can clearly be shown that Henry IV did not maintain close ties to the high aristocracy (except for his relationship with Archbishop Adalbert of Hamburg-Bremen) but rather sought his confidants among the lesser nobility, in comital circles, among prelates and chaplains in his vicinity, and among his own ministerials. Individuals from these groups, despised by his enemies, were the king's "intimate friends" (*amici, familiares*) and counselors (*consiliarii, consultores*). The relationship between Henry IV and his *familiares* must have been based on a special sense of bonding and mutual obligation as indicated by the inclusion of these men in the prayer memorials for the king's salvation.[9] In sum, his demeanor toward his associates projects a picture of rare constancy and trust.

A fairly accurate picture of Henry IV's physical appearance has come down to us. When his sarcophagus was opened on 25 August 1900, an untouched, perfectly preserved skeleton was revealed, permitting a close reconstruction of his frame and even his facial features. Based on the evidence, Henry must have been a sturdy man of perfect build and considerable height, at least six feet tall.

No residues indicating decease or illness can be found. The perfect curving of his cranium, including the temples, and the remarkable absence of bones with superfluous seams point, among other things, toward an undisturbed, robust constitution from birth on. An arched chest, broad shoulders, narrow loins, and energetic, well shaped bones in the long extremities, especially in the arms and hands, insinuate the frame of a slender, stalwart, almost athletic male, adept and well-versed in all skills expected of a knight. Virility paired with a touch of feminine charm graces his countenance. The large cranium, the delicately shaped forehead, the energetically protruding brow, and the characteristically elongated, aristocratic nose give the sharply chiseled, narrow face an energetic look which is further accented by a martial mustache. The large, receptive eyes, a finely shaped mouth, and an almost delicate chin provide his expression with a certain softness and rare beauty.[10]

When Henry IV became king in his own right in 1065, his vigorous and energetic appearance was paralleled by his determined actions. One of his first moves involved an unusually large transaction in which he transferred twelve royal monasteries and canonries to various ecclesiastical and secular princes.[11] The king was apparently trying to win these magnates' tacit ap-

proval for the uncompromising and autocratic royal policies he was planning to pursue.[12] Shortly thereafter, in an unprecedented demonstration of
power, he initiated a systematic and ruthless move against Saxony. From
Lampert of Hersfeld's *Annals* and Bruno's *Book of the Saxon War* we learn
that he ordered the construction of massive fortifications in strategic loca-
tions around the Harz mountains, in the very heart of Saxony. All of these
fortresses were so-called *Höhenburgen* (literally "high castles") (fig. 34).
Built on exposed mountain spurs or at the edge of inaccessible cliffs, they
constituted a radical departure from the design of traditional Saxon strongholds. The way their defenses were set up was also quite different; the
castle of Sachsenstein on the southern rim of the Harz mountains, for example, featured a large round tower in the center of an enclosed courtyard
and two towers flanking the entrance gate.[13] None of these massive royal
fortifications were garrisoned by Thuringians or Saxons, though, nor were
they conferred as fiefs; all of them remained at the direct disposition of
the king and were manned by "foreign" ministerials, predominantly from
Swabia. This permanent military presence thus served as a guarantor for
royal authority in Saxony.

The mightiest of these castles was the Harzburg, located east of Goslar.[14] Although conceived as a royal residence, its character differed sharply
from the open design of the palace in Goslar. Perched on a high ridge, the
Harzburg with its impregnable fortifications could only be reached over
a very precarious mountain path. This twin fortress, containing a smaller
and a larger castle complex, was secured by a system of moats and massive
ramparts that had been designed in conformity with the latest fortification
technology. The western portion of the castle contained a canonry where
the imperial insignia and royal treasures were kept when the king was in
residence. Henry IV had the remains of his brother Conrad (d. 1055) transferred to the collegiate church on the Harzburg and also buried his infant
son Henry (d. 1071) there.[15] These actions may have been an attempt to
establish yet another dynastic burial site, underscoring the residential character of this new Salian stronghold.

What was the purpose of these massive fortresses? A large complex
of fiscal lands already existed at the northern edge of the Harz mountains,
and Henry III, as we have seen, created an important center in this region
when he enlarged and embellished the palace at Goslar. Many scholars
have held the opinion that after 1065 Henry IV mainly strove to retrieve
royal estates and sovereign rights that had been alienated by powerful
nobles during Agnes's regency (*Revindikationspolitik*) and that this was the

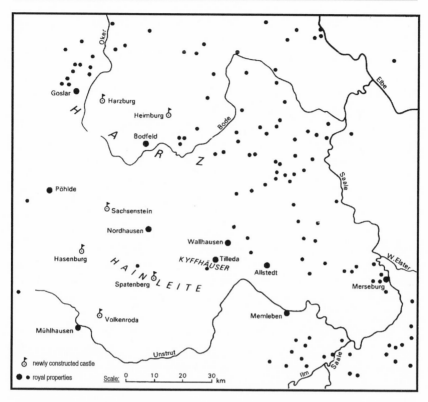

34. Fortifications in the Harz region and in Thuringia, built during the rulership of Henry IV (Deutsche Geschichte, Bd. 2, Berlin-Ost 1983, p. 20).

main reason for his focus on Saxony. Although this point of view cannot be discounted, systematic studies [16] have demonstrated that the loss of fiscal lands during the regency years was relatively small. Furthermore, there is no indication whatsoever that such losses had been more substantial in the Harz area of Saxony and Thuringia than elsewhere. The concept of re-vindication, therefore, hardly provides a satisfactory answer for the Salian king's unprecedented demonstration of power in this region.

In contrast, these fortifications and strongholds must be seen as part of a comprehensive effort to permeate this region with royal authority and to expand and solidify the king's territorial and political power. The existing fiscal lands evidently provided an excellent base for this purpose, allowing royal officials to accelerate the development of an efficient administrative system. For instance, we encounter Prefect Bodo of Goslar as head of an apparently newly constituted royal advocacy. In addition, royal clients (*clientes*) now frequently appear in the sources, such as royal ministerials and people from the lesser nobility; none of them, however, are rooted in Saxony but most stem from Swabia. "For the king loved these people [the Swabians] in particular; and he promoted many of them, men of low birth and almost without ancestry, to the highest offices and elevated them to the first rank at court." Thus we read in Lampert of Hersfeld's report for the year 1073. These men appear as mintmasters or mining supervisors, as foresters or palatial officials; and in this region, with its rich deposits of iron and silver, they organized the royal dominion ever more effectively.

During this period the administrators of the royal fortresses in Saxony became progressively more aggressive. Lampert of Hersfeld reports for the year 1073:

Since their provisions were insufficient, the king gave them [the royal officials] permission to procure booty from neighboring villages and crop lands, as if they were in enemy territory. The inhabitants of this region were forced to furnish their own work force to build castles, assemble construction materials, and provide services from the sweat of their brow like slaves. . . . The garrisons made daily sallies, pillaged whatever they could find in the fields and villages, extracted unbearable fees and taxes from forest and crop lands, and confiscated whole herds of cattle, ostensibly as tithes.[17]

The Saxon sources tell of many atrocities committed by these royal garrisons, composed of insolent and pugnacious young men. They also tell of countless commemorative stones that supposedly were erected along the road from Goslar to the Harzburg, covering a distance of almost two miles, to honor the large number of Goslar residents who had been slain. The sources further mention the abuse of Saxon women and the confiscation of properties belonging to persons who had dared to protest. Many of these allegations must be considered with caution, however, for the image of the evil adversary was definitely designed to conjure up the idea of evil a priori. Still, these Saxon accounts betray a fundamental outrage over the king's presumptuous actions which were considered not only arbitrary and unjust but also flagrant violations of time-honored Saxon liberties.

The Saxons complained bitterly that the king directed his vindictive campaign exclusively against them: "While the people (*gens*) in other parts of the realm were left alone and all of them were hardly disturbed, the king selected us [the Saxons] in particular to subject us to the 'threshing of iron carts,' as the prophet says. Once he [the king] had entered our region, he stayed on and first robbed us of our heritage and then of our freedom. Disregarding our birthright, he slew us with the yoke of bitter servitude."[18] Although Henry IV's focus on Saxony might have been motivated by his desire to benefit from the unusually dense cluster of fiscal properties in this region, the bitter struggle that ensued must have had much deeper roots. It seems that the king was intent on subjugating a duly constituted society that had a proud tradition of tying social status and privilege to consensual decisions and hereditary rights.[19] No other society—save the Frisians—displayed a stronger sense of personal, inalienable legal status and of a collectively determined consensus than the Saxons. Customary rights and liberties thus formed the twin pillars of the Saxon people's sense of justice and, to a degree, these were also embraced by their neighbors, the Thuringians.

Typical, for example, was the defiant stance of Magnus Billung, the son and successor (1073/74–1106) of the Saxon Duke Otto. When the king had him incarcerated in 1071 and demanded that he renounce forever his duchy and the rest of his rightfully inherited possessions (*hereditario iure*) if he wanted to be set free, Magnus Billung was shaken. This demand violated the very essence of his sense of justice and he purportedly declared that he would rather languish in prison and die by all manner of torture and torment than officially yield his inherited rights. Henry IV, on the other hand, consciously sought to break up the traditional bonds between hereditary powers and high office and, in particular, to reestablish the purely administrative character of the comital office. Significant changes may be observed in Saxony during this period, indicating the "tightening of royal authority over the appointment of officials, the rounding out of comital territories, and the establishment of a more hierarchical social structure."[20] Especially north of the Harz mountains the Salian monarch attempted to implement a far-reaching reorganization. This move, which included the redistribution of comital offices to royal administrators, proved particularly injurious to the Saxons' sense of justice.[21]

A comment in Lampert of Hersfeld's *Annals* for 1073 is very revealing in this context: "The king decided to pursue a monstrous course, a course none of his predecessors had ever attempted: namely to reduce all Saxons and Thuringians to servitude" (*in servitium redigere*). In the eyes of the Saxons, Henry IV's acts and decisions seemed to represent a programmatic effort to destroy their independence. Initially, the young king almost certainly took his lead from Archbishop Adalbert of Hamburg-Bremen when he moved against the Saxons. As previously mentioned, Adalbert's fiercest rival, the Saxon duke Magnus Billung, had created an ever-expanding power base there, and the archbishop hoped to gain further advantages in this region through the king's assistance. Several sources report that Henry IV ordered the construction of the impregnable mountain fortresses in the Harz region at Adalbert's recommendation. Bishop Benno II of Osnabrück (1068–1088) may also have played a leading role in these endeavors, as indicated in his *Vita*. He came from a ministerial family in Swabia, attended school at Strasbourg and the monastery of Reichenau, and later became a teacher at the cathedral school of Speyer and at the canonry of Saints Simon and Jude in Goslar. Subsequently, he was appointed to the post of provost at Hildesheim and eventually attained the prestigious office of *vicedominus* for the archdiocese of Cologne under Archbishop Anno II. The *vicedominus* was the chief administrator and manager of the metropolitan see's vast land holdings. Finally, at age forty-eight, he was elevated to the episcopal dignity of Osnabrück. Benno, an unusually gifted man, had without question a distinguished career in ecclesiastical and royal service. Later, he proved his talents as an architect and master builder during the expansion and reconstruction of the cathedral at Speyer. But even much earlier, in the late 1060s and 1070s, the king supposedly put Benno, "a genius in the art of stone masonry," in charge of "overseeing the expedient implementation of his construction projects" in Saxony.[22] Just as his colleague in Hamburg-Bremen, he had a personal interest in strengthening the episcopal authority in Saxony; and the similarities between the Harzburg and his own episcopal fortifications at the Iburg are probably no accident. No doubt, the king had prominent advisers who were ardent advocates of royal politics in Saxony. Nevertheless, the dramatic developments and dynamics that led to the "Saxon Wars" can only be understood in a much broader context. Beginning in the early eleventh century, the kings had become ever more insistent that a centralized, hierarchical command structure throughout the realm was a royal prerogative; it was this principle that fueled Henry IV's showdown with the Saxons. Comparable to Conrad II's confrontation with Duke Ernest of Swabia and to Henry III's unbending stance toward Duke Godfrey the Bearded, Henry IV now set out to demonstrate his power by demanding unconditional recognition of his supreme royal authority. Yet he no longer directed his action against an individual rival or a group of adversaries, but rather against a divergent constitutional principle per se, against a principle that was the embodiment of the Saxon people.

To be sure, the means that the king employed to underscore his royal authority were hardly innovative; for the practice of organizing and deploying administrative and military units of servile origin and of erecting castles on lofty mountain perches had long since been adopted by nobles and bishops alike. Indeed, closer scrutiny reveals that the aristocracy was in many ways ahead of the king in this process. The transformation of the traditional order into new hierarchical structures became ever more evident in the latter part of the eleventh century and affected the administration of every lordship. These general developments often came into direct conflict with royal ambitions, especially in Saxony, where Henry IV felt compelled to move against the heavily fortified strongholds of such defiant nobles as Margrave Dedi's castles at Beichlingen and Burgscheidungen (1069) and Otto of Northeim's castles at Hanstein and Desenberg (1070). No doubt, the newly constructed royal fortresses in the Harz mountains imposed severe limitations on the ability of Saxon magnates to expand their own lordships; in their eyes the king was a ruthless competitor who unfairly exploited his royal position to his own advantage.

A major clash was in the offing. The causes leading up to this confrontation were manifold, but obviously included the changing patterns within the lordships, as well as the king's heightened claims to absolute authority (*Befehlsherrschaft*). These conditions made it inevitable that the struggle in Saxony would eventually entangle the entire body politic, for the principal issue in this stand-off was the position and function of the king within the realm. Otto of Northeim (d. 1083), a Saxon who was duke of Bavaria, recognized the nature of these problems at an early stage and, therefore, was the first among the magnates who experienced harsh treatment at the hands of Henry IV. In 1070, based on rather dubious proceedings, Otto was stripped of the Bavarian duchy, which then was awarded to Welf IV. This prince had not shown any compunction about chasing away his wife, Ethelinda, his predecessor's daughter, to become duke of Bavaria. Otto of Northeim, on his part, refused to comply with a royal order to participate in a duel with his accuser, a notorious scoundrel, when the king denied him safe passage. Consequently, he was sentenced to death in absentia for high treason (*crimen maiestatis*). Northeim subsequently assumed the leadership of the Saxon resistance, which grew steadily and was joined by such eminent Saxon bishops as Burchard II of Halberstadt (1059–1088), Werner of Magdeburg (1063–1078), and Hezilo of Hildesheim (1054–1079). The protest movement further enjoyed the support of Margrave Udo II of the Nordmark (d. 1082), Margrave Dedi of Niederlausitz (d. 1075), and Magnus Billung (d. 1106).

In 1073 major preparations were underway for a general uprising against the king. The Saxons demanded that the Salian fortresses be immediately dismantled. In his *Book of the Saxon War*, Bruno assigns the following speech to Otto of Northeim:

Valiant warriors! . . . The injuries and indignities that our king has perpetrated against each and every one of you over a long time are grave and unbearable. But what else he intends to do, should God the Almighty allow it, will be even more frightful. . . . Are you, valiant men, willing to suffer all of this? Is it not better to fall in battle than to lose a miserable and shameful life in the disgraceful service of such scornful people? Not even servants that have been purchased for money will bear the unjust demands of their masters, yet you who were born free will suffer patiently this servitude? As Christians you may perhaps shy away from violating the oath that you have sworn to your king. All right, but you swore your oath to the king. As long as he was my king, I kept the oath I had sworn to him. However, when he ceased to be a king, he was no longer the person to whom I had pledged my loyalty. I take up arms, not against the king but against the unlawful robber of my liberty, not against the fatherland (*patria*) but *for* the fatherland and *for* the liberty that no man will give up except with his life; I ask you to do the same.[23]

This speech was, of course, not worded as it appears in Bruno's text, but it shows vividly how the notion had spread that Henry IV was no longer a king but rather a tyrant. In 1074 Lampert of Hersfeld mentions for the first time a concrete plan of action evolving from this situation. He writes: "After consulting with the remaining imperial princes, a consensus emerged to seek a ruler for the gravely endangered realm who would meet with the approval of everyone."[24] Shortly thereafter the Saxons supposedly urged Otto of Northeim "to assume the royal power over them." The "Salian king" who, during Conrad II's reign, had been the integrating force within the realm and who had provided unity and stability through his person, now became a liability to peace and unity. Under the leadership of the archbishops of Cologne and Mainz, the princes repeatedly attempted to negotiate and arbitrate between the two camps. However, the pressure to reach a decision kept mounting and, in the process, some magnates kept switching sides; among these were Rudolf of Rheinfelden, Duke of Swabia (1057–1079), Duke Berthold of Carinthia (1061–1077), and Godfrey the Hunchback of Lower Lotharingia (1069–1076). At a peace assembly at Gerstungen in 1074, the king, in the presence of fifteen bishops, seemed almost willing to yield to the demands of his "sworn opponents" (*sacramento obstricti*) and to give up his castles. But when it became known a short time later that Saxon peasants had looted and desecrated the Salian grave sites on the Harzburg, many princes disapproved of this scandalous deed and felt obliged to return to the king's camp. As a consequence, Henry IV commanded a sizable following when he called for the decisive battle against the Saxons in 1075.

It was the biggest battle ever fought between constituents of the realm within the confines of the East Frankish/German kingdom. The royal army assembled in the vicinity of Hersfeld early in June 1075. The host was so enormous, according to Lampert of Hersfeld, that "within human memory, no larger, more valiant, and militarily better equipped army had ever been raised for any battle on German soil. All the prominent personages in the realm, including bishops, dukes, and counts, ecclesiastical and secular dignitaries, were gathered here to direct their strength and power toward this war. No one was missing, unless he had been excused because of an urgent or compelling reason."[25] Royal scouts reported that the Saxon forces and their allies were hardly any weaker in numbers and arms and that the rest of their equipment seemed even superior; they also were extremely well supplied with auxiliary gear and provisions. A civil war of monstrous proportions was in the offing. The entire kingdom was drawn into this power struggle, and although superficially a showdown between the king and the Saxons, it was in essence fought over the Salian ruler's determination to impose his autocratic command structure throughout the realm.

The horrifying clash finally occurred on 9 June 1075, near Homburg on the Unstrut River. Once again on the king's side, Duke Rudolf of Swabia and his men led the royal army's attack directly from the marching column and, by doing so, surprised the Saxons who barely managed to array themselves for battle. A bloody carnage ensued, claiming many victims from the ranks of the magnates but above all wreaking havoc among the Saxon foot soldiers who were slaughtered like cattle. At sunset the king had achieved total victory; he was triumphant. When the Saxon princes submitted to Henry IV's mercy on 25 October 1075, his power seemed boundless and his authority in the realm permanently secured.

His victory, however, was deceptive, for probing questions regarding the position of the kingship vis-à-vis the realm had come to the fore during the first decade of Henry IV's reign. What was the ruler's function within the body politic in view of the changing role and self-perception of ecclesiastical and secular lords? The Salian period had reached a "turning point."[26] How could a king preserve peace and justice when his authority was increasingly challenged in large parts of the realm? Yet according to Henry IV's idea of kingship, adversaries and insurgents had to be subdued by force because the prestige of both ruler and realm were at stake.

Even though both ecclesiastical and secular leaders soon recognized that the king's deeply held convictions were ultimately directed against their personal interests, most were still willing to follow him in 1075 since their identity and princely authority depended on the recognition by and obedience of their own subjects. The Saxon peasants' willful destruction of the Salian grave sites on the Harzburg deeply troubled the powerful elite; and since this act of lawlessness occurred in the same year as the uprising of the citizens of Cologne, which was put down by Archbishop Anno II, their assistance in a rigorous crackdown seemed justified. Soon after the victory at the Unstrut River, though, the princes had second thoughts and began wondering whether their participation had actually furthered the realm and thus their own cause (*minimo rei publicae emolimento*, Lampert of Hersfeld). Their fight for the king did not seem to enhance the realm any longer. This realization basically sealed the verdict against Henry IV and his tyrannical rule long before the reform papacy's wrath descended upon him.

These considerations lead to the conclusion that the princes' election of Rudolf of Rheinfelden as anti-king in 1077 had been initiated much earlier and should not simply be understood as a consequence of Pope Gregory VII's deposition of Henry IV in 1076. Although some decisions may have been expedited through the king's excommunication, the anti-king was actually elected without the pope's permission. In spite of the presence of papal legates, the princes proceeded with their plan contrary to the papal will. They drew their strength from other sources. Lampert of Hersfeld lets Otto of Northeim utter these crucial words: "Thus is the difference between a king and a tyrant: a tyrant resorts to force and cruelty to extort obedience from unwilling participants; a king, on the other hand, guides his subjects according to the rights and customs of their ancestors and makes arrangements for the tasks at hand."[27] The people longed for a king who, according to *their* concept of justice and order, would act as an impartial and disinterested arbitrator in settling strife and discord throughout the realm and they elected Rudolf to be such a "just king, ruler and protector for the entire realm" (*in iustum regem, rectorem, et defensorem totius regni*).[28] Henry IV, in contrast, had been pursuing royal practices that were aimed at restructuring the realm in strictly hierarchical terms. Consequently, he emphasized his overall royal dominion and derived his sacrosanct authority from his position as God's vicar on earth and from the legitimacy of his dynastic claims. He thus followed closely in his father's footsteps and seemed oblivious to the fact that the social and political developments within the realm had reached a point where people were no longer willing to tolerate his pretensions.

Above all, the nobles sought to eradicate the Salians' claim to the establishment of a divinely ordained, everlasting kingship that was inseparable from their dynasty. The belief that the continued existence of the kingship within one and the same dynasty was beneficial and necessary for the realm's stability was now superseded by the idea that imperial unity could best be preserved if the princes freely elected the leader whom they deemed most suitable to rule. Royal elevation by election had always been an option, of course, but if the reigning king had sons, the very presence and power of a royal bloodline (*stirps regia*) determined the decision-making process; and the Salians had consciously cultivated this force. In the wake of increasing pressures by the Church to fill vacant ecclesiastical offices by means of free, canonical elections, Henry IV's opponents adopted similar principles when they elevated the anti-king in Forchheim on 15 March 1077. The princes who had assembled there included the southern German dukes Rudolf of Swabia (of Rheinfelden), Welf IV of Bavaria, and Berthold of Carinthia, as well as the archbishops Siegfried of Mainz, Gebhard of Salzburg, and Werner of Magdeburg. There was further a delegation of papal legates in attendance. In Bruno's *Book of the Saxon War* we find the following comments: "And it was approved by all and confirmed by the authority of the pope that royal power shall no longer fall to anyone through inheritance, as had been the custom. The son of a king, no matter how worthy, should become king in his own right through a spontaneous election rather than through rights of succession. But if a king's son is not worthy or if the people do not want him, it should be in the people's power to elevate to the kingship any person they want to choose."[29] By electing an anti-king, the princes established a new constitutional principle that was based on *their* understanding of their role within the realm and that stood in sharp contrast to the Salian ruler's concept of kingship.

The idea of choosing the king in a free and open election had considerable appeal and, as shall be seen, had a major impact on the way the kingship was transferred to Henry V, the last Salian king. But this principle, ardently supported by the bishops, gained special momentum at the royal elevation of 1125. Although Duke Frederick II of Swabia insisted on his right to succession because of his mother Agnes's Salian bloodline, the forces that favored a free election prevailed. King Henry IV, due to his luck on the battlefield, had managed to fend off this ominous menace to the Salian dynasty. On 15 October 1080 after several initial skirmishes, the king and Rudolf of Rheinfelden faced each other for the decisive battle on the Elster River. Although Rudolf's army was victorious under the able leadership of Otto of Northeim, the anti-king lost his right hand in battle and succumbed to his injuries on the following day. Many contemporaries viewed his fate as a manifestation of divine justice and, accordingly, Henry IV's *Vita* reads: "This was an important lesson that no one shall rise up against his lord. For Rudolf, through the loss of his right hand, received the just due for his perjury, as he had not hesitated to break the oath of fealty that he had sworn to his lord and king; and as if he had not received enough mortal wounds, his punishment was administered on this particular limb in order to make his guilt manifest in the way he was punished."[30] Nevertheless, the struggle between Henry IV and his adversaries had not yet come to an end, but continued in various degrees of violence clear to the end of his reign.

Many scholars have dealt with the developments that led to the confrontation between the Church and the Salian king in the 1070s. Contrary to his father, Henry IV spent little time cultivating his relationships with the church reformers, a fact that has been interpreted as incompetence. However, we need to consider that the way the reformers viewed the principles of hierarchical order had already undergone significant changes during the regency of the Empress Agnes and that, in their eyes, the king had long since lost his place of preeminence within the Church. Their concern for the salvation of human souls, their efforts on behalf of improved pastoral care, and their earnest pursuit of Christ's instructions to bishops and priests called for a higher authority. Divine law, in their view, manifested itself in canon law, that is in the decisions of the Church councils, the writings of the Church Fathers, and the papal decrees. Conciliar resolutions and papal decrees thus possessed universal validity; yet in those cases where ecclesiastical regulations contained contradictions, papal decisions would take precedence over any other authority. That is, in any case, how Peter Damian, the eminent theological scholar, had interpreted these matters; and from there he went on to conclude that that unconditional obedience to the pontiff was a *conditio sine qua non*. The Church's redemptive mission could ultimately only be fulfilled through strict obedience to the apostolic see.

Guided by this principle, Pope Leo IX already had developed a previously unprecedented ecclesiastical and political activism, interfering freely in ecclesiastical, political, and jurisdictional matters of individual churches and bishoprics. The pontiff's highest authority within the universal church and the obedience that it commanded came into play for the first time during his tenure. Leo's circle of reformers included the young Hildebrand who, through the power of his personality, was probably the most ardent promoter of ecclesiastical renovation.[31] Born between 1020 and 1025, probably in Soana in southern Tuscany, he had taken his vows in the Roman monastery of Saint Mary's on the Aventine in Rome where he had absorbed the spiritual legacy of the great monastic reforms. Before long Hildebrand became one of the closest advisers to the reform papacy. Under Pope Nicholas II (1058–1061) his influence gained so much currency that a popular saying affirmed: "Hildebrand feeds his Nicholas in the Lateran like a donkey in his stall." At the Lateran synod of 1059, he advocated radical clerical reform and demanded that the Church return to the simple life of the *ecclesia primitiva*, in other words, to the original Church as it had been established by Christ and his disciples or, to put it more accurately, to an "original" Christian community as conceived in the mind of eleventh-century reformers. Hildebrand's decisive nature and extraordinary sense of mission did not escape Peter Damian's attention who comments in a letter: "He comes at me like a furious north wind with a tempestuous breath."[32]

Hildebrand, taking the name Gregory VII, was elevated to the papacy in 1073, although, as his enemies later would allege, not entirely according to regulations. His pontificate was probably the most significant in all of papal history. He continued the fight against simony and nicolaitism with unmitigated severity and ordered the bishops to implement his instructions. Prohibition of priestly marriages had a long canonical tradition, but it rarely had been enforced below the episcopal level. Gregory now issued strict orders "that, according to canon law, priests were prohibited from having wives, that those who were married must dismiss their wives or would be removed from office, and that heretofore absolutely no one could be admitted to the priesthood who was unwilling to profess permanent abstinence and celibacy."[33] The pope made sure that the new rules were widely disseminated. But when Archbishop Siegfried of Mainz dutifully passed these instructions on to his suffragans at a provincial synod in Erfurt in 1074, he ran into a storm of protests and had to recognize "that it would take great pains to eradicate such established traditions as the cohabitation of priests with women."[34] Indeed, the pontiff's rebukes and directives as well as his demand for unconditional obedience initially seemed unbearable to the imperial bishops. The essence of this sentiment is summed up in a frequently quoted sentence from a letter which Archbishop Liemar of Hamburg-Bremen (1072–1101) sent to Bishop Hezilo of Hildesheim in the winter of 1074/75: "This dangerous man [Gregory VII] is trying to order bishops around at will, as if they were stewards, and if

they do not carry out everything exactly [as ordered], they are summoned
to Rome, or they are simply suspended from their office without judicial
recourse."[35] Soon an image of Hildebrand "casting about the flames of
hell" took root within the realm.

Initially, Gregory VII exhibited amazing patience toward Henry IV.
He sent the king a series of admonitions, rebuking him for his personal
conduct, his decisions in filling episcopal vacancies, or his handling of individual bishops. The situation became aggravated, however, when Henry
refused to yield to the pope's wishes in a dispute over a new metropolitan
for Milan and when Gregory felt compelled to banish five of the king's
councilors from the Lenten synod in spring 1075. Subsequently, the pope
raised serious charges against the king. A papal letter, dated 8 December 1075, begins with the ominous lines: "Bishop Gregory, servant of the
servants of God, sends King Henry greetings and apostolic blessings, provided that he [the king] obey the pope as behooves a Christian king."[36]
The writ then continues:

You should show more respect to the head of the Church. If you indeed belong to
the Lord's sheep, you are actually bound over to him [the pope] through the word
and power of the Lord. He [the pope] will then lead you to pasture, as Christ has
commanded him: Peter lead my sheep to pasture! . . . Since we, as holder of his
seat and his apostolic office . . . through God's will, represent his power, in reality
it is he, Christ himself, who receives whatever communication, written or oral, you
convey to us! . . . Therefore, you should take care that your words and messages to
us contain no willful disobedience since you would not deny due reverence to us
but to God the Almighty!

This wording was unequivocal: Christ himself acted and judged through
the pope alone, thus depriving the king of any direct access to and communion with God.

Such notions were outrageous and totally foreign to Henry IV's
thinking. When at the beginning of 1076 the papal epistle reached the royal
court in Worms, where numerous bishops had assembled, the king was
easily persuaded to support their refusal to follow the pope's instructions.
Although the papal letter was hardly the decisive factor in the bishops' defiant response to the Holy See,[37] it once more, for one last fleeting moment,
revived the idea at Worms that king and bishops were united by a common
cause. Henry IV, bolstered by his victory over the Saxons, felt called upon
to put the pope in his place and to emphasize his own role as protector of
the realm and as defender of the bishops who seemed threatened by papal
servitude. Summarizing their grievances, the twenty-six bishops sought to
justify their disobedience in a letter on 24 January 1076. They stated that

Gregory had introduced outrageous innovations in the Church, had suppressed the bishops, had deprived the episcopal office of its dignity, and had usurped unseemly authority over them. They went so far as to say: "None of us will recognize you as pope in the future" (*tu quoque nulli nostrum amodo eris apostolicus*).[38] Henry IV, correspondingly, alleged in his own reply that Gregory had not only shown disdain for the king's inherited regal dignity, but had not shied away either from laying hands on the venerable bishops and, contrary to divine and human justice, had offended them with arrogant insults and wicked abuse. He, Henry, concurred with the bishops' conclusions and hereby ordered the pope to step down from his throne.[39] The king thus met his obligation of protecting the episcopal *libertas*; in fact, had he not done so, he would have undermined his own authority. In 1076 he had no alternative but to support his bishops' actions.

Nevertheless, it soon became evident that Henry IV's move had triggered a bitter struggle for the highest rank on earth, a struggle in which the king was bound to lose. For when Gregory VII responded with the excommunication of Henry IV at the lenten synod in February 1076, it was immediately decided that the pontiff's argumentation had greater force. The pope justified his action with long-standing ecclesiastical traditions, particularly with the tenet that "the highest ecclesiastical office cannot be judged by anybody" (*prima sedes a nemini iudicatur*). Originating in the sixth century, this papal claim was paired with the conviction that whoever disagreed with the Roman Church, founded by Saint Peter, was by definition a heretic.[40] The pope cleverly couched his sentence of excommunication in form of a prayer to Saint Peter, the prince of the apostles:

I therefore believe that you in your grace—and not because of my good works—wish for the Christian community, which is especially entrusted to you, to show obedience to me because it is equally entrusted to me as your deputy; and I believe that God, for your sake, has granted me power to bind and absolve in heaven and on earth. In this firm conviction, for the glory and protection of your Church, in the name of God the Almighty, the Father, the Son, and the Holy Spirit, by force of your power and authority, I thus deprive King Henry, Emperor Henry's son, who rose up against your Church with unprecedented arrogance, of his regal lordship over Germany and Italy; and I absolve all Christians from the oath they have sworn to him or might swear to him in the future, and I deny him the honor of serving as king heretofore. . . . And since he has spurned to obey as a Christian should and has not returned to God, whom he has abandoned, I, as your deputy, strike him with the scourge of God's curse.[41]

These words had a very different ring than the pronouncements of the king and the bishops. Arising from the depth of conviction, this invocation re-

ferred to the highest level of responsibility for Christendom and spoke of
the exclusive truth of God's laws; its compelling sense of mission swept
away any objections and reservations that might have been voiced against
the pope's supreme authority on earth. Even an oath of fealty to the king
was now superseded by papal decisions, an issue that sparked great controversy and fueled heated discussions in the polemical writings of the late
eleventh century.[42] Gregory's authoritarian claims completely undermined
the legal position of the king and his supporters and caused the court historian (Petrus) Crassus in his *Defense of Henry IV*, 1083/84, to conjure up
the vision of a human race that had "strayed so far from loyalty, justice,
and truthfulness and all the other virtues that serve the salvation of the
soul that it [mankind] was either unfamiliar with these values, or, if it was
aware of them, despised them."[43] For the reformers, in contrast, the divine
truth as represented by the pope had become the sole measure and guiding
principle in all matters.

Gregory VII's deposition and banishment of the king stirred up deep
emotions among his contemporaries; for such an event had been unthinkable before this time. Its traumatic effects were graphically summarized by
the reformer Bonzio of Sutri in 1085/86: "When the message of the king's
banishment reached the people, our whole Roman universe began shaking!"[44] Now everyone became aware that their world order had undergone
a radical change. Now it also became evident that the joint effort of the
king and the bishops at Worms was no longer viable. Before long many of
the ecclesiastical princes sought a reconciliation with the pope, a second
group sat on the sidelines waiting, and only a small core of supporters remained loyal to the king. Scholars have repeatedly expressed amazement
over the bishops' hasty desertion of Henry IV and have sought expla-
nations.[45] It seems that the king had not always had the right touch in
selecting his bishops and that several of them lacked character and stature.

The underlying reasons for the bishops' behavior, however, must be
sought in the fact that principles similar to those used to justify the pope's
supremacy increasingly determined the hierarchical and spiritual views of
the episcopal office. Moreover, bishops could hardly challenge the idea
that spiritual matters should always take precedence over secular ones.
Consequently, the bishops did not hesitate long before they recognized
the preeminence and supreme authority of the pope; his exalted position,
after all, paralleled their own concept of the new order. Scholarly studies
have shown that the Gregorian church reform ultimately enhanced the
principles of a hierarchical episcopate.[46] Although the special papal pro-

tection granted to reformed monasteries (*libertas Romana*) at the expense of episcopal jurisdiction seems to contradict this analysis, it has been demonstrated that such measures were directed mostly against bishops who had rejected the authoritative claims of the reform papacy. By and large it became clear, though, that appeals to the primal authority of the pope (*auctoritas Sancti Petri*) could also become a powerful instrument for the bishops in the administration of their episcopal offices.

By the summer of 1076 Henry IV had been abandoned by all but a small core of his supporters. In mid-October, while the king was waiting in Oppenheim, an assembly of princes convened at Trebur just across the Rhine to deliberate about the further fate of the realm and the banished monarch. Finally, they informed him that if he wanted to reclaim his crown, he had to gain absolution from his ban prior to the anniversary of his excommunication. Once again decisive pressure on the part of the princes forced the Salian king's hand and compelled him to journey to Canossa in the winter of 1076/77. There, on the northern slopes of the Apennine mountains, Pope Gregory was a guest in the castle of Countess Matilda of Tuscany. After a treacherous crossing over the ice-coated Mont Cenis pass, in the western Alps, Henry appeared in penitent garb and barefoot at the interior castle gate of Canossa on 25 January 1077. He began his public penitence with bitter tears and persisted for three days until the pope's resistance had been broken. Gregory VII personally described these events in a letter to the German princes: "He did not desist from imploring the assistance and consolation of the apostolic mercy under tears until he had generated such compassion and pity among all those who were present or had received this news that all pleaded with many entreaties and tears on his behalf; and many showed amazement at the unusual harshness of our conviction. Some even complained that we did not represent the firm hand of apostolic justice but rather the cruelty of licentious tyranny."[47] Even Matilda of Tuscany advocated for him (fig. 35). Thus the pope finally absolved Henry from his banishment and once again received him into the community of the Church.

How should this penitent journey to Canossa be interpreted? Did it really represent the submission of the highest secular power to the supreme spiritual authority? Did it actually signify the precedence of the papacy over the kingship? It is unlikely that any such thoughts had crossed the mind of Henry IV! For him the whole exercise was primarily a shrewd tactical maneuver to forestall a potential showdown with the princes, just as it is related in his *Vita* of 1106: "When Henry recognized the extent of his

R ex ROGAT ABBATem. MATHILDIM SupplicATATQ; ;

35. Henry IV kneeling in front of Matilda of Tuscany in Canossa, pleading for her mediation in his dispute with Pope Gregory VII (to the left Abbot Hugh of Cluny) (Rome, Bibl. Vat. Lat. 4922, fol. 49).

troubles, he secretly conceived a crafty plan. Suddenly and unexpectedly he departed to meet the pope half-way and thus achieved two things in one: he received absolution from the banishment and, through his active interference, prevented the threatening prospect of the pope's meeting with his adversaries."[48] Recent scholarship has come to similar conclusions and has shown that Henry IV, even in his act of submission, did not at any time "recognize the pope's denial of his kingship or the dissolution of the oath of fealty for those who owed him loyalty."[49] At that time he further insisted on the royal prerogative that would allow him to swear an oath by proxy.[50] Politically, however, the real menace for Henry came from the antagonistic princes, who obviously were no longer willing to recognize his kingship, regardless of the fact that he had been absolved from his banishment. Rather, as previously mentioned, on 15 March 1077 the imperial magnates proceeded to elect an anti-king.

After years of strife and struggle, Henry IV eventually prevailed militarily against his adversaries in the kingship and against his nemesis Pope Gregory VII. Hermann of Salm from the house of Luxembourg (d. 1088), the second anti-king, elected in 1081, was never very viable. Gregory on his part damaged his prestige when he renewed the banishment of the Salian king in 1080 and prophesied that the latter would come to a bad end before the feast of Saint Peter Enchained on 1 August of that year. Then he went even further, asking for his own expulsion from the Holy See should his prophecy not come true. This arrogant demeanor persuaded many German bishops to participate in the election of an (anti-)pope at a synod in Brixen in June 1080. They chose Wibert, who had been archbishop of Ravenna since 1072; he assumed the name Clement III. This name established a link to Clement II, the pontiff who had been elevated by Henry III in 1046 to lead the papacy out of its troubles. It was from the hands of Clement III that Henry IV and his wife Bertha accepted the imperial crown in a Roman ceremony on Easter Sunday 1084 while Gregory VII was ensconced behind the stout walls of Castel Sant' Angelo. As soon as the German host had departed, Gregory requested assistance from the Norman prince Robert Guiscard. The Normans arrived promptly; however, they wrought such terrible devastation on Rome on 28 May 1084 that the reform pope was no longer safe in his own city. He followed Robert Guiscard to Salerno, where he died a year later on 25 May 1085.

But in spite of his successes, the Salian king could not prevent the ideas and mental attitudes of the Gregorian reform from spreading. Bishops such as Altmann of Passau (1065–1091), Gebhard of Salzburg (1060–

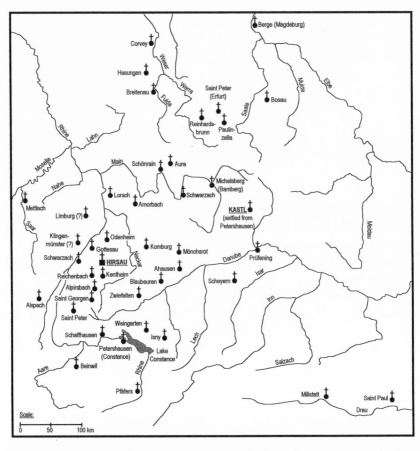

36. Monasteries reformed under the direct leadership of Hirsau (Deutsche Geschichte, Bd. 2, Berlin-Ost 1983, p. 53).

1088), or Burchard II of Halberstadt (1059–1088) were active supporters and promoters of clerical and monastic reforms. In addition, this movement found fertile ground among the ranks of the nobility and soon led to a close alliance between the princely opposition and the church reformers, especially in Swabia and Saxony. The forces of resistance were thus doubled, and aimed their efforts at the secular tyrant as well as the enemy of God and the Church: the Antichrist. Especially the latest monastic reform that had emanated from Cluny spread like wildfire all over southwestern Germany, establishing important centers at Hirsau (1076/79) (fig. 36) and Saint Blaise (1072). Although Henry IV had not opposed this movement initially, it now increasingly turned its venom against him and his followers. The king's time-honored function as the ultimate protector of life and liberty was blatantly disregarded when the reformed monasteries turned to the pope for their protection (*libertas Romana*) and transferred the authority over their affairs to Saint Peter's in Rome (*traditio Romana*). This is a further example of the changing nature of authority during this period. Acceptance of the *libertas Romana* meant that these monasteries were no longer in need of any lay support, not even that of the king. Indeed, he was actually on the verge of losing his traditional right of appointing advocates for monastic communities. These conflicts between the Salian camp and the reform movement were interpreted as harbingers of coming endtimes; for as Gregory VII wrote to his faithful: "The closer we come to the time of the Antichrist, the more he will engage in a life and death struggle to extinguish the Christian religion."[51] Images of the Antichrist roaming the globe with a deadly sword and tearing down churches became a common feature (fig. 37). The nobles who were sympathetic to the reform emerged as its self-styled protectors. Being deeply touched by the salutary truth of the Gregorian movement, these men saw themselves as the *militia sancti Petri*. In cooperation with the bishops, they remained the king's confirmed adversaries to the bitter end and in 1104, as we shall see, ultimately initiated the final downfall of King Henry IV.

The confrontation with the Gregorian reformers who, through their attacks on the idea of a divinely instituted kingship and their challenges to a dynastic right of succession, shook the foundation of the Salian concept of royal authority, forced Henry IV to find new ways of defending his legitimacy. As early as 1076 the king felt compelled to compose a propagandistic letter, charging that the pontiff had dared to deprive him of the power, duly bestowed on him by God, as if he, Henry, had received his kingship from the pope and as if the regal and imperial lordship lay in the pope's and not in God's hands.[52] Writing to the cardinals in 1082, Henry IV calls the pope's pronouncement a blasphemous presumption, adding: "God chose us to be king from the cradle!"[53]

The concept of a direct, divinely ordained mandate constituted the core of the ideological justification for the Salian kingship.[54] Gottschalk of Aachen, who wrote numerous documents and letters for Henry IV, played an important role in this respect. He later became provost of the chapter house at Saint Mary's in Aachen and eventually entered the monastery of Klingenmünster on the Haardt River. Especially between 1070 and 1085 he was actively involved at court and introduced Pope Gelasius I's (492–496)

37. The fury of the Antichrist (Paris, Bibl. Nat. MS Lat. 8878, fol. 155).

doctrine of the two swords in defense of the Salian ideal of regal authority. When the disciples handed Christ two swords in his decisive hour, he said: "This will do."[55] According to his will, therefore, a spiritual and a secular sword should exist side by side on this earth. Even if greater dignity may be assigned to the spiritual power, the secular one is in principle equal in rank.

In the past the doctrine of the two swords had been used to support the papal position, but had now been given up by Gregory VII and his promoters. They preferred different imagery, such as sun and moon, gold and lead, and soul and body, to illustrate the preeminence of the spiritual power (*sacerdotium*) over the secular lordship (*regnum*). Gottschalk charges that the papal representatives wanted to replace the two swords with one and, consequently, subordinate the secular power to the spiritual authority.[56]

It is noteworthy, though, that the Salian court used the doctrine of the two swords especially to emphasize the realm's autonomous standing vis-à-vis the Church, indicating that the concept of a unity embodied in the emperor as supreme protector could no longer be sustained. A pro-imperial propaganda tract written in the monastery of Hersfeld between 1091 and 1093, the *Book Concerning the Preservation of Ecclesiastical Unity*,[57] also assigns the Church to the spiritual domain. It states that Saint Peter was only empowered to bind and absolve in regard to sins and that the old order, instituted by God, could only be reestablished if the Church focused on its pastoral duties and left the secular order to the royal power. The two domains were thus delimited by their functions. But this argumentation did not really indicate an adherence to an outmoded universal order on the part of the Salian camp, as scholars have sometimes maintained. For Henry III's ideal of a realm of peace on earth, mandated by royal decree and encompassing both Church and secular polity, had long since been abandoned.

A further step toward the delineation between spiritual and worldly powers consisted of an attempt to emphasize the traditional rights of the secular rulers. The linkage to Roman imperial tradition was of crucial importance in this context: the realm (*regnum*) was seen as the continuity or renewal of the ancient Roman empire.[58] It is hardly accidental that chroniclers and annalists around this time began enumerating the emperors from Caesar Augustus clear through the Salians and that the title *rex Romanorum* appears much more frequently under Henry IV than previously. Henry V eventually used this title on a regular basis to counteract the rather pejorative and limiting designation *rex Teutonicorum* ("King of the Germans") preferred by the reform papacy.[59] Once again the *Book Concerning the Preservation of Ecclesiastical Unity* may serve to illustrate this point. The author states that Constantine, by moving his residence to Constantinople, had physically separated the secular from the spiritual power since the papacy remained in Rome. This move not only resulted in the temporal preeminence of the empire over the papacy but also in the fundamental precedence of the Roman emperors and their successors over the Church. The power (*potestas*) of the Roman emperors, consequently, emanated from a different source and was completely independent from the Church.

In 1081 in a letter addressed to the Romans, Henry IV also raises the idea of a hereditary imperial office that would be sanctioned by the citizens of Rome. After crushing his toughest enemies, so it reads, Henry would come to the Romans "in order to receive from your hands and with your consent and favorable approval the hereditary dignity that is due to us."[60] In his *Defense of King Henry IV* (1083/84), (Petrus) Crassus, the court historian, developed even more compelling arguments to prove the legitimacy of Salian hereditary claims. Besides considering canon law, he relies primarily on Roman law and quotes from the *Codex Iustinianus* and the *Institutes*. He claims that the hereditary right of kingship was already encoded in the Roman law. The king could not be deprived of it any more than a private person could be legally denied his customary rights—an argument that skillfully alluded to the strong sense of hereditary privileges among the Saxons. He further posited that the hereditary succession in the kingship was divinely ordained and therefore also rooted in canon law.

Like the focal rays in a burning glass, the various pursuits of legitimacy converged on the Salian cathedral church at Speyer. Around 1076 Henry IV started paying renewed attention to that city and the burial church of his ancestors. In the 1080s he made numerous substantial grants to the church of Saint Mary's. In addition to the Salian monasteries of Limburg on the Haardt River and Saint Lambrecht, which had been transferred to the episcopal church in 1065, Speyer now acquired control over the monasteries of Kaufungen and Hornbach, the house of canonesses at Eschwege and the priory of Naumburg; it was further granted estates in the Upper Rhine region, in the Remstal, in the Nahegau, and in Saxony, as well as counties in the Speyergau and on the right side of the Rhine in the area around Forchheim. In the charters where these donations were recorded, Henry IV never neglected to refer to the memory of his forebears, to Conrad II and his wife Gisela, as well as to Henry III, and occasionally to the latter's wife Agnes who had died in Rome on 14 December 1077. Except for Agnes, they were all buried in the cathedral at Speyer, and in Henry's eyes it was they who, through the will of God, mediated his legitimate claim to the kingship. The presence of his ancestors in the Salian burial site at Speyer became a legal precedent to justify his right to rule.

The king's position as a ruler who had been installed directly by God—without intercession of the clergy or mediation by the pope—was

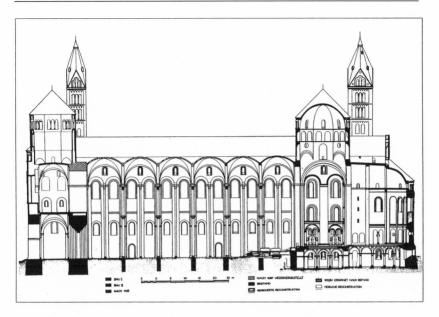

38. Longitudinal reconstruction of the imperial cathedral at Speyer under Henry IV (Edifice II) (D. Von Winterfeld).

to find its reflection in the cathedral of Speyer as well. Over a period of roughly twenty years, from circa 1080 to 1102/1106, the entire eastern section of the church was torn down and reconstructed. Initially Bishop Benno II of Osnabrück (1068–1088) was in charge of this gigantic building project; from 1097–1102 the royal chaplain Otto, the later bishop of Bamberg (1102–1139), supervised its completion.[61] The special shape and size of the Salian burial site no longer played the central role in the newly constructed cathedral but rather its splendor and magnificent appearance. Everything was changed to achieve the desired effect. Unprecedented technical skills were employed to restructure the walls, provide every space with vaulted ceilings, and decorate all horizontal lines with elaborately ornamented ledges. The heavy stone walls were broken up into elegant arches and arcades. Dwarf galleries, an architectural novelty consisting of rows of miniature arcades, were becoming popular in the Rhineland in that period. However, it was in Speyer where these elegant arcades were first used as a unifying device. Wrapped around the entire upper tier of the cathedral, they provided the gigantic edifice with a rare measure of proportion and harmony.

Hence originated the famous structure, sometimes called Speyer II, the imperial cathedral of Henry IV, which "more than any works of the old kings merits praise and admiration."[62] Its sheer size and physical beauty filled the world with amazement. This unique and magnificent cathedral, "our special and holy church at Speyer" (*nostra specialis sancta Spirensis ecclesia*),[63] towered above all other churches; none could measure up to it. The elements of Roman architecture combined with the purplish-red masonry works were unmistakable hallmarks of an imperial church of the highest order.

In addition to using his ancestral grave site to legitimize his rule and to bear witness to the impact of devine ordination on his royal and imperial office, Henry IV was also motivated by his deep-seated piety and the concern for his own salvation. Like his grandfather Conrad II in 1024, he commended his fate to the protection of the Virgin Mary, the patron saint of Speyer. He revered Mary above all the other saints and in his charters he calls her *sancta sanctorum* and the "Queen of Angels."[64] In 1080, prior to the decisive battle against the anti-king Rudolf of Rheinfelden, he placed his life in the hands of the Holy Virgin and endowed her with two important Salian estates in Waiblingen and Winterbach. In the arenga of the respective diploma he justifies his donation as follows: "Although we honor the virtues of all saints, we must especially implore the protection of the Virgin Mary who is ever constant and whose advocacy alone has swayed the Lord over heaven and earth to show mercy to all believers."[65] This text clearly indicates that Henry IV lived with the conviction that only the Holy Virgin could establish the crucial link between God and the king. The cathedral at Speyer with its Salian burial site and with Mary as its patron saint served now, as never before, not only as a demonstrative symbol but also as an anchor for the legitimacy and the continuance of the Salian dynasty's royal and imperial lordship as well as the personal salvation of Henry IV (fig. 38). From this point of view, legitimate kings could only come from the dynasty that was directly linked to *this* church.

8

Princes as Heads
of the Polity

ON 12 DECEMBER 1104, Henry V, eighteen years old and already designated as his father's successor, abandoned Henry IV in the middle of preparations for a Saxon campaign and journeyed south to Bavaria. There he joined a group of rebellious magnates assembled in Regensburg and celebrated Christmas with them.[1] According to the *Vita Heinrici IV*, the dissidents manipulated him with skillful arguments and persuasive innuendo. They told young Henry they could not understand how he could put up with such a harsh father (*quod tamen durum patrem pati posset*); by bearing his tyranny so obediently, he in fact made himself indistinguishable from a lowly servant. If he were planning to wait until his father's death to assume his kingship, someone would surely preempt him; and such a rival could count on many helpers because of the ill-will and hatred that had accumulated against his father. On the other hand, he could be assured of everyone's vote if he did not hesitate to exercise power over the kingdom now which, after all, had already been transferred to him. Such a move was especially necessary because his father lay under excommunication and had been banished by the church and rejected by the imperial princes long ago.[2]

Henry V then agreed to assume the leadership of the grumbling princes. The following year, 1105, both father and son began mobilizing their forces, but no decisive encounter ensued. Then Henry V resorted to a ruse: he came to meet his father feigning remorse and willingness to seek reconciliation. Thereupon the emperor reportedly embraced his son in tears and dismissed his army. As father and son were riding toward Mainz, Henry V supposedly suggested to the emperor that it might be wise if he sought refuge in the castle of Böckelheim on the Nahe River since a large force of Bavarians and Swabians had assembled in Mainz and might pose a great danger to him. Meanwhile he, the son, would proceed to the city and calm the excited crowd. Henry IV then rode on to the castle of Böckelheim with a small retinue. He had no sooner arrived there, however, than he was arrested and kept in custody. But Henry V, according to the *Vita Heinrici IV*, "returned to the assembly in Mainz, rejoicing over his successful deception; and, as if he had achieved a heroic feat, he boasted how cunning he had been in taking his father prisoner. The assembly, then, resounded in jubilation and applause; a crime was called justice, betrayal virtue."[3] Subsequently, the emperor was compelled to hand over crown, cross, and holy lance, as well as any other imperial insignia, and at the beginning of 1106 he was brought to the palace of Ingelheim as a prisoner and forced to resign. Once again the *Vita Heinrici IV* tells us of the aging emperor's sighs and tears and describes how he even threw himself at his son's feet, resorting to the same extreme form of self-inflicted royal humiliation as his grandfather Conrad II had done. For Henry, however, it was to no avail.

Late January or early February 1106, Henry IV managed to escape from custody at Ingelheim. On his flight he passed through the city of Cologne, where its citizens offered him shelter, and eventually he reached Liège. There he wrote a series of letters to prominent individuals, such as the abbot Hugh of Cluny, King Philip of France, his son Henry V, and the imperial princes. In these epistles he complained bitterly about "the enormity of the outrageous betrayal" and about his son's broken oath by which the latter had previously sworn to abstain from rebellion against his father. He further protested that he had only given up his rulership to save his life. In Liège he began rallying support for his own cause; before a decisive encounter between the opposing camps could take place, however, on 6 August 1106 Henry IV died.

At first glance, these events seem to indicate that the Salian house had experienced an unmitigated tragedy that was precipitated by Henry V's sheer ambition and lust for power. Indeed, this opinion still prevails in some scholarly circles: at the beginning of this century, the son's deceptive action against his father was proclaimed the "most heinous deed in all of German history,"[4] and even a recent biographical sketch of Henry V chastises him "for hiding his unscrupulous brutality under a cloak of feigned piety and behind a mask of attractive appearance."[5]

In order to judge these events fairly, though, we should not overlook the fact that Henry V was not the first son to rise up against his father. His older brother Conrad had done so before him. Although he had been crowned in Aachen as Henry IV's designated successor on 30 May 1087,

Conrad switched sides in 1093 by joining the camp of the church reformers, then headed by Pope Urban II (1088–1099).

Inspired by the spirit of the great reform pope Gregory VII, Urban II began pressing his fight against the Salian emperor as soon as he assumed office. In the announcement of his election to the German bishops, he stated programmatically: "I shall strive to follow in his [Gregory's] footsteps unequivocally. Whatever was damned by him, I shall damn as well; whatever commanded his love, I shall also embrace with love."[6] In one respect, however, Urban II differed substantially from his role model: he was the great pragmatist among the reformers. Because of his keen sense of reality and his gift for diplomacy, he succeeded in actually implementing the church reform and, ultimately, in securing its success.[7] From this point of view Urban II was much more dangerous to Henry IV than Gregory VII had ever been. A typical example of the new pope's pragmatic thinking was his involvement in 1089 in the arrangement of a marriage between the forty-three-year-old Countess Matilda of Tuscany and the eighteen-year-old Welf V of Bavaria. Although this union appeared somewhat extreme even to stalwart Gregorians, there was no denying that it formed an effective alliance of anti-Salian forces both north and south of the Alps. To strengthen this coalition even further, Pope Urban II also promoted the marriage of Henry IV's firstborn son Conrad, who had attained the crown of Italy in 1093, to Maximilla, daughter of the Norman count Roger II of Sicily (1061–1101).

The sources reveal little about the motives that might have persuaded the eighteen-year-old Conrad to switch parties. The author of the *Vita Heinrici IV* blames Countess Matilda of Tuscany for supposedly ensnaring the young Salian prince with "sweet words"—"for who could resist the seductive charms of a lady?"[8] But can we really assume that Conrad would carelessly and without any compelling reasons jeopardize his co-rulership that had been firmly established through his coronation? The only plausible explanation lies in the inference that the reformers' convictions must have had a profound impact on the young prince. If they considered the banned emperor's provisions for royal succession invalid, Conrad's own kingship stood on a shaky foundation. The reformers, conversely, were given the opportunity to strike at the very essence of the Salian kingship: its concept of regal authority tied to a divinely ordained succession. If Conrad's confidence in his legitimacy could be undermined, there was a real chance to curb the dynastic ambitions of the Salian house.

Under these circumstances it was crucial for Henry IV to secure the princes' approval when he took steps to disinherit his son Conrad. He sought a compromise with some of his opponents, especially with Welf V, who in 1095 had separated from Matilda, and with the latter's father Welf IV, whom he reinstated as duke of Bavaria. It is probable that the Welfs were promised hereditary rights to the Bavarian duchy at this time. A reconciliation with the powerful Zähringen family also put an old conflict to rest. In 1079 Henry IV had not only made Frederick I of Hohenstaufen his future son-in-law but had also appointed him duke of Swabia disregarding the fact that the anti-king's camp had previously awarded the Swabian duchy to Berthold II of Zähringen. Finally, in 1098 this thorny issue was resolved: while Frederick of Hohenstaufen remained Duke of Swabia, the lord of Zähringen was allowed to retain his ducal title for his own dominions which had been substantially enlarged by the addition of the royal advocacy of Zurich. As a consequence, there now existed a somewhat diminished Swabian duchy and a newly created duke of Zähringen, a title which appears in the records for the first time in the year 1100. The duchy of Zähringen comprised the extensive and concentrated dominions under the control of the powerful Zähringen dynasty and, thus, had a very different legal foundation than the traditional "stem" duchies. A new type of territorially based duchies appeared on the horizon.

In May 1098, at the assembly of Mainz, the princes finally acquiesced, though reluctantly, to support Conrad's disinheritance and to renounce him as their future king. The emperor purportedly argued that his son had committed an offense against the entire community rather than against his person and that it behooved the princes to interfere in the interest of the polity (*rei publicae causae*) when someone sought to gain power through crime and violence.[9] By using such rhetoric, Henry IV cleverly exploited for his own advantage the princes' growing sense of duty in regard to shared responsibilities for the welfare of the realm. It was also within this context that he eventually persuaded the nobility to recognize his younger son, the twelve-year-old Henry V, as his successor and to approve his coronation in Aachen on 6 January 1099. On this occasion Henry IV had his son swear an oath, promising to abstain from usurping power over the realm or from seizing any paternal possessions as long his father lived. Through such precautionary measures, the emperor hoped to insulate the Salian house from the corroding influence of his opponents: the clerical and princely adherents of the reform movement. In the long run these efforts proved to be futile, as we have already seen.

Initially, though, matters seemed to run smoothly for ruler, princes, and realm. The premature death of Conrad, Henry IV's older son, on 27 July 1101 eliminated the peril of fraternal discord. The emperor now turned his attention increasingly to the peace movement that had first made an impact in German lands when both Liège (1082) and Cologne (1083) established a *pax Dei* (*Gottesfrieden*) in their communities. These developments culminated in the regional peace associations (*Landfrieden*) of 1093/94, which issued a formal prohibition of feuds. Peace keeping now depended heavily on the commitment of the princes, contrasting sharply from Henry III's approach to the preservation of peace. Eventually, Henry IV entered into an alliance with the most powerful nobles and an agreement was sealed in the imperial *Landfrieden* of Mainz in 1103. The group of magnates included the dukes Welf V of Bavaria (1101–1120), Berthold II of Zähringen (1098–1111), and Frederick I of Swabia (1079–1105). They swore an oath promising to preserve peace throughout the realm (*per totum regnum*) and to set severe penalties for violators.[10] Once again it can be observed how Henry IV, around 1100, had become much more sensitive to the princes' altered perceptions of lordship and to their desire to participate in keeping order in the realm.

Accommodations with the papacy seemed possible as well when, following Urban II's death on 29 July 1098, the reformers elected the cardinal presbyter of Saint Clemente to the Holy See as Paschal II and when the anti-pope Clement III died on 8 September 1100. The princes, in particular, may have pushed for an early restoration of ecclesiastical unity (*reformanda unitas ecclesiastica*), a topic that was the subject of extensive discussions at the Christmas assembly in Mainz in the year 1100. Henry IV concurred with their desire to end the schism. Ekkehard of Aura states in his *Chronicle* for the year 1102 that the emperor even planned a trip to Rome in order "to discuss his own and the pope's case according to canon law and to restore harmony between the royal and the apostolic power sphere after many years of disunity."[11]

However, Paschal II would not be appeased by the emperor's simple recognition of his papacy. The schism, in the pontiff's view, had occurred because of the Salian ruler's endeavor to gain undue influence in the governance of the Church and by insisting on his right to invest high clerical officials. The investiture by the king, first formally prohibited by the reformers in 1078,[12] increasingly became the focal point in the dispute between emperor and pope. This struggle for preeminence on earth eventually culminated in the so-called investiture contest. Paschal assumed an uncompromising posture in these matters and developed a legal position that denied the emperor any authority whatsoever. The Lateran Synod in March 1102 renewed the prohibition of lay investiture and of the *hominium*, that is, the bishops' acceptance of the king as their overlord. The pope is said to have added:

Since he [Henry IV] did not cease to tear the cloak of Christ, in other words, to devastate the Church by ravage and arson and to besmirch it through licentiousness, perjury, and murder, he was excommunicated and condemned on account of his disobedience—first by the blessed pope Gregory, and, subsequently, by my predecessor, the saintly Urban. Supported by the judgment of the entire Church we, too, have proclaimed an everlasting banishment over him at our last Synod. According to our will, this shall be made known to all, especially to those north of the Alps, so that they may keep their distance from his sin.[13]

Subsequently, Paschal II attempted to draw the German princes back into his camp and urged them in letters to turn away from the "corrupted head" (*perverso capiti*), and to return to the saving bosom of the orthodox Church. The effect of this appeal should by no means be underestimated; for the core of nobles who had persuaded the adolescent Henry V to rebel against his father in 1104 was closely associated with the ecclesiastical and monastic reform movement. Among this group of prominent magnates we find Margrave Diepold III of Cham-Vohburg-Nabburg (1102–1112), Count Berengar I of Sulzbach (1099–1125), and Count Otto of Habsberg-Kastl (1102–1112). They all belonged to a kindred that was scattered widely throughout Bavaria, Swabia, and Saxony and whose exponents were among the founders of the monastery of Kastl in the Bavarian Nordgau, an institution that adhered strictly to the Hirsau reform.[14] Members of this family are also credited with the foundation of the reform abbeys of Berchtesgaden and Baumburg in Bavaria. Their circle further included Bishop Gebhard III of Constance (1084–1110) who, as legate, represented the reform papacy's interests in the German kingdom. A letter authored by Count Palatine Frederick of Saxony and other Saxon nobles at the turn of the year 1104/1105 provides a glimpse into the deep religiosity which motivated these reform-minded nobles. Addressed to a certain count B., who was probably identical with Berengar of Sulzbach and who must have belonged to King Henry V's inner circle, the letter states that these reforms were needed "because no one had been saved in the flood outside Noah's ark which bore the shape of the Church" (*Nullus salvatus est in diluvio extra archam, quae figuram gerebat ecclesiae*).[15] This very sentence sheds unexpected light on the religious sincerity that was driving the reform. This movement represented less a calculated bid for power than a deeply existential concern: the salvation of souls.

Whether such motives also played a role for Henry V would be hard to determine. But like his brother Conrad earlier, he must have had well-founded fears that a substantial opposition would arise against his father and that he would jeopardize the recognition of his own claims to the throne if he stayed by his side. He had no choice but to save his kingship, or to put it more succinctly: he had to save the kingship for the Salian dynasty. Addressing his followers in 1105, he supposedly said that he had no intention of fighting or, God forbid, killing his father and that he was not driven by the desire to rule (*regnandi cupiditas*); what mattered to him was to hold on to the kingship as heir and successor and to defend his paternal legacy (*regnum ut heres et successor augusti tenere; me . . . paterni regni propugnatorem noveritis*).[16] These passages, practically recorded as events were unfolding, indicate that Henry V did nothing more than implement the Salian principles of dynastic thinking, in fact, that he felt obligated to defend and preserve his dynasty's hereditary right to the kingship. Nowhere is this ideology more powerfully expressed than in the depiction of the Salian family tree (see frontispiece), as I have indicated in the opening pages of this book. This extraordinary illumination originated in all likelihood around 1106/1107 in close proximity to Henry V's inner circle. On this representation the brothers, Conrad and Henry V, are graphically embedded in the tradition of the Salian house, underscoring a theme which we also encounter in a miniature from the Evangelary of Saint Emmeram in Regensburg that shows Henry IV with both of his sons (fig. 39).[17] If this interpretation is correct, the Regensburger source may well be dated around the same time as the Salian family tree (ca. 1105/06). Another significant image in this context is Henry IV's handing over the regal insignia to his son (fig. 40). This illumination is included in the same Ekkehard manuscript as the Salian family tree and must have originated from the same period. In stark contrast to the turbulent events that marked the turn from 1105 to 1106, this picture evokes a peaceful transfer of power within the Salian house: the dynasty's continuity was secure.[18] A further sign of remarkable dynastic prowess was Henry V's shrewd move to secure control over Speyer through a member of the reform clergy. By choosing the abbot of Hirsau (1105–1107), Gebhard, as bishop to head the very center of Salian traditions, he managed to give his kingship additional credence. The personal rights of the ruler, namely Henry IV, had to yield to the higher priorities of the Salian dynasty and its divinely ordained continuity. These were in essence the reasons and motives for Henry V's rebellion against his father.

Only if we consider this background does it make sense that Henry V defied the princes' wishes after his father's death. They had the body of the

39. Henry IV (upper row, middle) with his sons Henry V and Conrad at his sides; (lower row) abbots of the monastery of Saint Emmeram in Regensburg; miniature originates circa 1105/1106 (Evangelary of Saint Emmeram in Regensburg, now located in Cracow, Bibliothek des Domkapitels 208, fol. 2).

excommunicated emperor buried near Liège. But his son, shortly thereafter, gave orders to transfer it to Speyer, where it was kept at Saint Afra's, a chapel not yet consecrated that was adjacent to the cathedral. As callously as Henry V seems to have rejected his father's pleas for mercy while still alive, as diligently and caringly he now sought his absolution from the Church's banishment. He finally achieved this goal in 1111 at his imperial

40. Transfer of royal insignia from Henry IV to Henry V in the *Chronicle* of Ekke-
hard of Aura, probably based on an earlier version in the Recensio II of 1106/1107
(Havelberger version, now in the Staatsbibliothek Berlin, Stiftung Preußischer
Kulturbesitz, Cod. lat. 295, fol. 99).

coronation in Rome. After his return, he arranged for his father's solemn burial in the cathedral of Speyer and laid him to rest at the side of his ancestors. On this occasion, Henry V granted the inhabitants of Speyer the famous privilege of 14 August 1111, which, in golden letters and graced with the emperor's portrait, was mounted above the main portal of the cathedral.[19] For the salvation of his "beloved father's" soul he transferred a number of rights and benefits to the people of Speyer. The grant stipulated that all the townspeople, including all those who lived there now and in the future and regardless of their origin or social status, would solemnly assemble each year on the anniversary of Henry IV's birth. All would hold candles in their hands and each household would donate a loaf of bread as alms for the poor. In death Henry IV was restored to the proper position within the Salian dynasty, and the prayer memorial on his behalf was elevated onto a new level of dignity by the fact that the whole urban community, a group characterized by its members' upward mobility, was obligated to participate in the commemoration of the Salian house.

Just as Henry IV had needed the princes' approval to disinherit his son Conrad, Henry V now depended on their support, particularly on the backing of the reformers among them, for the continuous recognition of the Salian kingship. He likewise appealed to the magnates' growing sense of responsibility in representing and safeguarding the interests of the realm. When his forces were beaten in an ambush laid by his father's troops and he was in need of military assistance, Henry V, at the end of March 1106, wrote to the imperial magnates:

This humiliation is not mine alone; you, too, were scorned by this occurrence. Those presumptuous people do not want to abide by your decisions; they value only their own precepts; in short, they aspire to hold the fulcrum of the realm (*totum regni pondus*) in their own hands. They mean to depose the king, whom you have elevated, in order to rescind your decisions. For these reasons, this injustice has been perpetrated less against my person than against the whole realm. Although the overthrowing of the head, even the highest, has undoubtedly adverse effects on the realm, such damage can be remedied. Disregarding the princes, in contrast, will bring certain ruin to the realm![20]

Such words were music to the ears of the princes, whose self-consciousness was growing and with it their confidence; for these words demonstrated that, even in the young king's own consciousness, the concepts of kingship and realm were increasingly becoming separate entities. Henry V's interpretation of lordship, in their eyes, seemed to be in harmony with their own ideas and many, such as Ekkehard of Aura, had great expectations for him. In 1106 or 1107 Ekkehard dedicated the second version of his chronicle to the young king. The dedication reads as follows: "In your golden years, my king—may you live in eternity—I, Ekkehard, an insignificant and small human being, perceive new yields after long years of misery. . . . Rising from the dust, the whole Roman orb from sea to sea, the whole world from sunrise to sunset, jubilantly, wishes you good fortune. The hearts of all wise men are directed toward you, the newly awakened scion of David. But especially God's servants, who are reemerging from their hiding places, view you as the light that has arisen in their darkness."[21] In this euphoric state many totally overlooked the fact that Henry V was from the very beginning guided by the Salian dynasty's concept of kingship and that he actually went even further in this respect than his father. The conflict was thus inherent in the foundation of his kingship. Consequently, it did not take long before many prominent nobles joined a resistance movement that haunted the last Salian ruler to the very end of his reign. In the last version of his chronicle, shortly after Henry V's death, Ekkehard noted rather sadly: "This one [Henry V], as described, took the realm away from his excommunicated father, initially by feigning piety. But once he was firmly established in his kingship, he changed his behavior."[22] In reality, though, Henry V's understanding and concept of the Salian kingship remained unaltered throughout his life.

Recent research has also demonstrated that Henry V had never been willing to make any concessions to the papacy in regard to the investiture.[23] A tract entitled *De investitura episcoporum* (Concerning the investiture of bishops), originating in 1109 in close proximity to the king, likewise reflects Henry V's views on this matter.[24] The text may actually represent a set of guidelines to be used by a royal emissary for conducting negotiations with the pope around the turn of the year 1109/1110. The tract states emphatically, though, that the king did not mean to confer anything spiritual (*nihil spirituale*) through the investiture of bishops and that he would not insist on retaining the ring as a symbol of the investiture since it pertained specifically to the spiritual office. Nevertheless, the investiture by the king must take place prior to the consecration of a bishop; for the kings must be able to rely on the bishops who would be entrusted with so many holdings as well as various movable goods (*in fundis et aliis mobilibus*) and with so many public privileges and *regalia*, such as rights of toll and coinage, authority over administrators and jurors, counties, advocacies, and jurisdictions (*in theloneis, monetis, villicis et scabinis, comitatibus, advocatis, synodalibus bannis*).[25]

This legalistic position seems to have influenced Pope Paschal II's further considerations. In August 1110 Henry V started on a Roman journey that was supposed to result in his imperial coronation. Early in 1111 he had almost reached Rome when the papal legates unexpectedly put forth a remarkable proposal during preliminary negotiations. On 4 February, in the church of Santa Maria at Turri, they stated that the Church intended to return all of the imperial *regalia* in Germany and Italy and that it would henceforth make do with those holdings that had not been obtained from the crown. As a precondition to this offer, the king was asked to renounce on his coronation day, in the presence of clergy and lay people, any further participation in the investiture of spiritual leaders. The pope, on the other hand, would pledge in writing and under threat of excommunication for potential offenders that his bishops would no longer attempt to control the *regalia*, "the towns, duchies, margraviates, counties, rights of coinage and tolls, markets, imperial advocacies, rights of lower jurisdictions, and royal manors (*curtes*) with all their appurtenances, armed followings and imperial castles." [26]

This proposal, which was accepted by Henry V at Sutri, on 9 February 1111, was just as revolutionary as it was legally consistent. The king's argumentation that it was his obligation to safeguard all imperial rights had become mute. Yet the pope's designs went even further. The imperial bishops who had shown aspirations of becoming territorial lords would now be restricted to their spiritual office and would be subordinated to papal authority more strictly than ever before. In a calculated move, the pope had made his plans without the involvement of the bishops, hoping to quash any resistance through means of spiritual coercion. Depriving the bishops of their secular power base would most certainly have weakened their position vis-à-vis the Holy See. The importance of this consideration in Paschal's scheme becomes obvious when we take a closer look at the text of the papal document that was read at Saint Peter's on 12 February 1111, just prior to the scheduled imperial coronation. It explicitly states that the rendering of royal services and military support by bishops and abbots, as practiced in Germany, was in violation of canon law. Since the acceptance of *regalia* obligated ecclesiastics to provide time-consuming and financially burdensome *servitium* to the king, the servants of God actually turned into servants of the crown. This fact had led to the custom of lay investiture by the ruler prior to consecration. Such practices would henceforth be forbidden; simultaneously a papal order would be issued demanding that bishops return their *regalia* to the realm and that, in the future, they live from their own holdings, from tithes, and from alms given by the faithful.[27] The root of all evil within the Church was, thus, no longer attributed to the meddling of laymen in ecclesiastical matters but rather to the bishops' secular aspirations and the concentration of political and judicial powers in their hands. Pope and king, as might be inferred from these events and negotiations, had formed an effective coalition against a powerful new force: the spiritual leaders' desire to create territorial lordships.

From the very beginning, however, the royal camp had been skeptical in regard to the implementation of such a plan and had insisted on securing the consent of the imperial princes. It was, therefore, no surprise that the assembled bishops rose in a storm of protest when the papal proposal was announced at Saint Peter's on 12 February 1111. Under no circumstances would they go along with the sacrifice the pope had ordered. Such a move would not only undermine their authority but also their protective and peace-promoting powers which assumed an ever-growing significance in a time of social and political change. These measures would further destroy their role as responsible participants in the shaping of the imperial order and in representing the realm's interests. The uproar at Saint Peter's took on such threatening dimensions that the coronation had to be canceled. When riots started spreading throughout the city of Rome, Henry V took Pope Paschal II and several cardinals prisoners in the night of 15–16 February and moved them outside the city walls. Presumably persuaded by the discomfort of his fellow captives and by fear of a schism, the pope eventually yielded to the king's demands. On 12 April 1111, he issued a privilege that affirmed the coronation—which took place the next day at Saint Peter's—and recognized the king's right of investiture.[28]

The concessions granted in this privilege, soon dubbed "Pravilege" (bad law) by the reformers, were in the king's eyes barely more than a scaling back of the far-reaching agreements of Turri and Sutri. Aside from the ring and staff, the two symbols which, according to the wording in the "Pravilege," were to be used in the investiture *after* the episcopal election by clergy and people but *before* the consecration, there is no substantial difference between the elevation of the bishop in this procedure and the one described in the Concordat of Worms in 1122, the agreement that finally brought the investiture contest to a close. Nevertheless, Henry V's actions unleashed a storm of outrage; for he had dared to do the unthinkable; he had dared to take into custody the sacrosanct pope, Christ's representative on earth and, hence, the supreme authority in all of Christendom; and he had dared to use coercion against him. Subsequently, the papal party succeeded in maligning Henry V in a series of writings. In the *Poem Concerning the Captivity of Pope Paschal* (*Rhythmus de captivitate Paschalis papae*), all Germans are denounced because of their great cruelty and Henry is seen as the standard bearer of the Antichrist, the leader of satanic people. In the end the author bursts out into a great lamentation: "O miserable Germany, what sort of madness has taken hold of you?"[29] These events led to a fundamental reappraisal of Henry V's image. His uprising against his father was no longer viewed as a laudable act against a schismatic ruler but rather as an infamous betrayal. From this vantage point, Henry had not only cheated his own father out of his kingship, but he had also robbed his Mother, the Holy Church, of her freedom. In the summer of IIII the cardinal legate Kuno of Praeneste proclaimed the Church's ban of excommunication over Henry V and in March III2 the Lateran council revoked the "Pravilege" because it had been obtained under coercion and because it was contrary to the Holy Spirit and canon law.

In spite of these reversals in the relationship between the Salian ruler and the pope, the models that were explored in IIII made a crucial contribution to the eventual resolution of the investiture contest. As demonstrated in the discussion of Paschal II's document of 12 February IIII, the pope now interpreted *regalia* as ecclesiastical rights and holdings that originated from the king and, thus, pertained to the realm. The realm's transpersonal nature, in addition, diffused the fear that the churches could become an instrument in the hands of the king. The royal camp, in contrast, adhered to the broader definition of the term *regalia* which comprised *all* secular possessions and rights of a church, in other words, all its temporalities, and which can be identified as the German concept of *regalia*.[30] In the "Pravilege" of 12 April IIII, it was used in this sense. The compromise that eventually resulted in the Concordat of Worms of II22 was basically determined by the fact that the divergence in the usage of the term *regalia* was consciously ignored.

The emperor and the pope—now Calixtus II—were to meet in Mouzon, on 24 October III9, to resolve the impasse in the investiture question. The papal side still feared, however, that based on the German concept of *regalia*, the ruler could illegally appropriate ecclesiastical holdings. If Henry V enfeoffed a bishop with all of the temporalities of his respective church, he presumably assumed personal power over church holdings that did not originate from the king or the realm. Once again the emperor was asked to renounce the right of royal investiture. When he refused to oblige, he was once more excommunicated. By now it had become clear that further fine-tuning of the term *regalia* seemed impossible. Eventually, the emperor and his supporters recognized the pope's own claim to the *regalia sancti Petri* which, based on the donations of Constantine, clearly did not belong to the realm but to Saint Peter. The pope's power over the *patrimonium Petri* existed in its own right and was totally independent of the emperor, a crucial criterion for legitimating the future papal state. At last, when the emperor acquiesced to give up ring and staff as symbols of the royal investiture, a compromise could be reached that concluded the bitter struggle over the investiture. On 23 September 1122, the agreement was publicly proclaimed outside the gates of Worms.[31] The divergent understanding of the term *regalia*, which had played such a crucial role in the course of the drawn-out negotiations, was now tolerated without any further discussions.

The Concordat of Worms, however, marks not simply the end of the investiture conflict, but is also an expression and hallmark of a radically altered constitutional framework. These closing episodes of the Salian era demonstrate once again how much the high political drama between pope and emperor was intricately interwoven with and actually determined by the changing dynamics within the realm. The eventual resolution of the conflict is unthinkable without the involvement and the commitment of the princes. After years of wrangling, the emperor and the influential magnates convened in 1121 at an assembly in Würzburg and concluded a peace agreement that is revealing in regard to the realm's power constellations and the general understanding of its political reality. The preamble to this document states: "This is the conclusion that the princes have reached regarding the controversies between the lord emperor and the realm." The first instruction says: "The lord emperor shall obey the Apostolic See. In regard to the damage that he has inflicted on the Church, the princes shall offer assistance and counsel in working out a compromise between him and the lord pope; and the peace that shall be concluded with the pope must be firm and inviolable so that the lord emperor will obtain whatever belongs to him and the realm, and so that the Church and everyone else will be able to enjoy his own in peace and tranquillity." The fifth point likewise addresses this problem: "In respect to the fact that the Church has filed a complaint against the emperor and the realm because of the investiture, the princes shall earnestly strive, without guile and without hypocrisy, to restore the realm's honor in this matter."[32]

The peace agreement of Würzburg is a document that shows clearly how, by the end of the Salian period, the dynamics between emperor, realm, and princes had been radically altered by a century of change. Emperor and kingship now stood in opposition to realm and princes and the term *regnum* no longer meant realm *and* kingship, as it had at the beginning of Salian rule, but signified *either* realm *or* kingship. Although the emperor was allowed to exercise certain rights within the realm, the preservation and continuity of these privileges was now primarily a responsibility of the princes. These rights were defined by the term *honor*. The peace agreement of Würzburg further settled several other disputes and cleared the way for bringing the perennial warfare between Henry V and the princes to a close. The emperor was apprised in no uncertain terms that the assembled magnates had joined in a sworn brotherhood to enforce his adherence to the negotiated settlement. Moved by this spirit, Ekkehard of Aura reported in his chronicle "that the disputed questions were not decided by his [Henry's] judgment or the efforts of his people, but according to the will of the princes."

One of the leading personalities in this princely circle was the archbishop Adalbert I of Mainz (1109–1137). He was a member of the comital family of Saarbrücken which had supported Henry V in the struggle against his father. Adalbert first appears in a document of 14 February 1106 as Henry's chancellor; in this capacity he was also provost of the canonries of Saint Servatius at Maastricht and Saint Mary's at Aachen. As chancellor he wielded considerable influence on Henry V's policy decisions, and he accompanied him to Italy in 1110/1111. Toward the end of 1109 already, Adalbert had been designated as archbishop of Mainz and on 15 August 1111, after his return from Rome, he was invested. Then surprisingly, in the summer of 1112, the archbishop and the emperor had a great falling out. He [Adalbert], "who had always been the second right behind the king in all affairs and without whose advice the king would not undertake anything, now unbelievably was suspected of having entered into a conspiracy with several princes; and when the matter became known, the king had him arrested."[33]

This unexpected switch warrants an explanation. Adalbert, no doubt, personified the new type of episcopal lord who pursued the systematic formation of an ecclesiastical territory. Seeking to justify his punitive action against Adalbert in a letter to the princes at the close of 1112, Henry V accused the archbishop of enriching himself at the expense of imperial estates and castles. "We gave them [the estates] to him in trust, but did not transfer them outright; yet he takes possession of them. He personally lays claim to the legacy of our forefathers, to ecclesiastical estates, fiscal lands, even the royal prerogatives on the left bank of the Rhine, and to rights and privileges pertaining to bishoprics and abbeys."[34] Worst of all, the new archbishop of Mainz appropriated the imperial fortress of Trifels which was situated on the road leading from the Saar area through the Pfälzer forest to the upper Rhine region south of Speyer. This move allowed him to garner control over several strategic strongholds between his archiepiscopal see and his family's power base around Saarbrücken; he further managed to strengthen his authority in this region through the acquisition of jurisdictional and seignorial rights, especially advocacies. Such blatant intermingling of episcopal politics and familial interests had never before been pursued with such intensity.

While Henry V kept Adalbert in custody, he attempted to exploit the city of Mainz and its episcopal resources for his own purposes. On 6 January 1114 he convened a magnificent assembly in Mainz and on the following day he celebrated there his marriage to the English princess Matilda (fig. 41). At the end of 1114 the Saxons rose up in a major rebellion. On 11 February 1115 their forces, under the able command of Duke Lothar (of Supplinburg) (1106–1137), inflicted such a devastating defeat on the imperial army at the battle of Welfesholz that Henry V was henceforth barred from entering Saxony. On 1 November of the same year the emperor scheduled an assembly at Mainz to negotiate with the princes. But the inhabitants of Mainz took up arms, as Ekkehard of Aura reports, and surrounded the palace; a large crowd pushed its way into the entrance hall and made it resound with the clatter of weapons. The intruders would have overwhelmed the palace if Henry V had not taken swift action by offering hostages and the release of their archbishop. Adalbert of Mainz thus regained his freedom after three years of dire captivity; it is reported that his skin "was barely clinging to his bones." Together with Bishop Reinhard of Halberstadt (1107–1123) and Archbishop Frederick I of Cologne (1100–1131), Adalbert I now became the most tenacious antagonist of the last Salian ruler.

On 24 July 1115, countess Matilda of Tuscany died, providing Henry V with a pretext to journey to Italy the following year to claim her inheritance for himself; preliminary hereditary agreements had been concluded in 1110 and 1111. It looks as if the Salian ruler wanted to seek new footholds outside of Germany to compensate for the losses he had suffered north of the Alps. He entrusted his nephew, the Hohenstaufen Duke Frederick II of Swabia (1105–1147), with the administration of Germany and appointed the Rhenish count palatine Godfrey of Calw (1113–1131) as

41. Wedding of Henry V and Matilda on 7 January 1114, *Chronicle* of Ekkehard of Aura (Cambridge, Corpus Christi College MS 373, fol. 95).

his assistant. Duke Frederick's brother, the Hohenstaufen prince Conrad, who later became King Conrad III (1138–1152), was installed as duke in Eastern Franconia where he emerged as the main rival of Bishop Erlung of Würzburg (1105–1121). The German kingdom thus lay in the hands of the Hohenstaufen brothers until Henry V's return from Italy in 1118. In the absence of the emperor they pursued their own territorial policies, calculated to strangle the aspirations of Archbishop Adalbert I of Mainz. Frederick began encroaching on the archbishop's territorial sphere and, in the process, as the chronicler Otto of Freising remarked so graphically,[35] he always "haul[ed] a fortress along at the tail of his horse," in other words, he had numerous substantial fortresses built. His eyes were cast on the vast expanse ranging from the Hunsrück mountains to Speyer and Limburg on the Haardt River and from there clear to Basel on the upper Rhine. But Adalbert too attempted to increase the archiepiscopal presence of Mainz in the region around the middle and upper Rhine and to extend his influence into the Salian heartland. Once again we encounter an example where diocesan concerns and familial interests were blended and merged with the political goals of the reform party and the high nobility.[36]

In 1118 Adalbert succeeded in taking the Hohenstaufen stronghold of Oppenheim, located south of Mainz on the Rhine, and in doing so freed his archiepiscopal domain from the Swabian duke who had posed a formidable threat. In the wake of this struggle, Adalbert granted the inhabitants of Mainz a privilege (1119/20) that became a monument to the close cooperation between the townspeople and their archbishop.[37] The people of Mainz had the text of this remarkable document engraved on the bronze portal of the Mariengreden church. This portal has been preserved and today it graces the Mainz cathedral facing the market square. The privilege promised the inhabitants of Mainz that they no longer needed to seek justice from an advocate outside the city, but would have their own court of law in town. No one, save the king or the emperor, had previously granted such privileges, as in the cases of Speyer in 1111 and Worms in 1114. Now we encounter an archbishop executing this act of sovereignty and assuming the position of the ruler, as it were. This is yet another illustration of the shifting distribution of power within the polity of the realm.

The years around 1120 were characterized by incessant hostilities between the emperor's camp and Adalbert and his following. The archbishop had formed an alliance with prominent Saxon princes, particularly with Duke Lothar of Saxony, as well as with Archbishop Frederick I of Cologne. In 1121 Henry V moved to regain control over Mainz, the stronghold of his fiercest enemy. He instituted a naval blockade on the Rhine and ordered an embargo on food and commerce. Faced with this threat, the archbishop assembled his Saxon allies and other princes to force a showdown with the emperor. Ekkehard of Aura reports in his chronicle:

Around the time of the summer solstice, when cereal had become dear already because of the general ravage of the land, two armies converged for your sake, you noble city of Mainz; one came from Alsace, the other from Saxony, and both endeavored—although with different intentions—to reach your proud and venerable walls. One aimed at your destruction, the other at your defense. And while you were lamenting: "My mother's sons are fighting against me," Christ answered you through his deed: "See, these are assembled once again and will come to your rescue!"[38]

But when the two armies were finally facing each other, reason prevailed and the two parties began negotiating. It was decided that the leadership of the opposing camps should gather in an assembly at Würzburg later in 1121 to find a resolution to these matters. At this convention, as was discussed previously, the emperor and the princes came to an agreement known as the Peace of Würzburg.

The settlement of Würzburg clearly shows the handwriting of Adalbert and his allies; they demanded restitution across the board and sought to emphasize the validity of hereditary principles. "All [expropriated] property was restored to those who had suffered expropriation; every hereditary entitlement was awarded to the [respective] heirs, and all persons of any [social] status were granted their rights."[39] The inherent principles of hereditary rights were once again pegged against the Salian concept of a strictly hierarchical order with the king at its apex (*Salische Befehlsherrschaft*). Henry V had no choice but to accept the princes' proposals; for how could he have opposed "so many heads of the public body" (*tot capita rei publice*).[40]

The princes now were viewed as the heads of the realm. That such a wording could become possible by the end of Salian rule is significant. The restructuring that occurred in the nature of lordship and kingship in the course of a century is truly amazing. Just prior to the Salian era, Bishop Thietmar of Merseburg (1009–1018) had referred to the princes of the realm as "collaborators" of the ruler and as "pillars of his lordship."[41] Wipo in his *Deeds of Emperor Conrad II* also describes a system where the king, relying on the princes' support, bears the responsibility for keeping the order in the realm. Of course, the king remained the primary mover in governmental affairs even at the end of the Salian era, but the idea of the realm as a separate entity had taken root and was now represented by the princes.

This state of affairs inevitably required new rules to define the relationship between the princes and the king. Exactly these concerns were addressed and settled in the Concordat of Worms in 1122, at least for the ecclesiastical sphere. The secular princes at the helm of their emerging territorial lordships were integrated into the new system in the course of the twelfth century (*Heerschildordnung*). The Concordat stated that, following his canonical election, a bishop in the German kingdom was to receive "the regalia through the scepter," that is, he was enfeoffed with it from the ruler, prior to his consecration. The status of an ecclesiastical lord vis-à-vis the king took on an objective nature and was henceforth defined by feudal law; their mutual allegiance rested entirely upon the bishop's enfeoffment. This altered constellation not only offered the bishops new possibilities for the development of episcopal lordships, but also allowed the king to employ feudal law to compensate for the loss of his sacral position and of the rights that had derived from it. In the course of the twelfth century the episcopate and the entire constitutional structure of the realm (*Reichsverfassung*) became progressively more feudalized,[42] in other words, determined and organized by feudal principles. The *servitium regis* which used to be imposed at the discretion of the royal court—often seen as a considerable burden for the bishoprics—was now replaced by legally defined obligations of the vassal. As crown vassals, the bishops were in a position to distance themselves even further from the king in the hierarchical order and to merge with the preeminent group of imperial princes, a body that was precisely defined along feudal lines. A new era of interaction between lordship and kingship had begun.

Concluding Remarks

EMPEROR HENRY V DIED on 23 May 1125 in Utrecht and was buried in the Salian grave site at Speyer. Shortly before his demise he had summoned his wife, Queen Matilda, his nephew, Duke Frederick II of Swabia, and other important princes "to advise them, as far as possible, on the condition of the realm and to entrust his possessions and his queen to the care of Frederick as his heir. He instructed them to safeguard the crown and the other royal insignia at Trifels, a secure fortress, until the assembly of princes could meet."[1] Since Henry V died without legitimate children, the royal succession was uncertain. But in sharp contrast to the panic that had gripped the polity after Henry II's death a century earlier, the realm showed no signs of disintegration and there seemed little concern for its stability.

The Salian concept of kingship with its powerful dynastic perspective, however, had a lasting impact. Although no records exist formally designating Frederick of Hohenstaufen as royal successor, there is no doubt that he, whose mother had been a Salian princess, was destined to assume Henry V's legacy. Frederick became not only responsible for the Salian patrimony but for the continuity of the dynasty's traditions as well. Confident of his legitimate claims to the royal crown, he appeared at the election assembly on 24 August 1125 at Mainz where Archbishop Adalbert presided. When Margrave Leopold III of Austria (1095–1136) and Duke Lothar of Saxony (1106–1137) were nominated in addition to his own candidacy, the Hohenstaufen prince was not willing to recognize the election of either of these rivals. Nothing could have been more important to him than his elevation to the kingship; for only the royal dignity would allow him to take charge of Henry V's entire dominion which consisted of an intricately intertwined web of fiscal lands and Salian allods. Just as significant, however, was the idea that the kingship could be continued only by a member of the Salian dynasty. Although the princes of the realm chose

the Saxon duke Lothar as their king at Mainz in 1125, it is telling that
Bishop Otto of Freising (1138–1158), the great historian of the twelfth century, considered Lothar III's royal tenure a historical fluke. In his opinion,
this unfortunate interlude was only remedied when Frederick of Hohenstaufen's brother, Conrad III (1138–1152) attained the kingship.[2] The Salian
dynasty lived on in the Hohenstaufen kings. It is further characteristic that
Otto of Freising assigned Emperor Frederick Barbarossa to the family of
the "Henrys of Waiblingen," that is, the Salians, "from whom the emperors are wont to arise."[3] Even Barbarossa himself supposedly stressed that
he had emerged from the royal family of Waiblingen (*de regia stirpe Waiblingensium*).[4]

From this vantage point we can hardly assert that the Salian kings
had been losers in their own era; for they had developed a concept of
kingship whose powerful impact became even more pronounced under
Hohenstaufen rule. Furthermore, Salian territorial policies, which under
Henry IV had assumed a distinctive focus, provided for the energetic development of fiscal lands during the Hohenstaufen period. Last but not
least, the Hohenstaufen rulers were able to build on the new constitutional
framework which Henry V had helped prepare through the feudalization
of the realm. The most prominent feature of the Salian era, however, was
the consolidation of the German kingdom. This process had been initiated
by Henry II's efforts to centralize power and had been further energized
by the dynamic forces that came into play under Salian rule. The innovative spirit of this age wrought radical changes in the structure of territorial
dominions, stressed a hierarchical order in church and society, and intensified and centralized administrative and economic activities. Overall these
trends led to a more functional government and a more legalistic system.
In short, a polity emerged that was strengthened rather than weakened
through the disputes over Salian ideology, and its foundation was to determine German history for centuries to come.

Appendix

Genealogy of the Salian Dynasty (ca. 936–1039)

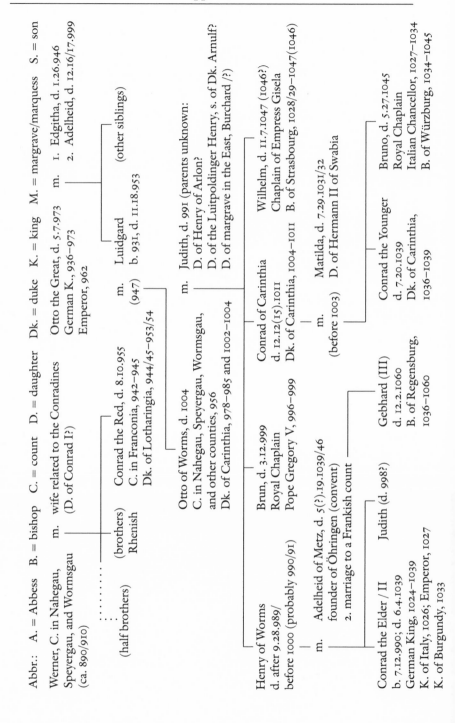

Genealogy of the Salian Dynasty (ca. 1024–1056)

Conrad II (the Elder)
b. 7.12.990; d. 6.4.1039
German K., 1024–1039
K. of Italy, 1026
Emperor, 1027
K. of Burgundy, 1033

m. (1016)

3. Gisela
b. 6.13.(ca. 990)
d. 2.15.1043
D. of Hermann II of Swabia

Gisela's previous marriages
1. m. C. Bruno of Brunswick
(of Brunonen family) d. before 1012

2. m. Dk. Ernest I of Swabia
(of the Babenberger family) d. 1015

Liudolf
d. 4.23.1038
C. of Brunswick

Margraves
of Meissen

Ernest II
d. 8.17.1030
Dk. of Swabia

Hermann IV
d. 7.28.1038
Dk. of Swabia

Henry III
b. 10.28.1017; d. 10.5.1056
German K., 1039–1056
Dk. of Bavaria, 1027–1042; Crowned King-elect,
1028; Dk. of Swabia, 1038–1045; Caretaker of the
duchy of Carinthia, 1039–1047; Emperor, 1046

Beatrix
d. 9.26.1036

Matilda, d. 1034
(1032) betrothal to
K. Henry I of France

1. m. (1036) Gunhild (Kunigunde) d. 7.18.1038; D. of K. Cnut of Denmark and England

2. m. (1043) Agnes of Poitou, d. 12.14.1077; D. of Dk. William of Aquitaine
Caretaker of the duchy of Bavaria, 1055–1061; Regent, 1056–1061

Beatrix
b. 1037
d. 7.13.1061
Abbess of
Quedlinburg
and
Gandersheim,
1044/45–1061

Adelheid
b. Fall 1045
d. 1.11.1096
Abbess of
Gandersheim,
1061–1096
and Quedlinburg (1063?)

Gisela
b. 1047
d. 5.6.(1053)

Matilda
b. 10.1048
d. 1.11.1060
m. (1060)
Rudolf of
Rheinfelden
Dk. of Swabia

(Conrad) Henry IV
b. 11.11.1050
d. 8.7.1106
German K., 1056–1106
Dk. of Bavaria, 1053–54
Co-regent, 1054
Emperor, 1084

Conrad
b. 9.10.1052
d. 4.10.1055
Dk. of Bavaria,
1054–55

Judith-Sophie
b. 1054(?), d. 3.14.(1092/96)
1. m. (not before 1066)
K. Salomon of Hungary
2. m. (1088)
Dk. Wladislaw-Hermann
of Poland

Genealogy of the Salian Dynasty (ca. 1039–1125)

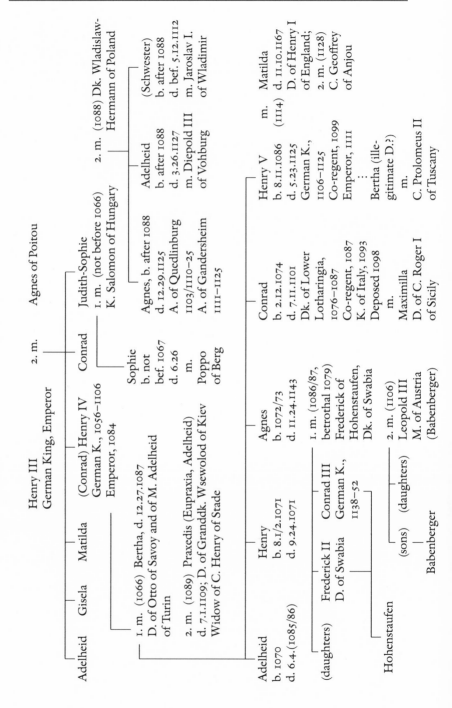

Abbreviations

AMRKG	*Archiv für mittelrheinische Kirchengeschichte*
AQDGM	Ausgewählte Quellen zur deutschen Geschichte des Mittelalters
DA	*Deutsches Archiv*
FMS	*Frühmittelalterliche Studien*
FS	Festschrift
HJ	*Historisches Jahrbuch*
HZ	*Historische Zeitschrift*
Investiturstreit	*Investiturstreit und Reichsverfassung.* Ed. J. Flecken-stein. Vorträge und Forschungen 17. Sigmaringen, 1973.
JB	Jahrbuch (Jahrbücher)
JEH	*Journal of Ecclesiastical History*
KHA	Kölner Historische Abhandlungen
MGH	Monumenta Germaniae Historica
MGH DD O II.	MGH Diplomata Ottonis II. Ed. T. Sickel. Berlin, 1888.
MGH DD O III.	MGH Diplomata Ottonis III. Ed. T. Sickel. Berlin, 1893.
MGH DD H II.	MGH Diplomata Heinrici II. Ed. H. Bresslau. Berlin, 1900–1903.
MGH DD K II.	MGH Diplomata Conradi II. Ed. H. Bresslau. Berlin, 1909.
MGH DD H III.	MGH Diplomata Heinrici III. Ed. H. Bresslau and Paul Kehr. Berlin, 1926–1931.
MGH DD H IV.	MGH Diplomata Heinrici IV. Ed. D. von Gladiss and A. Gawlik. 3 parts. Berlin, 1941; Weimar, 1959. Hanover, 1978.
MGH SS	MGH Scriptores
MGH SS rer. Germ.	MGH Scriptores rerum Germanicarum
MIÖG	*Mitteilungen des Institus für österreichische Geschichts-forschung*

NF	Neue Folge
RVJB	*Rheinische Vierteljahrsblätter*
Salier und Reich	*Die Salier und das Reich*, 3 vols. Vol. 1: *Salier, Adel und Reichsverfassung*. Vol. 2: *Die Reichskirche in der Salierzeit*. Vol. 3: *Gesellschaftlicher und ideengeschichtlicher Wandel im Reich der Salier*. Ed. S. Weinfurter. Sigmaringen, 1991.
VF	Vorträge und Forschungen
ZBLG	*Zeitschrift für bayerische Landesgeschichte*
ZGOR	*Zeitschrift für die Geschichte des Oberrheins*
ZKG	*Zeitschrift für Kirchengeschichte*
ZRG	*Zeitschrift für Rechtsgeschichte*

Notes

Foreword

1. Freed, "Reflections on the Medieval German Nobility."
2. Alfred Haverkamp, *Medieval Germany*, Horst Fuhrmann, *Germany in the High Middle Ages*, and Hagen Keller, *Zwischen regionaler Begrenzung und universalem Horizont*, are examples of German scholars who insist that the history of medieval Germany was not radically different from other European polities at that time. Unfortunately Keller's book has not yet been translated. See my review of Keller in *Speculum* 64 (1989). Susan Reynolds, a British scholar, also insists (*Kingship and Communities*) on the commonalty of German and European medieval history. On the question of Germany's unique historical development during the Middle Ages, see Reuter, "The Origins of the German *Sonderweg*."
3. Cf. Bowlus, "The Early *Kaiserreich*."
4. Eckhard Müller-Mertens, *Regnum Teutonicum*.
5. Freed, "Medieval German Social History," and "The Place of Local and Regional History in German and French Historiography."
6. Bowlus, "The Early *Kaiserreich*," though not concerned specifically with Weinfurter's book (which had not appeared at the time), makes the point that the dichotomy between social and political history is often too finely drawn.
7. Felix Gilbert, in *Ranke and Burckhardt*, shows that cultural and political history are not always as incompatible as they seem on the surface.
8. On this subject Weinfurter more fully develops his arguments in "Reformidee und Königtum in spätsalischen Reich."
9. Reynolds, *Fiefs and Vassals*.
10. On ministerials, the classic study was published by Karl Bosl in the 1950s. See Freed's critique, "The Origins of the Medieval Nobility: The Problem of the Ministerials." Arnold, *German Knighthood*. In spite of its title, Arnold's book deals primarily with the ministerials. Freed has called for more regional studies of this class and has recently published *Noble Bondsmen*, an in-depth analysis of the ministerials of the archiepiscopal see of Salzburg.
11. For an English translation of a classic study of the creation of a powerful territorial lordship through the clearing of forests and wastelands, see Theodor Mayer, "The State of the Dukes of Zähringen."

Introduction

1. This copy of Ekkehard of Aura's *Chronicle* is located in the Berlin State Library at the Foundation for Prussian Cultural Heritage.
2. Karl Schmid, "Haus und Herrschaftsverständnis," 21–54.
3. Karl Hampe, *Deutsche Kaisergeschichte*.
4. Ibid., 88, 3d ed., 1916.
5. Hagen Keller, *Propyläen Geschichte Deutschlands*, vol. 2; Egon Boshof, *Die Salier*; Horst Fuhrmann, *Deutsche Geschichte im Hohen Mittlealter*; Friedrich Prinz, *Grundlagen und Anfänge*; Alfred Haverkamp, *Aufbruch und Gestaltung*; Hermann Jakobs, *Kirchenreform und Hochmittelalter*; Eduard Hlawitschka, *Vom Frankenreich zur Formierung*.

Chapter 1. Origins and Lordship of the Salian Dynasty

1. Bruno became Pope Gregory V. He was the first German pope, assuming office at age twenty-four and holding it from 996 to 999.
2. Wipo, *Gesta Chuonradi*, chap. 2.
3. Hermann Schreibmüller, "Die Ahnen Kaiser Konrads II," 173–233; Heinrich Büttner, "Das Bistum Worms," 9–38; Büttner, "Die Widonen," 33–39; Wolfgang Metz, "Miszellen," 1–27.
4. The monastery was probably established in 742 or shortly before.
5. The sphere of influence of the Widonen roughly covered the area between Metz, Trier, Idar-Oberstein in Nahegau, and Pirmasens (the "place of Pirmin") east of Saarbrücken.
6. Widukind, *Rerum gestarum Saxonicarum*, III, 32.
7. The Lechfeld is located south of Augsburg in western Bavaria.
8. Widukind, *Rerum gestarum Saxonicarum*, III, 47.
9. Peter Classen, "Bemerkungen zur Pfalzenforschung," 475–501.
10. The counties between the Rhine and the Neckar Rivers included Elsenzgau, Kraichgau, Pfinzgau, and perhaps Uffgau.
11. MGH DD O II, 199.
12. Today known as Kaiserslautern between Mannheim and Saarbrücken.
13. *Vita Philippi presbyteri Cellensis*, chap. 1.
14. For a more detailed discussion of the function of advocacies in developing territorial lordships, see below and Chapter 4.
15. The "charter" was possibly crafted in the eleventh century while the actual events must have occurred during Otto III's regency, 983–996.
16. A. Stauber, "Kloster und Dorf Lambrecht," 49–227, addendum 1.
17. Hans Werle, "Titelherzogtum," 225–299.
18. Conrad of Carinthia was the uncle of the future King Conrad II, known as Conrad the Elder. Conrad of Carinthia had also a son named Conrad who was commonly known as Conrad the Younger.
19. *Vita Burchardi*, chaps. 7 and 21.

20. MGH DD H II, 34.

21. Henry II was declared a saint in the twelfth century.

22. Wipo, *Gesta Chuonradi*, chap. 2.

Chapter 2. The Dynamic Beginnings of the New Royal Dynasty

1. Franz-Josef Schmale, *Briefe*, no. 10.

2. Wipo, *Gesta Chuonradi*, chap. 1.

3. Ibid., chap. 2.

4. Franz-Josef Schmale, *Briefe*, no. 13.

5. Theodor Schieffer, "Heinrich II," 384–437.

6. Stefan Weinfurter, "Zentralisierung der Herrschaftsgewalt," 241–297; Hagen Keller, "Reichsstruktur und Herrschaftsauffassung," 74–128; Keller, "Charakter der 'Staatlichkeit'," 248–264.

7. Wipo, *Gesta Chuonradi*, chap. 13.

8. MGH DD K II, no. 64.

9. MGH DD H III, no. 31.

10. MGH DD K II, no. 129.

11. MGH DD K II, no. 195.

12. Wipo, *Gesta Chuonradi*, chap. 7.

13. Helmut Beumann, "Transpersonale Staatsvorstellungen," 185–204.

14. Anton Doll, "Überlegungen," 9–25; Karl Schmid, "Die Sorge der Salier," 666–726; Stefan Weinfurter, "Die Salier und ihr Dom in Speyer," 55–56.

15. MGH DD K II, no. 4.

16. *Vita Bischof Benno II von Osnabrück*, MGH SS 30/II, 871–892.

17. MGH DD O III, no. 130.

18. Péter Váczy, "Thietmar von Merseburg," 29–53.

19. Hans Erich Kubach and Walter Haas, *Der Dom zu Speyer*. See also Dethard von Winterfeld's illustrations.

20. Otto Gerhard Oexle, "Die Gegenwart der Toten," 19–77.

Chapter 3. Royal Prerogatives and Authority Under Conrad II

1. Theodor Bitterauf, *Die Traditionen des Hochstifts Freising*, 2, no. 1422.

2. Wipo, *Gesta Chuonradi*, chap. 34.

3. It is noteworthy in this context that this was the same Patriarch Poppo who in 1028 had commissioned the aforementioned splendid fresco in honor of the new imperial family in the apse of his cathedral in Aquileia.

4. MGH DD K II, no. 244.

5. Wipo, *Gesta Chuonradi*, chap. 6.

6. Ibid., chap. 21.

7. Ibid., chap. 30.

8. Egon Boshof, *Die Salier*.

9. Brygida Kürbis, "Die Epistola Mathildis."

10. Hansmartin Schwarzmaier, "Reichenauer Gedenkbucheinträge," 19–28.

11. Wipo, *Gesta Chuonradi*, chap. 20.

12. The Kyburg family holdings were located northeast of Zurich, Switzerland.

13. Gerd Althoff, "Königsherrschaft und Konfliktbewältigung," 265–290.

14. Wipo, *Gesta Chuonradi*, chap. 25.

15. Hans Constantin Faußner, *Königliches Designationsrecht*.

16. Walther Bulst, *Die ältere Wormser Briefsammlung*, no. 27.

17. Ingrid Heidrich, "Die Absetzung Herzog Adalberos," 70–94.

18. These practices can be documented since Henry III's reign at the latest.

19. Josef Fleckenstein, "Problematik und Gestalt," 87–98; Timothy Reuter, "Imperial Church System," 347–374; Odilo Engels, "Der Reichsbischof," 41–94; Engels, "Der Reichsbischof in ottonischer und frühsalischer Zeit," 135–175.

20. Walther Bulst, *Die ältere Wormser Briefsammlung*, no. 13.

21. Leo Santifaller, *Zur Geschichte des Reichkirchensystems*.

22. Hagen Keller, *Adelsherrschaft*.

23. Rudolf Schieffer, "Der ottonische Reichsepiskopat," 291–301.

24. Berent Schwineköper, "Christus-Reliquien-Verehrung," 183–281.

25. Ibid.; Mechtild Schulze-Dörrlamm, *Die Kaiserkrone Konrads II*.

Chapter 4. Realm and Society in Transition

1. Johannes Fried, "Endzeiterwartung," 381–473.

2. Gisela Grupe, "Umwelt und Bevölkerungsentwicklung," 24–34.

3. Rodulfus Glaber, *Historiarum libri V*, III, 4.

4. Wolfgang Giese, "Zur Bautätigkeit von Bischöfen," 388–438; Gerhard Streich, *Burg und Kirche*.

5. Erich Herzog, *Die ottonische Stadt*.

6. Manfred Balzer, "Zeugnisse für das Selbstverständnis," 267–296.

7. *Vita Bischof Meinwerks*, chap. 186.

8. Helmut Maurer, "Kirchengründung," 47–59; Günther Binding, *Städtebau*; Stefan Weinfurter, "*Sancta Aureatensis Ecclesia*," 3–40.

9. Franz Staab, "Die Mainzer Kirche," 31–77.

10. *Anonymus Haserensis*, chap. 9.

11. Manfred Groten, "Von der Gebetsverbrüderung zum Königskanonikat," 1–34.

12. Johannes Laudage, *Priesterbild und Reformpapsttum*.

13. Karl Schmid, "Zur Problematik von Familie," 1–62; Wilhelm Störmer, "Adel und Ministerialität," 84–152.

14. Hermann Jakobs, *Der Adel in der Klosterreform*; Karl Schmid, "Adel und Reform," 295–319.

15. Stefan Weinfurter, "Der Aufstieg der frühen Wittelsbacher," 13–47.

16. Lampert von Hersfeld, *Annalen*, a. 1074.

17. Carl Erdmann, *Ausgewählte Briefe*, no. 10.

18. *Anonymus Haserensis*, chap. 37.

19. Viktor Achter, *Die Geburt der Strafe*.

20. Carl Erdmann, *Die Briefe Heinrichs IV.*, no. 4.

21. Harry Bresslau, "Ein Brief," 623 f.

22. *Das Register Gregors VII.*, III, 10.

23. Thomas Zotz, "Die Formierung der Ministerialität," 3–50.

24. Philipp Jaffé, *Bibliotheca rerum Germanicarum*, vol. 5, 50–52.

25. *Vita Heinrici IV*, Chap. 8.

26. Horst Fuhrmann, *Papst Urban II.*

27. Hanna Vollrath, "Herrschaft und Genossenschaft," 33–71.

28. MGH DD K II. 216.

29. Anton Doll, "Zur Frühgeschichte, der Stadt Speyer," 133–200.

30. MGH DD K II. 41.

31. Karl Bosl, "Die Sozialstruktur," 93–213.

32. Knut Schulz, "Die Ministerialität als Problem," 184–219; Schulz, "Zensualität und Stadtentwicklung," 73–93.

33. Manfred Groten, "Die Kölner Richerzeche," 1–34; Hugo Stehkämper, "Die Stadt Köln in der Salierzeit," 75–152.

34. Lampert von Hersfeld, *Annalen*, a. 1074.

35. Matthew 24, Luke 17.

36. Adalbero von Laon, *Lied an König Robert (Carmen ad Robertum regem)*.

37. Edmond Ortigues, "L'élaboration de la théorie," 27–43; Otto Gerhard Oexle, "Die funktionale Dreiteilung," 1–54; Oexle, *"Tria genera hominum,"* 483–500; Oexle, "Deutungsschema der sozialen Wirklichkeit," 65–117.

Chapter 5. Henry III

1. Wipo, *Gesta Chuonradi*, chap. 39.

2. Franz Staab, "Die Mainzer Kirche," 31–77; Peter Johannek, "Die Erzbischöfe von Hamburg-Bremen," 79–112; Rudolf Schieffer, "Erzbischöfe und Bischofskirche von Köln," 1–29; Manfred Balzer, "Zeugnisse," 267–296; Stefan Weinfurter, *"Sancta Aureatensis Ecclesia,"* 3–40.

3. Franz-Josef Schmale, *Die Briefe des Abtes Bern von Reichenau*, no. 27.

4. Paul Gerhard Schmidt, "Heinrich III.," 582–590.

5. Romuald Bauerreiß, "War Günther von Niederaltaich Dichter?"

6. Karl Schmid, "Heinrich III.," 79–97; Franz-Josef Schmale, "Die 'Absetzung' Gregors VI.," 55–103; Heinz Wolter, *Die Synoden im Reichsgebiet*.

7. Anselm von Lüttich, *Gesta episcoporum Leodiensium*, chap. 66.

8. This valuable codex was produced in the monastery of Echternach in Lotharingia around 1050 and is currently kept in Uppsala, Sweden.

9. Helmut Beumann, "Reformpäpste als Reichsbischöfe," 21–37.

10. The episcopal see of Brixen is in northern Italy, formerly southern Tyrol; the Italian name of the town is Bressanone.

11. Kurt Reindel, *Die Briefe des Petrus Damiani*, no. 88.

12. Josef Fleckenstein, *Die Hofkapelle der deutschen Könige*.

13. Wipo, *Tetralogus*, 185ff.

14. *Ruodlieb*, Faksimile Ausgabe.

15. Johannes Spörl, "Pie rex caesarque future!" 331–353; Karl Schnith, "Recht und Friede," 22–57.

16. Franz-Josef Schmale, *Die Briefe des Abtes Bern von Reichenau*, no. 27.

17. Ibid., no. 24.

18. Monika Minninger, "Heinrichs III. interne Friedensmaßnahmen," 33–52.

19. Heinz Thomas, "Abt Siegfried von Gorze," 11–44.

20. Otloh von St. Emmeram, *Liber Visionum*, vision no. 15.

21. MGH *Constitutiones* 1, no. 54.

22. Hermann von Reichenau, *Chronik*, a. 1053.

23. Trebur was a royal palace south of Mainz on the right bank of the Rhine.

24. Egon Boshof, "Lothringen," 63–127.

25. Matthias Werner, "Der Herzog von Lothringen," 367–473.

26. Carlrichard Brühl, *Deutschland—Frankreich*.

27. Gerd Althoff, "Die Billunger," 309–329.

28. *Chronik des Klosters Petershausen*, II, chap. 31.

29. Lampert von Hersfeld, *Annalen*, a. 1057.

30. Wilhelm Störmer, "Bayern und der Bayerische Herzog," 31–77.

31. Lampert von Hersfeld, *Annalen*, a. 1056.

32. Friedrich Prinz, "Kaiser Heinrich III," 529–548; Prinz, "Die Grenzen des Reiches," 159–173.

Chapter 6. The Coup

1. He had originally been named Conrad after his paternal grandfather. See Gertrud Thoma, *Namensänderungen*.

2. Wilhelm Berges, "Gregor VII.," 189–209.

3. Das Register Gregors VII, *Gregorii VII Registrum*, IV, 3.

4. *Annalen von Niederaltech*, a. 1060.

5. Carl Erdmann, *Ausgewählte Briefe*, no. 5.

6. MGH DD H IV, 71, 75, 85.

7. Lampert von Hersfeld, *Annalen*, a. 1062.

8. Carl Erdmann, *Ausgewählte Briefe*, no. 68.

9. Ibid., no. 70.

10. Tilman Schmidt, "Hildebrand," 299–309.

11. Uta-Renate Blumenthal, *Der Investiturstreit*.

12. *Annalen von Niederaltech*, a. 1062.

13. Lampert von Hersfeld, *Annalen*, a. 1062.

14. Georg Jenal, *Erzbischof Anno II*. The following motives for Anno's actions can be found in the sources: lust for power, concern for the young king's education, criticism of the empress's regency, restoration of order in the realm.

15. Eberhard Nellmann, *Die Reichsidee*.
16. *Das Annolied*, ed. Eberhard Nellmann, chaps. 34, 37.
17. Adam von Bremen, *Hamburgische Kirchengeschichte*, III, chap. 34.
18. Ibid., chap. 35.
19. Ursula Lewald, "Die Ezzonen," 120–168.
20. Manfred Groten, *Priorenkolleg und Domkapitel*.
21. Josef Semmler, *Die Klosterreform von Siegburg*.
22. MGH DD H IV. 104.
23. Ibid., 88 and 89.
24. Ibid., 89 and 101.
25. Adam von Bremen, *Hamburgische Kirchengeschichte*, III, chap. 47.
26. Ibid., chap. 34.
27. Bruno von Magdeburg, *Buch vom Sachsenkrieg*, chap. 2.
28. Hans-Joachim Freytag, *Die Herrschaft der Billunger*.
29. MGH DD H IV, 112, 113, 115.
30. Walther Lammers, *Das Hochmittelalter*; Peter Johanek, *Die Erzbischöfe von Hamburg-Bremen*.
31. Adam von Bremen, *Hamburgische Kirchengeschichte*, III, chap. 78.

Chapter 7. Henry IV

1. *Annalen von Niederaltaich*, a. 1065.
2. Lampert von Hersfeld, *Annalen*, a. 1065.
3. Gerd Tellenbach, "Der Charakter Kaiser Heinrichs IV.," 345–367.
4. *Ebonis Vita Ottonis episcopi Bambergensis*, I, chap. 6.
5. *Vita Heinrici IV. imperatoris*, chap. 1.
6. Bruno, *Buch vom Sachsenkrieg*, chaps. 1 and 5.
7. Ibid., chaps. 7 and 8.
8. Gerd Tellenbach, "Der Charakter Kaiser Heinrichs IV.," 345–367; Hanna Vollrath, "Konfliktbewältigung," 279–296.
9. Karl Schmid, "Salische Gedenkstiftungen," 245–264.
10. Johannes Ranke and Ferdinand Birkner, "Die Kaisergräber im Dom zu Speyer," 1065.
11. These included Polling, Malmedy, Benediktbeuern, Limburg an der Haardt, Saint Lambrecht, Corvey, Lorsch, Kornelimünster, Vilich, Niederaltaich, Kempten, and Rheinau.
12. Hubertus Seibert, "Libertas und Reichsabtei," 503–569.
13. Lutz Fenske, *Adelsopposition*.
14. Konrad Weidemann, "Burg, Pfalz und Stadt," 11–50.
15. The infant Henry died shortly after being baptized in the cathedral of Mainz.
16. Hans Krabusch, *Untersuchungen zur Geschichte des Königsgutes*; Sabine Wilke, *Das Goslarer Reichsgebiet*.
17. Lampert von Hersfeld, *Annalen*, a. 1073.

18. Lampert von Hersfeld, *Annalen*, a. 1073.

19. Georg Droege, *Landrecht und Lehnrecht*; Wolfgang Giese, *Der Stamm der Sachsen*.

20. Georg Droege, *Landrecht*, 175.

21. Hans K. Schulze, *Adelsherrschaft und Landesherrschaft*.

22. *Vita Bischof Bennos II*, chap. 9.

23. Bruno, *Buch vom Sachsenkrieg*, chap. 25.

24. Lampert von Hersfeld, *Annalen*, a. 1074.

25. Ibid., a. 1075.

26. Odilo Engels, "Das Reich der Salier," 479–541.

27. Lampert von Hersfeld, *Annalen*, a. 1076.

28. Berthold von Reichenau, *Annalen*, a. 1077.

29. Bruno, *Das Buch vom Sachsenkrieg*, chap. 91.

30. *Vita Heinrici IV*, chap. 4.

31. Rudolf Schieffer, *Die Entstehung des päpstlichen Investiturverbots*.

32. *Epistles* I, 16; Jacques Paul Migne, *Patrologia Latina*, 144, Sp. 236B; Kurt Reindel, *Die Briefe des Petrus Damiani*, no. 107.

33. Lampert von Hersfeld, *Annalen*, a. 1074.

34. Ibid.

35. Erdmann, *Ausgewählte Briefe*, no. 15.

36. *Das Register Gregors VII*, III, 10.

37. Uta-Renate Blumenthal, *Der Investiturstreit*.

38. Carl Erdmann, *Die Briefe Heinrichs IV*, appendix A.

39. Ibid., no. 11.

40. *Dictatus Papae*, sentences 19 and 26. Brian Pullan, ed., *Sources*. "Dictatus Papae," lines 19 and 26, 137.

41. *Das Register Gregors VII*, III, 6, and III, 10a.

42. Tilman Struve, "Das Problem der Eideslösung," 107–132.

43. Petrus Crassus, *Defensio Heinrici IV. regis*, chap. 1.

44. Bonzio von Sutri, *Liber ad amicum*, VIII.

45. Josef Fleckenstein, "Hofkapelle und Reichsepiskopat," 117–140.

46. Hermann Jakobs, *Die Hirsauer*; Jakobs, "Rudolf von Rheinfelden," 87–115.

47. *Das Register Gregors VII*, IV, 12.

48. *Vita Heinrici IV*, chap. 3.

49. Gerd Tellenbach, *Die westliche Kirche*, 193.

50. Werner Goez, ". . . iuravit in anima regis," 517–554.

51. H. E. J. Cowdrey, *Epistolae vagantes*, no. 54.

52. Carl Erdmann, *Die Briefe Heinrichs IV.*, no. 12.

53. Ibid., no. 17.

54. Gottfried Koch, *Auf dem Weg zum Sacrum Imperium*.

55. Luke, 22:38.

56. Carl Erdmann, *Die Briefe Heinrichs IV.*, nos. 13 and 17.

57. *Liber de unitate ecclesiae conservanda*, 184–284.

58. Tilman Struve, "Kaisertum und Romgedanke," 424–454.

59. Eckhard Müller-Mertens, *Regnum Teutonicum*.

60. Carl Erdmann, *Die Briefe Heinrichs IV.*, no. 16.

61. Wolfgang Giese, "Otto von Bamberg und der Speyerer Dombau," 105–113.

62. *Vita Heinrici IV.*, chap. 1.

63. MGH D H IV. 466.

64. Ibid., 350, 464, 466.

65. Ibid., 325.

Chapter 8. Princes as Heads of the Polity

1. *Annalen von Hildesheim*, a. 1104.

2. *Vita Heinrici IV.*, chap. 9.

3. *Vita Heinrici IV.*, chap. 10.

4. Karl Hampe, *Deutsche Kaisergeschichte*, 74.

5. Carlo Servatius, "Heinrich V.," 140.

6. Jaffé and Loewenfeld, *Regesta*, no. 5348.

7. Alfons Becker, *Papst Urban II*.

8. *Vita Heinrici IV.*, chap. 7.

9. Ibid.

10. Elmar Wadle, "Heinrich IV."

11. Ekkehard von Aura, *Chronik*, a.1102.

12. Rudolf Schieffer, *Die Entstehung des päpstlichen Investiturverbots*.

13. Ekkehard von Aura, *Chronik*, a.1102.

14. Karl Bosl, "Das Nordgaukloster Kastl," 3–186.

15. Philipp Jaffé, *Bibliotheca* 5, no. 116.

16. Ekkehard von Aura, *Chronik*, a.1105.

17. This illumination is in the Episcopal Library of Cracow.

18. Karl Schmid, "Zum Haus- und Herrschaftsverständnis," 21–54.

19. Hans Wibel, "Die ältesten deutschen Stadtprivilegien," 234–262, Beilage.

20. *Vita Heinrici IV.*, chap. 130.

21. Ekkehard von Aura, *Chronik*, a.1106 or 1107.

22. Ekkehard von Aura, *Chronik*, a.1125.

23. Carlo Servatius, "Heinrich V.," 135–154.

24. The tract possibly was authored by Siegebert of Gembloux.

25. Jutta Krimm-Beumann, "Der Traktat 'De investitura episcoporum,'" 37–83, lines 166 ff.

26. *MGH Constitutiones* 1, nos. 83–86.

27. Ibid., no. 90.

28. Ibid., no. 96.

29. MGH *Libelli de lite*, 2.

30. Johannes Fried, "Der Regalienbegriff," 450–528.

31. *MGH Constitutiones* 1, nos. 107 and 108.

32. Ibid., no. 106.

33. Ekkehard von Aura, *Chronik*, 1112.

34. *Mainzer Urkundenbuch* 1, no. 45.
35. Otto von Freising, *Gesta Frederici imperatoris*, book I, chap. 12.
36. Heinrich Büttner, "Erzbischof Adalbert von Mainz," 395–410; Odilo Engels, "Die Stauferzeit," 199–296.
37. *Mainzer Urkundenbuch* 1, no. 600.
38. Ekkehard von Aura, *Chronik*, a. 1121.
39. Ibid.
40. Ibid.
41. Thietmar von Merseburg, *Chronik*, VIII, chap. 34.
42. Peter Classen, "Das Wormser Konkordat," 411–460.

Concluding Remarks

1. Ekkehard von Aura, *Chronik*, a. 1125.
2. Otto von Freising, *Gesta Frederici imperatoris*.
3. Ibid., book 2, chap. 2.
4. Burchard von Ursberg, *Chronik*, p. 24.

Bibliography

A list of selected readings in English prepared by Charles R. Bowlus appears on p. 215.

SOURCES

Adalbero von Laon. *Lied an König Robert*. Ed. C. Carrozzi, *Poème au roi Robert*. Paris, 1979.

Adam von Bremen. *Hamburgische Kirchengeschichte*. Ed. B. Schmeidler, MGH SS rer. Germ. [2], 3d. ed. Hanover, 1917. Ed. with Ger. trans. W. Trillmich. In *Quellen des 9.-11. Jahrhunderts zur Geschichte der hamburgischen Kirche und des Reiches*. AQDGM 11. 5th ed. Darmstadt, 1978: 160–499.

Annalen des Klosters Sankt Gallen (Annales Sangallenses maiores). Ed. C. Henking, "Die annalistischen Aufzeichnungen des Klosters St. Gallen." In *Mitteilungen zur vaterländischen Geschichte* (St. Gallen) NF 9, 1884: 265–323.

Annalen von Hildesheim. Ed. Georg Waitz. MGH SS rer. Germ. [8], Hanover, 1878.

Annalen von Niederalteich. Ed. E. L. B. von Oefele. MGH SS rer. Germ. [4] 2d ed. Hanover, 1891.

Das Annolied. Ed., trans., and commentary E. Nellmann (Reclam 1416). Stuttgart, 1975.

Anselm von Lüttich. *Lütticher Bischofsgeschichte* (Gesta episcoporum Leodiensium). Ed. R. Köpke. MGH SS 7. Hanover, 1846: 210–234.

Anton, H. H. *Der sogenannte Trakt "De ordinando pontifice." Ein Rechtsgutachten im Zusammenhang mit der Synode von Sutri* (1046). Bonner Historische Forschungen 48. Bonn, 1982.

Augsburger Annalen (Annales Augustani maiores). Ed. G. H. Pertz. MGH SS 3. Hanover, 1839: 124–136.

Berthold von Reichenau. *Annalen*. Ed. G. H. Pertz. MGH SS 5. Hanover, 1844: 267–326.

Bitterauf, T. *Die Traditionen des Hochstifts Freising*. 2 vols. Quellen und Erörterungen zur bayerischen und deutschen Geschichte, NF 4 and 5. Munich, 1905 and 1909.

Bonzio von Sutri. *Liber ad amicum*. Ed. E. Dümmler. MGH Libelli de lite 1. Hanover, 1891: 571–620.

Bresslau, H. "Ein Brief des Erzbishof Anno von Köln." In *Neues Archiv* 14 (1889): 623 ff.

Bruno (von Magdeburg/Merseburg). *Buch vom Sachsenkrieg*. Ed. H.-E. Lohmann. MGH Deutsches Mittelalter. Leipzig, 1937. Ed. with Ger. trans. F.-J. Schmale.

In *Quellen zur Geschichte Heinrichs IV*. AQDGM 12. 3d ed. Darmstadt, 1974: 191–405.

Bulst, W. *Die ältere Wormser Briefsammlung*. MGH Briefe der deutschen Kaiserzeit 3. Weimar, 1949.

Burchard von Ursberg. *Chronik*. Ed. O. Holder-Egger and B. von Simson. MGH SS rer. Germ. [16]. 2d ed., Hanover, 1916.

Carmina Cantabrigiensia. Ed. K. Stretcher. MGH SS rer. Germ. [40]. Berlin 1926. German trans. of fourteen pieces by K. Langosch, *Hymnen und Vaganten-lieder*. 1954: 91–145.

Chronik des Klosters Petershausen. Ed. O. von Feger. Schwäbische Chronik der Stauferzeit 3. 2d ed. Sigmaringen, 1978.

Codex Caesareus Upsaliensis. Faksimile. Ed. C. Nordenfalk. Stockholm, 1971.

Cowdrey, H. E. J. *The "Epistolae Vagantes" of Pope Gregory VII*. Oxford, 1972.

Ebonis Vita Ottonis episcopi Bambergensis. Ed. P. Jaffé. Bibliotheca rer. Germ. Vol. 5. Berlin, 1869: 588–692.

Ekkehard von Aura. *Chronik*. See: Frutolf and Ekkehard. *Chroniken*.

Erdmann, C. *Ausgewählte Briefe aus der Salierzeit*. Texte zur Kulturgeschichte des Mittelalters 7. Rome and Leipzig, 1933.

———. *Die Briefe Heinrichs IV*. MGH Deutsches Mittelalter 1. Leipzig, 1937.

———. *Briefsammlungen der Zeit Heinrichs IV*. Die Briefe der deutschen Kaiserzeit 5. Weimar, 1950.

Evangelistar Kaiser Heinrichs III. Faksimile. Ed. G. Knoll. Wiesbaden, 1981.

Frutolf and Ekkehard. *Chroniken und die anonyme Kaiserchronik*. Ed. F.-J. Schmale and I. Schmale-Ott. AQDGM 15. Darmstadt, 1972.

Gesta episcoporum Cameracensium. Ed. L. C. Bethmann. MGH SS 7. Berlin, 1846: 402–489.

Heribert von Eichstätt. *Hymnen*. Ed. G. M. Dreves. Analecta Hymnica Medii aevi 50. Leipzig, 1907: 290–296.

Hermann von Reichenau. *Chronik*. Ed. G. H. Pertz. MGH SS 5. Hanover, 1844: 74–133. Ed. with Ger. trans., ed. R. Buchner. In *Quellen des 9.-11. Jahrhunderts zur Geschichte der hamburgischen Kirche und des Reiches*. AQDGM 11. 5th ed. Darmstadt, 1978: 628–707.

Jaffé, P. *Bibliotheca rer. Germ.*, Vol 5. Berlin, 1869.

Jaffé, P., S. Loewenfeld, et al. *Regesta Pontificum Romanorum*, 2 vols. Leipzig, 1885 and 1888.

Krimm-Beumann, J. "Der Traktat 'De investitura episcoporum' von 1109." *DA* 33 (1977): 37–83.

Lampert von Hersfeld. *Annalen*. Ed. O. Holder-Egger. MGH SS rer. Germ. [38]. Hanover, Leipzig, 1894: 3–304. Germ. trans. A. Schmidt. Ed. W. D. Fritz. AQDGM 13. Darmstadt, 1957.

Liber de unitate ecclesiae conservanda. Ed. W. Schwenkenbecher. MGH Libelli de lite 2. Hanover 1892: 184–284. Ed. with Ger. trans. I. Schmale-Ott. In *Quellen zum Investiturstreit*, part 2. AQDGM 12b. Darmstadt, 1984: 272–579.

Mainzer Urkundenbuch. Vol. 1. Ed. M. Stimmung. Darmstadt, 1932.

MGH Constitutiones. Vol. 1. Ed. L. Weiland. Hanover, 1893.

MGH Diplomata Ottonis II. Ed. T. Sickel. Berlin, 1888.

MGH Diplomata Ottonis III. Ed. T. Sickel. Berlin, 1893.

MGH Diplomata Heinrici II. Ed. H. Bresslau. Berlin, 1900–1903.

MGH Diplomata Conradi II. Ed. H. Bresslau. Berlin, 1909.

MGH Diplomata Heinrici III. Ed. H. Bresslau and Paul Kehr. Berlin, 1926–31.

MGH Diplomata Heinrici IV. Ed. D. von Gladiss and A. Gawlik, 3 parts. Berlin, 1941; Weimar, 1959; Hanover, 1978.

Migne, J. P. *Patrologia Latina* 144. Paris, 1853.

Miracula sancti Priminii Hornbacensia. Ed. O. Holder-Egger, MGH SS 15/I. Hanover, 1887: 31–35.

Nekrolog von St. Gallen. MGH Necrologia, Vol. 1. Ed. F. L. Baumann. Berlin, 1888: 464–487.

Otloh von St. Emmeram. *Liber Visionum.* Ed. P. G. Schmidt. MGH Quellen zur Geistesgeschichte des Mittelalters 13. Weimar, 1989.

Otto von Freising. *Gesta Frederici imperatoris.* Ed. F.-J. Schmale. AQDGM 17. 2d ed. Darmstadt, 1974.

(Petrus) Crassus. *Defensio Heinrici IV. regis.* Ed. L. von Heinemann. MGH Libelli de lite 1. Hanover, 1891: 433–453. Ed. with Ger. trans. I. Schmale-Ott. In *Quellen zum Investiturstreit,* part 2. AQDGM 12b. Darmstadt, 1984: 174–239.

Das "Pontifikale Gundekarianum." Faksimilie und Kommentar. Ed. A. Bauch and E. Reiter. Wiesbaden, 1987.

Das Register Gregors VII. Gregorii VII Registrum. Ed. E. Caspar. 2 vols. MGH Epistolae selectae 2. Berlin, 1920–23.

Reindel, K. *Die Briefe des Petrus Damiani,* MGH Die Briefe der deutschen Kaiserzeit 4, Vol. 2 (Nos. 41–90). Munich, 1988.

Rhythmus de captivitate Paschalis pape. Ed. E. Dümmler. MGH Libelli de lite 2. Hanover, 1892: 673–675.

Rodulfus Glaber. *Fünf Bücher der Geschichte.* Historiarum libri V. Ed. M. Prou and R. Glaber. Les cinq livres de ses histoires. Paris, 1886.

Ruodlieb. Faksimile-Ausgabe des Codex Latinus Monacensis 19486 der Bayerischen Staatsbibliothek München und der Fragmente von St. Florian. Intro. W. Haug, Vol. 1, I–II. Wiesbaden, 1974. Vol. 2, I, critical ed., ed. B. K. Vollmann. Wiesbaden, 1985.

Schmale, F.-J. *Die Briefe des Abtes Bern von Reichenau.* Veröffentlichungen der Kommission für geschichtliche Landeskunde in Baden-Württemberg, Series A: Sources, Vol. 6. Stuttgart, 1961.

Siegfried von Gorze. *Brief an Abt Poppo von Stablo.* Ed. W. von Giesebrecht. Geschichte der deutschen Kaiserzeit, Vol. 2. 5th ed. Leipzig, 1885: 714–718.

Stauber, A. "Kloster und Dorf Lambrecht. Beilagen." In *Mitteilungen des historischen Vereins der Pfalz* 9 (1880): 207–227.

Thietmar von Merseburg. *Chronik.* Ed. R. Holtzmann. MGH SS rer. Germ. NS 9. 2d ed. Berlin, 1955. Ed. with Ger. trans. W. Trillmich. AQDGM 9. 5th ed. Darmstadt, 1974.

Triumphus sancti Remacli Stabulensis de coenobio Malmundariensi. Ed. W. Wattenbach. MGH SS 11. Berlin, 1854: 433–461.

Vita Erzbischof Annos von Köln. Ed. R. Köpke, MGH SS 11. Berlin, 1854: 462–514.

Vita Bischof Bennos II. von Osnabrück. Ed. H. Bresslau, MGH SS 30, II. Leipzig,

1934: 871–892. Ed. with Ger. trans. H. Kallfelz. Lebensbeschreibungen einiger Bischöfe des 10.–12. Jahrhunderts. AQDGM 22. Darmstadt, 1973: 372–441.

Vita Bischof Burchards von Worms. Ed. H. Boos, Monumenta Wormatiensia. Quellen zur Geschichte der Stadt Worms 3. Berlin, 1893: 99–126.

Vita Heinrici IV. imperatoris. Ed. W. Eberhard. MGH SS rer. Germ. [58]. 3d ed. Hanover, 1899. Ed. with Ger. trans. I. Schmale-Ott. In *Quellen zur Geschichte Kaiser Heinrichs IV*. AQDGM 12. 3d ed. Darmstadt, 1974: 407–467.

Vita Bischof Meinwerks von Paderborn. Ed. F. Tenckhoff. MGH SS rer. Germ. [59]. Hanover and Leipzig, 1921.

Vita Philippi presbyteri Cellensis. Ed. A. Hofmeister. MGH 30, II. Leipzig, 1934: 796–803.

Walther von Speyer. *Vita Christophori*. Ed. K. Strecke. MGH Poetae latini 5. 2d ed. Munich, 1978: 10–79.

Weinfurter, S. *Geschichte der Eichstätter Bischöfe des Anonymus Haserensis*. Ed., trans., and commentary. Eichstätter Studien NF 24. Regensburg, 1987.

Wibel, H. "Die ältesten deutschen Stadtprivilegien, insbesondere das Diplom Heinrichs V. für Speyer." In *Archiv für Urkundenforschung* 6. (1918): 234–262.

Widukind von Corevey. *Rerum gestarum Saxonicarum libri III*. Ed. P. Hirsch. Die Sachsengeschichte des Widukind von Korvei. MGH SS rer. Germ. [60]. 5th ed. Hanover, 1935. Ed. with Ger. trans. A. Bauer and R. Rau. In *Quellen zur Geschichte der sächsischen Kaiserzeit*. AQDGM 8. Darmstadt, 1971: 12–83.

Wipo. *Proverbia*. Ed. H. Bresslau. In *Die Werke Wipos*. MGH SS rer. Germ. [61]. 3d ed. Hanover and Leipzig, 1915: 66–74.

———. *Taten Kaiser Konrads II*. Gesta Chuonradi imperatoris. Ed. H. Bresslau. In *Die Werke Wipos*. MGH SS rer. Germ. [61]. 3d ed. Hanover and Leipzig, 1915: 1–62. Ed. with Ger. trans. W. Trillmich. *Quellen des 9. und 11. Jahrhunderts zur Geschichte der hamburgischen Kirche und des Reiches*. AQDGM 11. Darmstadt, 1978.

———. *Tetralogus*. Ed. H. Bresslau. In *Die Werke Wipos*. MGH SS rer. Germ. [61]. 3d ed. Hanover and Leipzig, 1915: 75–86.

Secondary Works

Achter, V. *Geburt der Strafe*. Frankfurt, 1951.

Althoff, G. "Königsbereich und Konfliktbewältigung im 10. und 11. Jahrhundert." *FMS* 23 (1989): 265–290.

———. "Die Billunger in der Salierzeit." In *Salier und Reich*, vol. 1. Sigmaringen, 1991: 309–329.

Anton, H. H. "Bonifaz von Canossa, Markgraf von Tuszien, und die Italienpolitik der frühen Salier." *HZ* 214 (1972): 529–556.

———. *Der sogenannte Traktat "De ordinando pontifice." Ein Rechtsgutachten im Zusammenhang mit der Synode von Sutri (1046)*. Bonner Historische Forschungen 48. Bonn, 1982.

———. "Beobachtungen zur heinrizianischen Publizistik: die Defensio Heinrici

IV. regis." In *Historiographia mediaevalis. Studien zur Geschichtsschreibung und Quellenkunde des Mittelalters. FS für Franz-Josef Schmale zum 65. Geburtstag*. Ed. D. Berg and W. Goetz. Darmstadt, 1988: 149–167.

Baldes, H. *Die Salier und ihre Untergrafen in den Gauen des Mittelrheins*. Marburg, 1913.

Balzer, M. "Zeugnisse für das Selbstverständnis Bischofs Meinwerk von Paderborn." In *Tradition als historische Kraft*. Ed. N. Kamp and J. Wollasch. Berlin, 1982: 267–296.

Banniza von Bazan, H. *Die Persönlichkeit Heinrichs V. im Urteil der zeitgenössischen Quellen*. Berlin, 1927.

Barth, R. E. *Der Herzog in Lothringen im 10. Jahrhundert*. Sigmaringen, 1990.

Bauerreiß, R. "War Günther von Niederaltaich Dichter?" *Studien und Mitteilungen zur Geschichte des Benediktiner-Ordens und Seiner Zweige* 49 (1931): 465–468.

Becker, A. *Papst Urban II. (1088–1099)*. 2 parts (Schriften der MGH 19, I und II) Stuttgart, 1964 and 1988.

Benz, K. J. "Kaiser Konrad II. (1024–1039) als kirchlicher Herrscher. Der Straßburger Adventstreit und die Synode von 1038 im Kloster Limburg an der Haardt." In *Archiv für Liturgiewissenschaft* 20–21 (1978–79): 56–80.

Berges, W. "Gregor VII, und das deutsch Designationsrecht." In *Studi Gregoriani* 2. Rome, 1947: 189–209.

Beumann, H. "Zur Entwicklung transpersonaler Staatsvorstellungen." In *Das Königtum. Seine geistigen und rechtlichen Grundlagen* VF 3. 4th ed. Sigmaringen, 1973: 185–204.

———. "Die Bedeutung des Kaisertums für die Entstehung der deutschen Nation im Spiegel der Bezeichnungen von Reich und Herrscher." In *Aspekte der Nationenbildung im Mittelalter. Ergebnisse der Marburger Rundgespräche, 1972–1975*. Ed. H. Beumann and W. Schröder. Nationes 1. Sigmaringen, 1978: 317–65.

———. *Der deutsche König als Romanorum Rex*. Wiesbaden, 1981.

———. "Reformpäpste als Reichsbischöfe in der Zeit Heinrichs III. Ein Beitrag zur Geschichte des ottonisch-salischen Reichskirchensystems." In *FS für Friedrich Hausmann*. Ed. H. Ebner. Graz, 1977: 21–37.

———. "Die Auctoritas des Papstes und der Apostelfürsten in Urkunden der Bischöfe von Halberstadt. Vom Wandel des bischöflichen Amtsverständnisses in der späten Salierzeit." In *Salier und Reich*, vol. 3. Sigmaringen, 1991: 333–353.

Binding, G. *Städtebau und Heilsordnung. Künstlerische Gestaltung der Stadt Köln in ottonischer Zeit*. Düsseldorf, 1986.

Blumenthal, U.-R. *Der Investiturstreit*. Urban Paperback 335. Stuttgart, Berlin, Cologne, and Mainz, 1982.

Böhme, H. W., ed. *Burgen der Salierzeit*, 2 vols. Sigmaringen, 1991.

———. *Siedlungen und Landesausbau zur Salierzeit*. 2 vols. Sigmaringen, 1991.

Böhn, G. F. "Salier, Emichonen und das Weistum des pfalzgräflichen Hofes zu Alzey." In *Alzeyer Kolloquium 1970. Geschichtliche Landeskunde 10*. Wiesbaden, 1974: 72–96.

Bornscheuer, L. *Miseriae Regum. Untersuchungen zum Krisen-und Todesgedanken in den herrschaftstheologischen Vorstellungen der ottonisch-salischen Zeit. Arbeiten zur Frühmittelalterforschung* 4. Berlin, 1968.

Boshof, E. *Die Salier*. Urban Paperback 387. Stuttgart, Berlin, Cologne, and Mainz, 1987.

———. "Lothringen, Frankreich und das Reich in der Regierungszeit Heinrichs III." *RVJB* 43 (1978): 63–127.

———. "Das Reich in der Krise. Überlegungen zum Regierungsausgang Heinrichs III." *HZ* 228 (1979): 265–287.

———. *Heinrich IV. Herrscher an einer Zeitwende*. Göttingen, 1979.

Bosl, K. "Die Sozialstruktur der mittelalterlichen Residenz- und Fernhandelsstadt Regensburg. Die Entwicklung ihres Bürgertums vom 9.–14. Jahrhundert." In *Untersuchungen zur gesellschaftlichen Struktur der mittelalterlichen Städte in Europa*, VF 11. 2d ed. Sigmaringen, 1974: 93–213.

———. "Die Markengründungen Kaiser Heinrichs III. auf bayerischösterreichischem Boden." *ZBLG* 14 (1944): 177–247.

———. "Das Nordgaukloster Kastl (Gründung, Gründer, Wirtschafts- und Geistesgeschichte)." *Verhandlungen des Historischen Vereins von Oberpfalz und Regensburg* 89 (1939): 3–186.

Brühl, C. *Deutschland—Frankreich. Die Geburt zweier Völker*. Cologne and Vienna, 1990.

Büttner, H. "Das Bistum Worms und der Neckarraum während des Früh-und Hochmittelalters." *AMRKG* 10 (1958): 9–38.

———. "Die Widonen. Der Wanderweg eines fränkischen Adelsgeschlechtes von Mosel und Saar nach dem Speyergau." *Saarbrücker Hefte* 3 (1956): 33–39.

———. "Erzbischof Adalbert von Mainz, die Kurie und das Reich in den Jahren 1118 bis 1122." In *Investiturstreit*. Sigmaringen, 1973: 395–410.

Cantarella, C. M. "La costruzione della verità. Pasquale II, un papa alle strette." Instituto Storico Italiano per il Medievò. *Studi Storici*, Fasc. 178–179. Rome, 1987.

Classen, P. "Bemerkungen zur Pfalzforschung am Mittelrhein" (1963). Reprinted in *Ausgewählte Aufsätze*. Ed. J. Fleckenstein. VF 28. Sigmaringen, 1983: 475–501.

———. "Das Wormser Konkordat in der deutschen Verfassungsgeschichte." In *Investiturstreit*. Sigmaringen, 1973: 411–460.

Doll, A. "Das Pirminkloster Hornbach." *AMRKG* 5 (1953): 108–140.

———. "Überlegungen zur Grundsteinlegung und zu den Weihen des Speyrer Domes." *AMRKG* 24 (1972): 9–25.

———. "Zur Frühgeschichte der Stadt Speyer. Eine topographische Untersuchung zum Prozess der Stadtwerdung Speyers vom 10. bis 13. Jahrhundert." *Mitteilungen des Historischen Vereins der Pfalz* 52 (1954): 133–200.

Droege, G. *Landrecht und Lehnrecht im hohen Mittelalter*. Bonn, 1969.

Engels, O. "Der Dom zu Speyer im Spiegel des salischen und staufischen Selbstverständnisses." *AMRKG* 32 (1980): 27–40.

———. "Der Reichsbischof (10. und 11. Jahrhundert)." In *Der Bischof in seiner Zeit. Festgabe für Joseph Kardinal Höffner*. Ed. P. Berglar and O. Engels. Cologne, 1986: 41–94.

———. "Der Reichsbischof in ottonischer und frühsalischer Zeit." In *Beiträge zu*

Geschichte und Struktur der mittelalterlichen Germania Sacra. Ed. I. Crusius. Göttingen, 1989: 135–175.

———. "Das Reich der Salier—Entwicklungslinien." In *Salier und Reich*, vol. 3. Sigmaringen, 1991: 479–541.

———. "Die Stauferzeit." In *Rheinische Geschichte*, vol. 2, part 3: *Hohes Mittelalter.* Ed. F. Peter and G. Droege. Düsseldorf, 1983: 199–296.

———. *Die Staufer.* Urban Paperback 154. 4th ed. Stuttgart, Berlin, Cologne, and Mainz, 1989.

———. *Stauferstudien, Beiträge zur Geschichte der Staufer im 12. Jahrhundert. Festgabe zu seinem 60. Geburtstag.* Ed. E. Meuthen and S. Weinfurter. Sigmaringen, 1988.

Erdmann, Carl, and Dietrich von Gladiss. "Gottschalk von Aachen im Dienste Heinrichs IV." *DA* 3 (1939): 115–174.

Erkens, F.-R. "Die Bistumsorganisation in den Diözesen Trier und Köln—ein Vergleich." In *Salier und Reich*, vol. 2. Sigmaringen, 1991: 267–302.

Faussner, H. C. *Königliches Designationsrecht und herzogliches Geblütsrecht. Zum Königtum und Herzogtum in Baiern im Hochmittelalter.* Österreichische Akademie der Wissenschaften, phil.-hist. KL SB 429. Vienna, 1984.

Fenske, L. *Adelsopposition und kirchliche Reformbewegung im östlichen Sachsen. Entstehung und Wirkung des sächsischen Widerstandes gegen das salische Königtum während des Investiturstreites.* Veröffentlichungen des Max-Planck-Instituts für Geschichte 47. Göttingen, 1977.

Fink von Finckenstein, Albrecht Graf. *Bischof und Reich. Untersuchungen zum Integrationsprozss des ottonisch-frühsalischen Reiches (919–1056).* Studien zur Mediävistik 1. Sigmaringen, 1989.

Fleckenstein, J. "Problematik und Gestalt der ottonisch-salischen Reichskirche." In *Reich und Kirche vor dem Investiturstreit. Vorträge beim wissenschaftlichen Kolloquium aus Anlaß des achtzigsten Geburtstags von Gerd Tellenbach.* Ed. K. Schmid. Sigmaringen, 1985: 70–94.

———. *Die Hofkapelle der deutschen Könige,* vol. 2: *Die Hofkapelle im Rahmen der ottonisch-salischen Reichskirche.* Schriften der MGH 16, II. Stuttgart, 1966.

———. "Hofkapelle und Reichsepiskopat unter Heinrich IV." In *Investiturstreit.* Sigmaringen, 1973: 117–140.

Freytag, H.-J. *Die Herrschaft der Billunger in Sachsen.* Göttingen, 1951.

Fried, J. "Endzeiterwartung um die Jahrtausendwende." *DA* 45 (1989): 381–473.

———. "Der Regalienbegriff im 11. und 12. Jahrhundert." *DA* 29 (1973): 450–528.

Fritze, W. *Frühzeit zwischen Ostsee und Donau.* Berlin, 1982.

Fuhrmann, H. *Deutsche Geschichte im hohen Mittelalter von der Mitte des 11. Jahrhunderts bis zum Ende des 12. Jahrhunderts.* 2d rev. ed. Göttingen, 1983.

———. *Papst Urban II. und der Stand der Regularkanoniker.* Bayerische Akademie der Wissenschaften, phil.-hist. Klasse, SB Jg. 1984, Heft 2. Munich, 1984.

———. "Das Reformpapstum und die Rechtswissenschaft." In *Investiturstreit.* Sigmaringen, 1973: 175–203.

———. "'Volkssouveränität' und 'Herrschaftsvertrag' bei Manegold von Lautenbach." In *FS für Hermann Krause.* Ed. S. Gagnér, H. Schlosser, and W. Wiegand. Cologne, Vienna, 1975: 21–42.

———. "Papst Gregor VII. und das Kirchenrecht. Zum Problem des Dictatus Papae." In *Studi Gregoriani* 13 (1989): 123–149.

Gaettens, R. "Das Geburtsjahr Heinrichs V. 1081 oder 1086? Rechtsgeschichtliche und numismatische Erörterungen." *ZRG*, Germ. Abt. 79 (1962): 52–71.

Giese, W. "Zur Bautätigkeit von Bischöfen und Äbten des 10. bis 12. Jahrhunderts." *DA* 38 (1982): 388–438.

———. *Der Stamm der Sachsen und das Reich in ottonischer und salischer Zeit. Studien zum Einfluss des Sachsenstammes auf politische Geschichte des deutschen Reiches im 10. und 11. Jahrhundert und zu ihrer Stellung im Reichsgefüge mit einem Ausblick auf das 12. und 13. Jahrhundert.* Wiesbaden, 1979.

———. "Otto von Bamberg und der Speyerer Dom." *Berichte des historischen Vereins Bamberg* 125 (1989): 105–113.

———. "Reichsstrukturprobleme unter den Saliern—der Adel in Ostsachsen." In *Salier und Reich*, vol. 1. Sigmaringen, 1991: 273–208.

Goettert, K. "Mittelalterliche Bauten in der Achse des Doms." *Kölner Domblatt* 18–19 (1960): 139–150.

Goez, W. ". . . iuravit in anima regis: Hochmittelalterliche Beschränkung königlicher Eidesleistung." *DA* 42 (1986): 517–554.

Grafen, H. "Spuren der ältesten Speyerer Necrologüberlieferung. Ein verlorenes Totenbuch aus dem 11. Jahrhundert." *FMS* 19 (1985): 379–431.

Groten, M. "Von der Gebetsverbrüderung zum Königskanonat. Zur Vorgeschichte und Entwicklung der Königskanonate und den Dom- und Stiftskirchen des deutschen Reiches." *HJ* 103 (1983): 1–34.

———. "Die Kölner Richerzeche im 12. Jahrhundert. Mit einer Bürgergemeindeliste." *RVJB* 48 (1984): 34–85.

———. *Priorenkolleg und Domkapitel von Köln im Hohen Mittelalter. Zur Geschichte des kölnischen Erzstifts und Herzogtums.* Rheinisches Archiv 109. Bonn, 1980.

Grupe, G. "Umwelt- und Bevölkerungsentwicklung im Mittelalter." In *Mensch und Umwelt im Mittelalter*. Ed. B. Herrmann. Stuttgart, 1986: 24–34.

Hampe, K. *Deutsche Kaisergeschichte in der Zeit der Salier und der Staufer.* 3d ed. Leipzig, 1916.

Haverkamp, A. *Aufbruch und Gestaltung. Deutschland 1056–1273.* Neue Deutsche Geschichte 2. Munich, 1984.

———. "Die Städte Trier, Metz, Toul und Verdun: Religiöse Gemeinschaften im Zentralitätsgefüge eine Städtelandschaft zur Zeit der Salier." In *Salier und Reich*, vol. 3. Sigmaringen, 1991: 165–190.

Heidrich, I. "Die Absetzung Herzog Adalberos von Kärnten durch Kaiser Konrad II. 1035." *HJ* 91 (1971): 70–94.

Heinemeyer, K. "Erzbischof Luitpold von Mainz—pontifex antique discipline, 1051–1059." In *Geschichte und ihre Quellen. FS für Friedrich Hausmann zum 70. Geburtstag.* Ed. R. Härtel. Graz, 1987: 59–76.

Herzog, E. *Die ottonische Stadt. Die Anfänge der mittelalterlichen Stadtbaukunst in Deutschland.* Berlin, 1964.

Hlawitschka, E. *Vom Frankenreich zur Formierung der europäischen Staaten-und Völkergemeinschaft 840–1046. Ein Studienbuch zur Zeit der späten Karolinger, der Ottonen und der frühen Salier in der Geschichte Mitteleuropas.* Darmstadt, 1986.

————. "Die Thronkandidaturen von 1002 und 1024. Gründeten sie im Verwandte-nanspruch oder in Vorstellungen von freier Wahl?" *Reich und Kirche vor dem Investiturstreit. Vorträge beim wissenschaftlichen Kolloquium aus Anlaß des acht-zigsten Geburtstags von Gerd Tellenbach.* Ed. K. Schmid. Sigmaringen, 1985: 49–64.

————. *Untersuchungen zu den Thronwechseln der ersten Hälfte des 11. Jahrhun-derts und zur Adelsgeschichte Süddeutschlands. Zugleich klärende Forschungen um "Kuno von Öhningen."* VF, special edition 35. Sigmaringen, 1987.

————. "Zur Bleitafelinschrift aus dem Grab der Kaiserin Gisela." *HJ* 97–98 (1978): 439–445.

Hoffmann, H. "Böhmen und das deutsche Reich im hohen Mittelalter." *JB für Geschichte Mittel-und Ostdeutschlands* 18 (1969): 1–62.

Jakobs, H. *Kirchenreform und Hochmittelalter, 1046–1250.* Oldenburg Grundriss der Geschichte 7. Munich 1984, 2d ed. 1989.

————. *Der Adel in der Klosterreform von St. Blasien.* KHA 16. Cologne and Graz, 1968.

————. *Die Hirsauer. Ihre Ausbreitung und Rechtsstellung im Zeitalter des Investi-turstreites.* KHA 4. Cologne and Graz, 1961.

————. "Rudolf von Rheinfelden und die Kirchenreform." In *Investiturstreit.* Sig-maringen, 1973: 87–115.

Jasper, D. *Das Papstwahldekret von 1059. Überlieferung und Textgestalt.* Sigmaringen, 1986.

Jenal, G. *Erzbischof Anno II. von Köln (1056–75) und sein politisches Wirken. Ein Bei-trag zur Reichs- und Territorialpolitik im 11. Jahrhundert.* Monographien zur Geschichte des Mittelalters 8. Stuttgart, 1974.

Johanek, P. "Die Erzbischöfe von Hamburg-Bremen und ihre Kirche im Reich der Salierzeit." In *Salier und Reich*, vol. 2. Sigmaringen, 1991: 159–173.

Kahl, H.-D. "Die Angliederung Burgunds an das mittelalterliche Imperium." *Schweizerische Numismatische Rundschau* 48 (1968): 13–105.

Keller, H. *Zwischen regionaler Begrenzung und universalem Horizont. Deutschland im Imperium der Salier und Staufer, 1024–1250.* Propyläen Geschichte Deutsch-lands, vol. 2. Berlin, 1986.

————. "Reichsstruktur und Herrschaftsauffassung in ottonisch-frühsalischer Zeit." *FMS* 16 (1982): 74–128.

————. "Zum Charakter der 'Staatlichkeit' zwischen karolingischer Reichsreform und hochmittelalterlichem Herrschaftsaufbau." *FMS* 23 (1989): 248–264.

————. *Adelsherrschaft und städtische Gesellschaft in Oberitalien, 9.–10. Jahrhundert.* Tübingen, 1979.

————. "Schwäbische Herzöge als Thronbewerber: Herzog Hermann II. (1002), Rudolf von Rheinfelden (1077), Friedrich von Staufen (1125). Zur Entwick-lung von Reichsidee und Fürstenverantwortung, Wahlverständnis und Wahl-verfahren im 11. und 12. Jahrhundert." *ZGOR* 131 (1983): 123–162.

Koch, G. *Auf dem Wege zum Sacrum Imperium. Studien zur ideologischen Herrschafts-begründung der deutschen Zentralgewalt im 11. und 12. Jahrhundert.* Vienna, Cologne, and Graz, 1972.

Kost, O.-H. *Das östliche Niedersachsen im Investiturstreit. Studien zu Brunos Buch vom Sachsenkrieg*. Studien zur Kirchengeschichte Niedersachsens 13. Göttingen, 1962.

Krabusch, H. "Untersuchungen zur Geschichte des Königsgutes unter den Saliern (1024–1125)." Unpublished dissertation. Heidelberg, 1949.

Krah, A. *Absetzungsverfahren als Spiegelbild von Königsmacht*. Untersuchungen zur deutschen Staats- und Rechtsgeschichte, New Series 26. Aachen, 1987.

Krimm-Beumann, J. "Der Traktat 'De investitura episcoporum' von 1109." *DA* 33 (1977): 37–83.

Kubach, H. E. *Der Dom zu Speyer*. Darmstadt, 1974.

Kubach, H. E., and W. Haas. *Der Dom zu Speyer*, 3 vols. Die Kunstdenkmäler von Rheinland-Pfalz 5. Munich, 1972.

Kürbis, B. "Die Epistola Mathildis Suevae an Mieszko II. in neuer Sicht. Ein Forschungsbericht. Mit einem Anhang von E. Freise und M. Weidner. Auf der Suche nach der verschollenen Widmungsminiatur des Cod. C91 der Düsseldorfer Universitätsbibliothek." *FMS* 23 (1989): 318–343.

Lammers, W. *Das Hochmittelalter bis zur Schlacht von Bornhöved*. Geschichte Schleswig-Holsteins 4, 1. Neumünster, 1981.

Lange, K.-H. *Der Herrschaftsbereich der Grafen von Northeim 960–1144*. Studien und Vorarbeiten zum historischen Atlas Niederschsens 24. Göttingen, 1969.

Laudage, J. *Priesterbild und Reformpapsttum im 11. Jahrhundert*. Beihefte zum Archiv für Kulturgeschichte 22. Cologne and Vienna, 1984.

Lewald, U. "Die Ezzonen, Das Schicksal eines rheinischen Fürstengeschlechts." *RVJB* 43 (1979): 120–168.

Ludat, H. *Slawen und Deutsche im Mittelalter*. Berlin, 1982.

Maurer, H.-M. "Die Entstehung der hochmittelalterlichen Adelsburg in Südwestdeutschland." *ZGOR* 117 (1969): 295–332.

Maurer, H. *Der Herzog von Schwaben. Grundlagen, Wirkungen und Wesen seiner Herrschaft in ottonischer, salischer und staufischer Zeit*. Sigmaringen, 1978.

———. "Kirchengründung und Romgedanke am Beispiel des ottonischen Bischofssitzes Konstanz." In *Bischofs- und Kathedralstädte des Mittelalters und der frühen Neuzeit*. Ed. F. Petri. Städteforschung Reihe A, vol. 1. Cologne and Vienna, 1976: 47–59.

Märtl, C. "Regensburg in den geistigen Auseinandersetzungen des Investiturstreits." *DA* 42 (1986): 145–191.

Metz, W. "Miszellen zur Geschichte der Widonen und Salier, vornehmlich in Deutschland." *HJ* 85 (1965): 1–27.

Millotat, P. *Transpersonale Staatsvorstellungen in den Beziehungen zwischen Kirchen und Königtum der ausgehenden Salierzeit*. Historische Forschungen 26. Rheinfelden, Freiburg i. Br. and Berlin, 1989.

Minninger, M. "Heinrichs III. interne Friedensmaßnahmen und ihre etwaigen Gegner in Lothringen." *JB für westdeutsche Landesgeschichte* 5 (1979): 32–52.

———. *Von Clermont zum Wormser Konkordat. Die Auseindersetzungen zwischen König und Episkopat*. Forschungen zur Kaiser- und Papstgeschichte des Mittelalters 2. Cologne and Vienna, 1978.

Moraw, P. *Das Stift St. Philipp zu Zell in der Pfalz*. Heidelberg, 1964.

Müller-Mertens, E. "Reich und Hauptorte der Salier: Probleme und Fragen." In *Salier und Reich*, vol. 1. Sigmaringen, 1991: 139–158.

———. *Regnum Teutonicum. Aufkommen und Verbreitung der deutschen Reichs- und Königsauffassung im frühen Mittelalter*. Vienna, Cologne, and Graz, 1970.

Nellmann, E. *Die Reichsidee in deutschen Dichtungen der Salier- und frühen Stauferzeit. Annolied—Kaiserchronik—Rolandslied—Eraclius*. Philologische Studien und Quellen 16. Berlin, 1963.

Neumeister, P. "Heinrich V. 1106–1125." In *Deutsche Könige und Kaiser des Mittelalters*. Leipzig, Jena, and Berlin, 1989: 129–138.

Oexle, O. G. "Die Gegenwart der Toten." In *Death and Burial in the Middle Ages*. Ed. H. Braet and W. Verbeke. Louvain, 1983: 19–77.

———. "Die Gegenwart der Lebenden und Toten. Gedanken über Memoria." In *Gedächtnis, das Gemeinschaft stiftet*. Ed. K. Schmid. Munich and Zurich, 1985: 74–107.

———. "Die funktionale Dreiteilung der 'Gesellschaft' bei Adalbero von Laon. Deutungsschemata der sozialen Wirklichkeit im frühen Mittelalter." *FMS* 12 (1978): 1–54.

———. "Tria genera hominum. Zur Geschichte eines Deutungsschemas der sozialen Wirklichkeit in Antike und Mittelalter." In *Institutionen, Kultur und Gesellschaft im Mittelalter. FS für Josef Fleckenstein zu seinem 65. Geburtstag*. Ed. L. Fenske, W. Rösener, and T. Zotz. Sigmaringen, 1984: 483–500.

———. "Deutungsschemata der sozialen Wirklichkeit im frühen und hohen Mittelalter. Ein Beitrag zur Geschichte des Wissens." In *Mentalitäten im Mittelalter. Methodische und inhaltliche Probleme*. Ed. F. Graus. VF 35. Sigmaringen, 1987: 65–117.

Ortigues, E. "L'élaboration de la théorie des trois ordres chez Haymon d'Auxerre." *Francia* 14 (1986): 27–43.

Peters, W. "Coniuratio facta est pro libertate. Zu den coniurationes in Mainz, Köln und Lüttich in den Jahren 1105/06." *RVJB* 51 (1987): 303–312.

Petke, W. *Kanzlei, Kapelle und königliche Kurie unter Lothar III. (1125–1137)*. Forschungen zur Kaiser- und Papstgeschichte des Mittelalters 5. Cologne and Vienna, 1985.

Pischke, G. *Herrschaftsbereiche der Billunger, der Grafen von Stade, der Grafen von Northeim und Lothars von Supplingenburg*. Studien und Vorarbeiten zum Historischen Atlas Niedersachsens 29. Hildesheim, 1984.

Plotzek, J. M. *Das Perikopenbuch Heinrich III. in Bremen und seine Stellung innerhalb der Echternacher Buchmalerei*. Dissertation, Cologne, 1970.

Prinz, F. *Grundlagen und Anfänge. Deutschland bis 1056*. Neue Deutsche Geschichte 1. Munich, 1985.

———. "Kaiser Heinrich III. Seine widersprüchliche Beurteilung und deren Gründe." *HZ* 246 (1988): 29–548.

———. "Die Grenzen des Reiches in frühsalischer Zeit: Ein Strukturproblem der Königsherrschaft." In *Salier und Reich*, vol. 1. Sigmaringen, 1991: 159–173.

Ranke, J., and F. Birkner. "Die Kaisergräber im Dom zu Speyer." In *Der Dom zu Speyer*, text volume. Ed. H. E. Kubach and W. Haas. Munich, 1972: 1065.

Rassow, P. "Der Kampf Kaiser Heinrichs des IV. mit Heinrich V." *ZKG* 47 (1928): 451–465.

Reuling, U. "Zur Entwicklung der Wahlformen bei den hochmittelalterlichen Königserhebungen im Reich." In *Wahlen und Wählen im Mittelalter*. Ed. R. Schneider and H. Zimmermann. VF 37. Sigmaringen, 1990: 227–270.

Reuter, T. "The 'Imperial Church System' of the Ottonian and Salian Rulers: A Reconsideration." *JEH* 33 (1982): 347–374.

Rösener, W. "Bauern in der Salierzeit." In *Salier und Reich*, vol. 3. Sigmaringen, 1991: 51–73.

Santifaller, L. *Zur Geschichte des ottonisch-salischen Reichskirchensystems*. 2d ed. Graz, Vienna, and Cologne, 1964.

Scheibelreiter, G. "Der Regierungsantritt des römisch-deutschen Königs (1056–1138)." *MIÖG* 81 (1973): 1–62.

Schieffer, R. "Der ottonische Reichsepiskopat zwischen Königtum und Adel." *FMS* 23 (1989): 291–301.

———. "Erzbischöfe und Bischofskirche von Köln." In *Salier und Reich*, vol. 2. Sigmaringen, 1991: 1–29.

———. "Heinrich III. 1039–1056." In *Kaisergeschichte des Mittelalters*. Ed. H. Beumann. Munich, 1984: 98–115.

———. "Die Zeit der späten Salier (1056–1125)." In *Rheinische Geschichte*, vol. 1, part 3: *Hohes Mittelalter*. Ed. F. Petri and G. Droege. Düsseldorf, 1983: 121–198.

———. *Die Entstehung des päpstlichen Investiturverbots für den deutschen König*. Schriften der MGH 28. Stuttgart, 1981.

———. "Gregor VII. — ein Versuch über historische Größe." *HJ* 97–98 (1978): 87–107.

Schieffer, T. "Heinrich II und Konrad II. Die Umprägung des Geschichtsbildes durch die Kirchenreform des 11. Jahrhunderts." *DA* 8 (1951): 384–437.

Schimmelpfennig, B. "Zölibat und Lage der 'Priestersöhne' vom 11. bis zum 14. Jahrhundert." *HZ* 227 (1978): 1–44.

Schmale, F.-J. "Die 'Absetzung' Gregors VI. in Sutri und die synodale Tradition." In *Annuarium Historiae Conciliorum* 11 (1979): 55–103.

Schmeidler, B. "Heinrichs IV. Absetzung 1105/06, kirchenrechtlich und quellenkritisch untersucht." *ZRG* kan. Abt. 43. (1922): 168–222.

Schmid, K. "Zum Haus- und Herrschaftsverständnis der Salier." In *Salier und Reich*, vol. 1. Sigmaringen, 1991: 21–54.

———. "Die Sorge der Salier um ihre Memoria. Zeugnisse, Erwägungen und Fragen." *Memoria. Der geschichtliche Zeugniswert des liturgischen Gedenkens im Mittelalter*. Ed. K. Schmid and J. Wollasch. Münstersche Mittelalter-Schriften 48. Munich, 1984: 666–726.

———. "Zur Problematik von Familie, Sippe und Geschlecht, Haus und Dynastie beim mittelalterlichen Adel." *ZGOR* 105 (1957): 1–62.

———. "Adel und Reform in Schwaben." In *Investiturstreit*. Sigmaringen, 1973: 295–319.

———. "Heinrich III. und Gregor VI. im Gebetsgedächtnis von Piacenza des Jahres 1046. Bericht über einen Quellenfund." *Verbum et signum*, vol. 2: *Beiträge zur mediävistischen Bedeutungsforschung. Studien zu Semantik und Sinn-*

tradition im Mittelalter. Ed. H. Fromm, W. Harms, and U. Ruberg. Munich, 1975: 79–97.

———. *Kloster Hirsau und seine Stifter*. Freiburg i. Br., 1959.

———. "Salische Gedenkstiftungen für fideles, servientes und milites." In *Institutionen, Kultur und Gesellschaft im Mittelalter. Festschrift für Josef Fleckenstein zu seinem 65. Geburtstag*. Ed. L. Fenske, W. Rösener, and T. Zotz. Sigmaringen, 1984: 345–64.

———. Editor. *Die Zähringer. Schweizer Vorträge und Forschungen*. Veröffentlichungen zur Zähringer-Ausstellung III. Sigmaringen, 1991.

———. "De regia stirpe Waiblingensium. Bemerkungen zum Selbstverständnis der Staufer. *ZGOR* 124 (1976): 63–73.

Schmidt, P. G. "Heinrich III.—Das Bild des Herrschers in der Literatur seiner Zeit." *DA* 39 (1983): 582–590.

Schmidt, R. "Königsumritt und Huldigung in ottonisch-salischer Zeit." In *VF* 6. Ed. T. Mayer. 2d ed. Sigmaringen, 1981: 97–233.

Schmidt, T. "Kaiser Konrads II. Jugend und Familie." In *Geschichtsschreibung und geistiges Leben im Mittelalter. FS für Heinz Löwe*. Ed. K. Hauck and H. Mordek. Cologne and Vienna, 1978: 312–324.

———. "Hildebrand, Kaiserin Agnes und Gandersheim." In *Niedersächsisches Jahrbuch für Landesgeschichte* 46–47 (1974–75): 299–309.

Schneider, C. *Prophetisches sacerdotium und heilsgeschichtliches regnum im Dialog 1073–1077. Zur Geschichte Gregors VII. und Heinrichs IV*. Münstersche Mittelalter-Schriften 9. Munich, 1972.

Schneider, R. "Das Königtum als Integrationsfaktor im Reich." In *Ansätze und Diskontinuität deutscher Nationsbildung im Mittelalter*. Ed. J. Ehlers. Nationes 8. Sigmaringen, 1989: 59–82.

———. "Landerschließung und Raumerfassung durch salische Herrscher." In *Salier und Reich*, vol. 1. Sigmaringen, 1991: 117–138.

Schnith, K. "Recht und Friede. Zum Königsgedanken im Umkreis Heinrichs III." *HJ* 81 (1962): 22–57.

———. " 'Kaiserin' Mathilde." In *Großbritannien und Deutschland. Europäische Aspekte der politisch-kulturellen Beziehungen beider Länder in Geschichte und Gegenwart. FS für John P. Bourke*. Ed. Ortwin Kuhn. Munich, 1974: 166–182.

Schramm, P. E., and F. Mütherich. *Denkmale der deutschen Könige und Kaiser. Ein Beitrag zur Herrschergeschichte von Karl dem Großen bis Friedrich II. 768–1250*. 2d rev. ed. Munich, 1981.

Schreibmüller, H. "Die Ahnen Kaiser Konrads II. und Bischof Brunos von Würzburg." In *Herbipolis Jubilans. 1200 Jahre Bistum Würzburg. FS zur Säkularfeier der Erhebung der Kiliansreliquien*. Würzburger Diözesangeschichtsblätter 14–15, 1952–53. Würzburg, 1952: 173–233.

Schulz, K. "Die Ministerialität als Problem der Stadtgeschichte. Einige allgemeine Betrachtungen, erläutert am Beispiel der Stadt Worms." *RVJB* 32 (1968): 184–219.

———. "Zensualität und Stadtentwicklung im 11./12. Jahrhundert." In *Beiträge zum hochmittelalterlichen Städtewesen*. Ed. B. Diestelkamp. Cologne and Vienna, 1982: 73–93.

Schulze, H. K. *Grundstrukturen der Verfassung im Mittelalter*. 2 vols. Urban Paperback 371 and 372. Stuttgart, Berlin, Cologne, and Mainz, 1985 and 1986.

———. *Adelsherrschaft und Landesherrschaft. Studien zur Verfassungs und Besitzgeschichte der Altmark, des ostsächsischen Raumes und des hannoverschen Wendenlandes im hohen Mittelalter*. Mitteldeutsche Forschungen 29. Cologne and Graz, 1963.

———. "Königsherrschaft und Königsmythos. Herrscher und Volk im politischen Denken des Hochmittelalters." In *FS für Berent Schwineköper zu seinem 70. Geburtstag*. Ed. H. Maurer and H. Patze. Sigmaringen, 1982: 177–186.

Schulze-Dörrlamm, M. *Die Kaiserkrone Kaiser Konrads II (1024–1039). Neue Untersuchungen zu Alter und Herkunft der Kaiserkrone*. Sigmaringen, 1991.

Schwarzmaier, H. "Reichenauer Gedenkbucheinträge aus der Anfangszeit der Regierung König Konrads II." *Zeitschrift für württembergische Landesgeschichte* 22 (1963): 19–28.

Schwineköper, B. "Christus-Reliquien-Verehrung und Politik. Studien über die Mentalität der Menschen des frühen Mittelalters, insbesondere über die religiöse Haltung und sakrale Stellung der früh- und hochmittelalterlichen Kaiser und Könige." In *Blätter für deutsche Landesgeschichte* 117 (1981): 183–281.

Seibert, H. "Libertas und Reichsabtei. Zur Klosterpolitik der salischen Herrscher." In *Salier und Reich*, vol. 2. Sigmaringen, 1991: 503–569.

Semmler, J. *Die Klosterreform von Siegburg. Ihre Ausbreitung und ihr Reformprogramm im 11. und 12. Jahrhundert*. Bonn, 1959.

Servatius, C. *Paschalis II. Studien zu seiner Person und seiner Politik*. Päpste und Papsttum 14. Stuttgart, 1979.

———. "Heinrich V." In *Kaisergestalten des Mittelalters*. Ed. H. Beumann. Munich, 1984: 135–154.

Speer, L. *Kaiser Lothar III. und Erzbischof Adalbert I. von Mainz. Untersuchung zur Geschichte des deutschen Reiches im frühen zwölften Jahrhundert*. Dissertationen zur mittelalterlichen Geschichte 3. Cologne and Vienna, 1983.

Spier, H. "Die Harzburg Heinrichs IV. Ihre geschichtliche Bedeutung und ihre besondere Stellung im Goslarer Reichsbezirk." In *Harz Zeitschrift* 19–20 (1967–68): 185–204.

Spörl, J. "Pie rex caesaresque future! Beiträge zum hochmittelalterlichen Kaisergedanken." In *Unterscheidung und Bewahrung. FS für Hermann Kunisch zum 60. Geburtstag*. Ed. K. Lazarowicz and W. Kron. Berlin, 1961: 331–353.

Staab, F. "Die Mainzer Kirche. Konzeption und Verwirklichung in der Bonifatius- und Theonesttradition." In *Salier und Reich*, vol. 2. Sigmaringen, 1991: 31–77.

Stauber, A. "Kloster und Dorf Lambrecht." *Mitteilungen des historischen Vereins der Pfalz* 9 (1880): 49–227.

Stehkämper, H. "Die Stadt Köln in der Salierzeit." In *Salier und Reich*, vol. 3. Sigmaringen, 1991: 75–152.

Steinbach, F. "Die Ezzonen. Ein Versuch territorialpolitischen Zusammenschlusses der fränkischen Rheinlande." In *Das erste Jahrtausend Kultur und Kunst im werdenden Abendland an Rhein und Ruhr*. Text volume 2. Ed. V. H. Elbern. Düsseldorf, 1964: 848–866.

Störmer, W. "Adel und Ministerialität im Spiegel der bayerischen Namengebung (bis zum 13. Jahrhundert). Ein Beitrag zum Selbstverständnis der Führungs-schichten." *DA* 33 (1977): 84–152.

———. "Bayern und der bayerische Herzog im 11. Jahrhundert. Fragen der Herzogsgewalt und der königlichen Interessenpolitik." In *Salier und Reich*, vol. 1. Sigmaringen, 1991: 503–547.

Streich, G. *Burg und Kirche während des deutschen Mittelalters. Untersuchungen zur Sakraltopographie von Pfalzen, Burgen und Herrensitzen.* VF, special edition 129. Sigmaringen, 1984.

Struve, T. "Zwei Briefe der Kaiserin Agnes." *HJ* 104 (1984): 411–424.

———. "Die Romreise der Kaiserin Agnes." *HJ* 105 (1985): 1–29.

———. "Kaisertum und Romgedanke in salischer Zeit." *DA* 44 (1988): 424–454.

———. "Das Problem der Eideslösung in den Streitschriften des Investiturstreites." *ZRG*, Kan. Abt. 75 (1989): 107–132.

Stüllein, H.-J. *Das Itinerar Heinrichs V*. In *Deutschland*, dissertation. Munich, 1971.

Tellenbach, G. "Der Charakter Heinrichs IV. Zugleich ein Versuch über die Erkennbarkeit menschlicher Individualität im hohen Mittelalter." In *Personen und Gemeinschaft. Karl Schmid zum 65. Geburtstag*. Ed. G. Althoff, D. Geuenich, O. G. Oexle, and J. Wollasch. Sigmaringen, 1988: 345–367.

———. *Die westliche Kirche vom 10. bis zum frühen 12. Jahrhundert*. Kirche in ihrer Geschichte 2. Göttingen, 1988.

Thoma, G. *Namensänderungen in Herrscherfamilien des mittelalterlichen Europa*. Münchener Historische Studien. Abt. mittelalterliche Geschichte 3. Kallmütz, 1985.

Thomas, H. "Abt Siegfried von Gorze und die Friedensmaßnahmen Heinrichs III. vom Jahre 1043." In *Jahres-Chronik 1976 des Staatlichen Regino-Gymnasiums*. Prüm, 1976: 125–137.

Toussaint, I. *Die Grafen von Leiningen. Studien zur leiningischen Genealogie und Territorialgeschichte bis zur Teilung von 1317/18*. Sigmaringen, 1982.

Váczky, P. "Thietmar von Merseburg über die ungarische Königskrönung." In *Insignia Regni Hungaria I. Studien zur Machtsymbolik des mittelalterlichen Ungarn*. Ed. Hungarian National Museum. Budapest, 1983: 29–53.

Vogel, J. *Gregor VII. und Heinrich IV. nach Canossa. Zeugnisse ihres Selbstverständnisses*. Arbeiten zur Frühmittelalterforschung 9. Berlin and New York, 1983.

Vollrath, H. "Herrschaft und Genossenschaft im Kontext frühmittelalterlicher Rechtsbziehungen." *HJ* 102 (1982): 33–71.

———. "Kaisertum und Patriziat in den Anfängen des Investiturstreits." *ZKG* 85 (1974): 11–44.

———. "Konfliktbewältigung und Konfliktdarstellung in erzählenden Quellen des 11. Jahrhunderts." *Salier und Reich*, vol. 3. Sigmaringen, 1991: 279–296.

Waas, A. *Heinrich V. Gestalt und Verhängnis des letzten salischen Kaisers*. Munich, 1967.

Wadle, E. "Heinrich IV. und die deutsche Friedensbewegung." In *Investiturstreit*. Sigmaringen, 1973: 141–173.

Weidemann, K. "Burg, Pfalz und Stadt als Zentrum der Königsherrschaft am Nordharz." In *Führer zu vor- und frühgeschichtlichen Denkmälern 35* (Goslar, Bad Harzburg). Mainz, 1978: 11–50.

Weinfurter, S. "Reformidee und Königtum in spätsalischer Zeit. Überlegungen zu einer Neubewertung Kaiser Heinrichs V." In *Reformidee und Reformpolitik in spätsalischer und frühstaufischer Zeit*. Ed. S. Weinfurter. (Quellen und Abhandlungen zur mittelheinischen Kirchengeschichte.) Mainz, 1992, 1–45.

———. "Die Zentralisierung der Herrschaftsgewalt im Reich durch Kaiser Heinrich II." *HJ* 106 (1986): 241–297.

———. "Herrschaftslegitimation und Königsautorität im Wandel: Die Salier und ihr Dom zu Speyer." In *Salier und Reich*, vol. 1. Sigmaringen, 1991: 55–96.

———. "Der Aufstieg der frühen Wittelsbacher." *Geschichte in Köln* 14 (1983): 13–47.

———. "Sancta Aureatensis Ecclesia. Zur Geschichte Eichstätts in ottonisch-salischer Zeit." *ZBLG* 49 (1986): 3–40.

Werle, H. "Das Erbe des salischen Hauses. Untersuchungen zur staufischen Hausmachtpolitik im 12. Jahrhundert vornehmlich am Mittelrhein. Unpublished dissertation. Mainz, 1952.

———. "Titelherzogtum und Herzogsherrschaft." *ZRG* Germ. Abteilung 73 (1956): 225–299.

———. "Die salische Obervogtei über die Reichsabtei Weißenburg." *AMRKG* 8 (1956): 333–338.

Werner, E. *Pauperes Christi. Studien zu sozial-religiösen Bewegungen im Zeitalter des Reformpapsttums*. Leipzig, 1956.

Werner, M. "Das Herzogtum von Lothringen in salischer Zeit." In *Salier und Reich*, vol. 1. Sigmaringen, 1991: 367–473.

Wibel, H. "Die ältesten deutschen Stadtprivilegien, insbesondere das Diplom Heinrichs V. für Speyer." *Archiv für Urkundenforschung* 6 (1918): 234–262.

Wilke, S. *Das Goslarer Reichsgebiet und seine Beziehungen zu den territorialen Nachbargewalten. Politische, verfassungs- und familiengeschichtliche Untersuchungen zum Verhältnis von Königtum und Landesherrschaft am Nordharz im Mittelalter*. Veröffentlichungen des Max-Planck-Instituts für Geschichte 32. Göttingen, 1970.

Winterfeld, D. von. *Untersuchungen zur Baugeschichte des Bamberger Domes*. Berlin, 1972.

Wolter, H. *Die Synoden im Reichsgebiet und in Reichsitalien von 916 bis 1056*. Paderborn, 1988.

Zielinski, H. *Der Reichsepiskopat in späottonischer und salischer Zeit (1002–1125)*. Wiesbaden, 1984.

Zimmermann, H. "Heinrich IV." In *Kaisergestalten des Mittelalters*. Ed. H. Beumann. Munich, 1984: 116–134.

———. "Die 'gregorianische Reform' in deutschen Landen." *Studi Gregoriani* 13 (1989): 263–279.

Zotz, T. "Die Formierung der Ministerialität." In *Salier und Reich*, vol. 3. Sigmaringen, 1991: 3–50.

Selected Readings for Anglo-Americans

These titles will give the English reader an introduction to medieval Germany and (especially) to the Salian period. To give the tenacious reader a sense of how interpretations of German medieval history have changed in the last half century, some older works are included. Also listed are a few studies of general importance (such as those of Susan Reynolds) which emphasize Germany's place in a broader European framework. For comments on these works, the reader is encouraged to consult historiographical articles by Bowlus, Freed, and Peters in *Central European History*, 23, 25, 28, and Reuter's bibliographical notes to his translation of Fuhrmann, *Germany in the High Middle Ages*.

Abbreviations

Communications	Karl J. Leyser, *Communications and Power in Medieval Europe*. Vol. 2: *The Gregorian Revolution and Beyond*. London and Rio Grande, 1994.
EHR	*English Historical Review*
Kings and Kingship	Anne J. Duggan, ed., *Kings and Kingship in Medieval Europe*. King's College London Medieval Studies. Exeter, 1993.
Leyser, *Medieval Germany*	Karl J. Leyser, *Medieval Germany and Its Neighbours, 900–1250*. London, 1982.
Lordship and Community	Frederic L. Cheyette, ed., *Lordship and Community in Medieval Europe*. New York, 1968.
Medieval Germany	Geoffrey Barraclough, *Medieval Germany, 911–1250*. 2 vols. Oxford, 1938.
Medieval Nobility	Timothy Reuter, ed., *The Medieval Nobility: Studies on the Ruling Classes of France and Germany from the Sixth to the Twelfth Centuries*. Amsterdam, 1978.
Renaissance and Renewal	*Renaissance and Renewal in the Twelfth Century*. Ed. Robert L. Benson and Giles Constable. Cambridge, Mass., 1982.
Warriors	*Warriors and Churchmen in the High Middle Ages: Essays Presented to Karl Leyser*. Ed. Timothy Reuter. London and Rio Grande, 1992.

Sources in English Translation

Adam of Bremen. *History of the Archbishops of Hamburg-Bremen*. Trans. F. J. Tchan. Columbia Records of Civilization 53. New York, 1959.
Pullan, B., ed. *Sources for the History of Medieval Europe from the Mid-Eighth to the Mid-Thirteenth Century*. 2d ed. Oxford, 1980.

The Correspondence of Pope Gregory VII: Selected Letters from the Registrum. Trans. E. Emerton. Columbia Records of Civilization 14. New York, 1932.

Cowdrey, H. E. J., ed. and trans. *The "Epistolae vagantes" of Pope Gregory VII.* Oxford Medieval Texts. Oxford, 1972.

Ecbasis cuisdam captivi per tropologiam: Escape of a Certain Captive Told in a Figurative Manner, an Eleventh-Century Latin Beast Epic. Ed. and trans. E. H. Zeydel. North Carolina Studies in the Germanic Languages and Literatures 46. Chapel Hill, 1964.

Mommsen, Theodor E., and Karl F. Morrison, ed. and trans. *Imperial Lives and Letters of the Eleventh Century.* New York, 1962.

Rodulfi Glabri Historiarum Libri Quinque: Rudolfus Glaber. The Five Books of the Histories. Ed. and trans. John France and Paul Reynolds. Oxford, 1989.

Ruodlieb: Ruodlieb, the Earliest Courtly Novel. Ed. and trans. E. H. Zeydel. North Carolina Studies in the Germanic Languages and Literatures. Chapel Hill, 1959.

The Ruodlieb, the First Medieval Epic of Chivalry from Eleventh-Century Germany. Ed. and trans. Gordon B. Ford, Jr. Leiden, 1965.

Secondary Literature

Airlie, Stuart. "After Empire—Recent Work on the Emergence of Post-Carolingian Kingdoms." *Early Medieval Europe* 2 (1993): 153–161.

Arnold, Benjamin. *German Knighthood, 1050–1300.* Oxford, 1985.

———. *Princes and Territories in Medieval Germany.* Cambridge, 1991.

———. *Count and Bishop in Medieval Germany: A Study of Regional Power, 1100–1350.* Philadelphia, 1991.

———. "Episcopal Authority Authenticated and Fabricated: Form and Function in Medieval German Bishops' Catalogues." *Warriors*: 63–78.

Cowdrey, H. E. J. *The Cluniacs and Gregorian Reform.* Oxford, 1970.

———. "The Papacy, the Patarens and the Church of Milan." *Transactions of the Royal Historical Society,* 5th series 18 (1968), 25–48.

Duggan, Lawrence G. *Bishop and Chapter: The Governance of the Bishopric of Speyer to 1552.* New Brunswick, N.J., 1978.

Freed, John B. *Noble Bondsmen: Ministerial Marriages in the Archdiocese of Salzburg, 1110–1334.* Ithaca, 1995.

———. *The Counts of Falkenstein: Noble Self-Consciousness in Twelfth-Century Germany.* Transactions of the American Philosophical Society 74.6. Philadelphia, 1984.

———. "The Origins of the Medieval Nobility: The Problem of the Ministerials." *Viator* 7 (1976): 211–241.

———. "The Formation of the Salzburg Ministerialage in the Tenth and Eleventh Centuries: An Example of Upward Social Mobility in the Early Middle Ages." *Viator* 9 (1978): 67–101.

———. "The Place of Local and Regional History in German and French Historiography: Some General Reflections." *Australian Journal of French Studies* 16 (1979): 447–478.

———. "Reflections on the Medieval German Nobility." *American Historical Review* 91 (1986): 553–575.

———. "Nobles, Ministerials, and Knights in the Archdiocese of Salzburg." *Speculum* 62 (1987): 575–611.

———. "Medieval German Social History: Generalization and Particularism." *Central European History* 25 (1992): 1–26.

———. "Review of Rösener." *Central European History* 26 (1993): 115–117.

Fleckenstein, Joseph. *Early Medieval Germany.* Trans. Bernard S. Smity. Amsterdam, 1978.

Fuhrmann, Horst. *Germany in the High Middle Ages c. 1050–1200.* Trans. Timothy Reuter. Cambridge, 1986.

———. "*Quis Teutonicos constituit iudices nationum?* The Trouble with Henry." *Speculum* 69 (1994): 344–358.

Gilbert, Felix. *Ranke and Burckhardt.* Princeton, 1990.

Gillingham, John. *The Kingdom of Germany in the High Middle Ages.* London, 1971.

———. "Elective Kingship and the Unity of Medieval Germany." *German History* 9 (1991): 124–135.

Goetz, Hans-Werner. *Life in the Middle Ages from the Seventh to the Thirteenth Century.* Ed. Steven Rowan, trans. Albert Wimmer. Notre Dame, Ind., 1993.

Hampe, Karl. *Germany Under the Salian and Hohenstaufen Emperors.* Trans. Ralph Bennett. 1909; reprint Totowa, N.J., 1973.

Hauck, Karl. "The Literature of House and Kindred Associated with Medieval Noble Families, Illustrated from Eleventh- and Twelfth-Century Writers on the Nobility." In *Medieval Nobility*: 61–86.

Haverkamp, Alfred. *Medieval Germany 1056–1273.* Trans. Helga Braun and Richard Mortimer. Oxford, 1988.

Hill, Boyd. *The Rise of the First Reich.* New York, 1969.

———. *Medieval Monarchy in Action: The German Empire from Henry I to Henry IV.* London, 1971.

Hirsch, Hans. "The Constitutional History of the Reformed Monasteries During the Investiture Contest." In *Medieval Germany*: 131–174.

Joachimsen, Paul. "The Investiture Contest and the German Constitution." In *Medieval Germany*: 95–130.

Johnson, J. N. "Adalbert of Hamburg-Bremen." *Speculum* 9 (1934): 147–179.

———. "Bishop Benno II of Osnabrück." *Speculum* 16 (1941): 389–403.

Kantorowicz, Ernst. *The King's Two Bodies: A Study in Medieval Political Theology.* Princeton, 1957.

Kern, Fritz. *Kingship and Law in the Middle Ages.* Trans. and intro. S. B. Chrimes. New York, 1956.

Ladner, Gerd B. "Gregory the Great and Gregory VII: A Comparison of Their Concepts of Renewal." *Viator* 4 (1973): 1–27.

———. "Terms and Ideas of Renewal." In *Renaissance and Renewal*: 1–33.

Leyser, Karl J. "The German Aristocracy from the Ninth to the Early Twelfth

Century: A Historical and Cultural Sketch." In Leyser, *Medieval Germany*: 161–190.

———. "The Polemics of the Papal Revolution." In Leyser, *Medieval Germany*: 138–160.

———. "On the Eve of the First European Revolution." In *Communications*: 1–20.

———. "The Crisis of Medieval Germany." In *Communications*: 21–50.

———. "From Saxon Freedom to the Freedom of Saxony: The Crisis of the Eleventh Century." In *Communications*: 51–68.

———. "Gregory VII and the Saxons." In *Communications*: 69–76.

———. "The Crisis of Medieval Germany." *Proceedings of the British Academy* 69 (1983): 409–443.

Mayer, Theodor. "The State of the Dukes of Zähringen." In *Medieval Germany*: 175–202.

———. "The Historical Foundations of the German Constitution." In *Medieval Germany*: 1–34.

Medieval Germany, 911–1250. Trans. Geoffrey Barraclough. Oxford, 1938.

Mitteis, Heinrich. *The State in the Middle Ages: A Comparative Constitutional History of Feudal Europe*. Trans. H. F. Orton. New York, 1975.

———. "Feudalism and the German Constitution." In *Medieval Germany*: 235–280.

Morrison, Karl F. "Canossa: A Revision." *Traditio* (1962): 121–48.

Peters, Edward. "More Trouble with Henry: The Historiography of Medieval Germany in the Angloliterate World, 1888–1895." *Central European History* 28 (1995): 47–72.

Reuter, Timothy. *Germany in the Early Middle Ages*. London and New York, 1991.

———, ed. and trans. *The Medieval Nobility: Studies on the Ruling Classes of France and Germany from the Sixth to the Twelfth Century*. Amsterdam and New York, 1978.

———. "A New History of Medieval Germany." *History* 66 (1981): 440–444.

———. "The 'Imperial Church System' of the Ottonian and Salian Rulers: A Reconsideration," *Journal of Ecclesiastical History* 33 (1982): 347–374.

———. "Otto III and the Historians." *History Today* 41 (1991): 21–27.

———. "*Episcopi cum sua milita*: The Prelate as Warrior in the Early Staufer Era." In *Warriors*: 79–94.

———. "The Origins of the German *Sonderweg*? The Empire and Its Rulers in the High Middle Ages." In *Kings and Kingship*: 179–212.

Reynolds, Susan. *Kingdoms and Communities in Western Europe*. Oxford, 1984.

———. *Fiefs and Vassals: The Medieval Evidence Reassessed*. Oxford, 1994.

Robinson, I. S. *Authority and Resistance in the Investiture Contest: The Polemical Literature of the Late Eleventh Century*. Manchester, 1978.

———. "The Friendship Network of Gregory VII." *History* 63 (1978): 1–22.

———. "*Periculosus Homo*: Pope Gregory VII and Episcopal Authority." *Viator* 9 (1978): 103–132.

———. "Pope Gregory VII, the Princes and the Pactum, 1077–1080." *EHR* 94 (1979): 721–756.

Rörig, Fritz. *The Medieval Town*. Berkeley and Los Angeles, 1967.

Rösener, Werner. *Peasants in the Middle Ages*. Champaign-Urbana, 1992.

Rotondo-McCord, Jonathan. "Body Snatching and Episcopal Power: Archbishop Anno II of Cologne (1056–75), Burials in St. Mary's *ad gradus*, and the Minority of King Henry IV." *Journal of Medieval History* 22: 297–312.

Schlesinger, Walter. "Lord and Follower in Germanic Institutional History." In *Lordship and Community*: 64–99.

Schmid, Karl, "The Structure of the Nobility in the Earlier Middle Ages." In *Medieval Nobility*: 37–60.

Sheehan, James J. "What Is German History? Reflections on the Role of the *Nation* in German History and Historiography." *Journal of Modern History* 53 (1981): 1–23.

Strait, Peter. *Cologne in the Twelfth Century*. Gainesville, Fla., 1974.

Tellenbach, Gerd. *Church, State and Christian Society at the Time of the Investiture Contest*. Trans. R. F. Bennett. Oxford, 1938; reprint, 1948.

Thompson, James Westfall. *Feudal Germany*. Chicago, 1928; reprint, New York, 1962.

Tierney, Brian. *The Crisis of Church and State, 1050–1300*. Englewood Cliffs, N.J., 1964.

Ullmann, Walter. *The Growth of Papal Government in the Middle Ages*. 3d ed. London, 1970.

Wilks, M. J. "*Ecclesiatica* and *Regalia*: Papal Investiture Policy from the Council of Guastalla to the First Lateran Council (1106–23)." *Studies in Church History* 7 (1971): 69–86.

Zotz, Thomas. "Carolingian Tradition and Ottonian-Salian Innovation: Comparative Observations on Palatine Policy in the Empire." In *Kings and Kingship*: 69–100.

Index

Bruno (bishop of Toul, 1026–1051). *See* Leo IX (pope)

Bruno (bishop of Trier, 1101–1124), 66

Bruno (Saxon cleric; author of *Das Buch vom Sachsenkrieg*), 132, 140, 143

Burchard II (bishop of Halberstadt, 1059–1088), 125, 139, 143

Burchard (bishop of Worms, 1000–1025), 13

Burchard (prior of Ursberg; chronicler), 181 (note 4)

Burghausen. *See* Sighard (count)

Burgscheidungen (castle in Saxony), 139

Burgundy, Burgundian (region), 26, 49, 51, 72, 84; kingdom, 47–50 (*see also* Conrad; Rudolph III; Arelat); legacy, 46, 48, 51; chancellorship, 97; nobles, 49–50; *pax Dei* and *treuga Dei*, 101; Upper Burgundy, 49

Busdorf (canonry). *See* Paderborn

Byzantine: emperors, 28 (*see* Constantine the Great, Justinian; Constantine VIII; Romanos III Argyros); territories, 117; traditions, 28–29, 35, 38, 58

Byzantium, 28–29, 35, 58

Cadalus (bishop of Parma, 1045–1071/72), 117. *See also* Honorius II (anti-pope)

Calixtus II (pope, 1119–1124), 172

canon law, 24, 91, 102, 143, 144, 145, 156, 178

Canossa (castle in Tuscany), 107, 149–150

capitanei, 45–47

Capua (principality in southern Italy). *See* Richard (prince of Capua)

Carinthia, Carinthian (duchy), 55, 109–110, 114; dukes of, 11, 54–56. *See also* Henry II the Wrangler; Otto; Conrad I, Adalbero of Eppenstein; Conrad II the Younger; Henry (III, king and emperor); Welf III; Conrad III; Berthold I (of Zähringen)

Carmina Cantabrigiensia, 98

Carolingian(s), 7, 54, 63, 89

Cham (margraviate), 110, 164

Champagne (county). *See* Odo I; Odo II

Charlemagne (king and emperor, 768–814), 26–27

Chartres (county). *See* Theobald III

Chur (bishopric), 22

Church [Roman] (as institution), 26, 56–57, 58, 90–91, 93–94, 96, 98, 100, 116–117, 118, 143, 144–149, 155, 164–166, 170, 172–173

Clement II (pope, 1046–1047), 93, 151

Clement III (anti-pope, 1080–1100), 151, 163

Clovis I (Frankish king, 481–511), 6

Cluny (monastery in Burgundy), 124, 153. *See also* Odilo; Hugh

Cnut II (the Great) (king of England, Denmark, 1017/18–1035, and Norway, after 1028), 28

Cochem (castle on the Moselle River), 122 (map), 123

Codex Caesareus, 92–93. *See* Henry III

Codex Iustinianus, 156

Cologne: location, 80, 85, 123; archbishopric, 88, 119–124, 138; archbishops of, 24, 80, 140 (*see also* Brun; Pilgrim; Hermann II; Anno II; Frederick I); archchancellorship for Italy, 96; college of priors, 124; coronation of Gisela (1024), 24, 26; coronation privilege of the archbishop, 24; episcopal lordship, 121, 124–125, 138; peace and truth of God (1083), 163; popular uprising (1074), 80, 142; *Richerzeche* (guild of the privileged), 80; royal assembly (1056), 107, 112; "sacred landscape," 64; Saint Mary in the Capitol (convent/ladies' canonry), 123; Saint Pantaleon, 124; townspeople, 72, 80; *vicedominus*, 138

Como (bishopric in northern Italy), 18. *See also* Alberich (bishop)

Conrad I (king, 911–918), 9

Conrad the Elder. *See* Conrad II

Conrad II (king and emperor, 1024–1039), 5–6, 16–17, 18–60, 84, 87, 89, 101, 111, 138, 140, 156, 160

Conrad [III] (son of King Henry IV; king, 1087–1098; d. 1101), 160–162, 165, 168

Conrad III (king, 1138–1152), 176, 181

Conrad (king of Burgundy, 937–993), 16

Conrad I (duke of Bavaria, 1049–1053; member of the Ezzonen family), 109–110

Conrad II (duke of Bavaria, 1054–1055; infant son of King Henry III), 113, 135

Conrad I (duke of Carinthia, 1004–1011; father of Conrad the Younger), 20

Conrad the Younger, II (duke of Carinthia, 1036–1039), 5–6, 20–21, 46, 48, 50, 52

Conrad III (duke of Carinthia, 1056–1061; member of the Ezzonen family), 113

Conrad the Red (duke of Lotharingia,